The Duel

The Duel

A History of Duelling
by Robert Baldick

Spring Books
London · New York · Sydney · Toronto

Original edition published 1965 by Chapman & Hall Ltd., London

This edition published 1970 by
The Hamlyn Publishing Group Limited
London · New York · Sydney · Toronto
Hamlyn House, Feltham, Middlesex, England

Printed in England by Fletcher & Son Ltd., Norwich, and bound by
Richard Clay (The Chaucer Press) Ltd., Bungay, Suffolk

ISBN 0 600 32837 6

Preface

'A duel', wrote Jules Janin in the last century, 'makes of every one of us a strong and an independent power, and constitutes out of each individual life the life of all; it grasps the sword of justice, which the laws have dropped, punishing what no code can chastise – contempt and insult. Those who have opposed duelling are either fools or cowards; and those who have both condemned and advocated the practice, are on both sides sophists and liars. It is to duelling alone that we owe the remains of our civilization.'

On the other hand, Paley could argue that 'duelling, as a punishment, is absurd, because it is an equal chance whether the punishment falls on the offender or the person offended; nor is it much better as a reparation – it being difficult to explain in what the satisfaction consists, or how it tends to undo the injury or afford a compensation for the injury sustained.'

This argument on the rights and wrongs of duelling, which has gone on for nearly a thousand years, is now merely academic, for the duel, condemned by popes and councils, banned by sovereigns and parliaments, and finally damned by public opinion, has become virtually non-existent.

Yet the fascination of the subject remains, and the sinister phrase 'Pistols for two and coffee for one' still sends a shudder down the spine. This work is an attempt to trace the history of this remarkable, sanguinary institution.

R. B.

Acknowledgments

The author and publishers wish to express their thanks to the following sources for their kind permission to reproduce material for the illustrations of this book:

The Bayerische Staatsgemäldesammlungen, for the frontispiece
The Mansell Collection, London, for illustrations 1, 2, 4, 9, 10a, 10b, 12, 13, 16, 17a, 17b, 23b, and the line drawings on pages 110, 111, and 171
The British Museum for illustrations 3, 11a, 11b, 27, and the line drawings on pages 12, 14, 15, 19, 24, 28, 53, 66, 68, 69, 74, 79, 82, 92, 98, 99, 121, 132, 140, 148, 149, 153, 156, 159, and 181
Bildarchiv Foto Marburg for illustrations 5a and 5b, and the line drawing on page 143
Photographie Giraudon, Paris, for illustrations 6, 7, 8, 15 and 28a
The Radio Times Hulton Picture Library for illustration 14 and the line drawing on page 85
John R. Freeman, London, for illustrations 18a, 18b, 19a, 19b, 20a, 20b, and the line drawings on pages 34 and 46
Museum Press, London, for illustration 21a
Culver Pictures, New York, for illustrations 21b and 22
Deutsche Fotothek, Dresden, for illustrations 23a, 23b and the line drawings on pages 50 and 164
Ullstein Bilderdienst, Berlin, for illustrations 24, 28b and the line drawing on page 172
Schweiz. Landesmuseum for illustration 25
H. Roger Viollet, Paris, for illustrations 26a and 26b
Paris Match for illustrations 31a, 31b, 31c and 31d
Editions Rencontre, Lausanne, for the drawing on page 190
Rodney Shackell for the motif which appears on the front board of the binding and on page 203

Contents

Illustrations

The half-tone reproductions listed above illustrate, for the most part, actual episodes referred to in the text. The book is also adorned with forty-three line drawings, which are not captioned, as their function is less specific. They have been taken from many and various sources – early woodcuts and prints, medieval manuscripts and Victorian vignettes – and they are intended to provide diversion and decoration appropriate to the chapters in which they occur.

The drawings printed on coloured paper are from an unusually fine set of eighteenth-century engravings illustrating duelling postures.

1 · The Judicial Duel

Early historians of the duel were fond of tracing it back to ancient and even Biblical times. More than one actually pointed to its origin in the story of Cain and Abel, ingeniously arguing that the Scriptural words 'And Cain talked with Abel his brother' referred to a challenge given and accepted, and pointing out that there was nothing in the Biblical text to exclude the supposition that Abel defended himself in the encounter. Several maintained that the famous conflicts of antiquity, held in the presence of opposing armies between two warriors or rival bands, were in fact early duels; and they cited the combats between Achilles and Hector, Turnus and Aeneas, the defeat of Polynices with seven comrades in arms by Eteocles with an equal number of followers, the conflict between the Horatii and the Curiatii, and the encounter between Pittacus of Mitylene and the Athenian general Phrynon. Some suggested that the combats of the Roman gladiators were really duels. And others even argued that each and every fight between two human beings since the beginning of time could legitimately be described as a duel.

In point of fact, if these arguments are examined at all carefully, they are seen to be untenable. While there is nothing to prove that Cain did not issue a formal challenge to Abel, it seems highly unlikely that he did. The warriors who fought on behalf of their armies, tribes or nations, engaged in combat as part of a larger unit, and not on grounds of personal honour. The gladiators have even less cause to be regarded as duellists, since they felt no personal hostility towards one another. As for the theory that all single combats are duels, it is important to make a distinction between the hot-blooded combat, fought on the spur of the moment, and the duel proper, which is fought in cold blood, before witnesses, with a certain ceremony and in accordance with a strict code of law or honour.

The origins of the duel cannot, indeed, be traced further back than A.D. 501, when Gundebald, King of the Burgundians, legally established the trial by combat, or judicial duel. This was a variation on the earlier forms of the so-called 'Judgement of God', the ordeal and the oath. The trial by ordeal consisted of such painful exercises as holding a heated plate of iron for a time in one hand or taking a consecrated ring from a vessel filled with boiling

water; the defendant's hand was then bandaged, and if, when the dressing was removed three days later, a burn was apparent, his cause was considered lost. Since it was not always possible to find a proxy with hands so calloused as to be virtually fire-proof, defendants not unnaturally preferred to take a simple oath as to the justice of their cause, and many committed perjury in the hope or conviction that God would not strike them down. It was gradually borne in upon the worthy Gundebald that deciding cases by oath was not entirely satisfactory, since so many of his subjects 'suffered themselves to be corrupted by their avarice, or impelled by their obstinacy, so as to attest by oath what they knew not, or what they knew to be false'; and he decided that they 'might as well risk their bodies as their souls'. He accordingly prescribed that 'whenever two Burgundians are at variance, if the defendant shall swear that he owes not what is demanded of him, or that he is not guilty of the crime laid to his charge; and the plaintiff, on the other hand, not satisfied therewith, shall declare that he is ready to maintain, sword in hand, the truth of what he advances; if the defendant does not then acquiesce, it shall be lawful for them to decide the controversy by dint of sword'. He added that 'this is likewise understood of the witnesses of either party, it being just that every man should be ready to defend with his sword the truth which he attests, and to submit himself to the judgement of Heaven'.

Gundebald's example was followed all over western Europe, and gradually 'Trial by Battel' became an accepted part of the medieval theory of divine and human justice. Ironically enough, however, the institution failed in its immediate object of abolishing perjury, for as it was formalized, fearful oaths were introduced into the prescribed ceremonial, so that at least one of the two combatants must have perjured himself. In England, for example, the appellee, when accused of a felony, would plead 'Not guilty', throw down his glove, and declare that he would defend it with his body. The appellant would then take up the glove and reply that he was ready to make good the appeal or accusation, body for body. After that the appellee would take the Bible in his right hand, and his antagonist's right hand in his left, and swear an oath in the following vein:

'Hear this, O man whom I hold by the hand, who callest thyself John by the name of baptism, that I who call myself Thomas by the name of baptism, did not feloniously murder thy father, William by name, nor am in any way guilty of the said felony; so help me God and the saints; and this I will defend against thee by my body, as this court shall award.'

To this the appellant, holding the Bible and his antagonist's hand in the same way as the other, would reply:

'Hear this, O man whom I hold by the hand, who callest thyself Thomas by name of baptism, that thou art perjured; and therefore perjured because that thou feloniously didst murder my father, William by name; so help me God and the saints; and this I will prove against thee by my body as this court shall award.'

A day was then fixed for the fight, weapons chosen – at first 'two staves or bastons tipt with horn, of an ell long, both of equal length' but later lances and swords for men of gentle birth – and oaths administered against the use of amulets and sorcery. In theory, accused and accuser had to fight in person, but women, invalids and men over sixty were exempt, and eventually priests were excused from trial by combat. In England, too, the Crown took to using 'approvers' or informers to accuse their fellow criminals and fight on the Crown's behalf, generally on the understanding that they would thereby save their own lives. Gradually a whole class of proxy fighters known as 'champions' came into existence, to engage in trials by combat for one side or the other. It was a dangerous trade, since if a champion was worsted, his right hand was chopped off, ostensibly because he was legally supposed to have been a witness of the offence, but possibly to encourage him and his kind to fight zealously for their clients. As for the principals in a capital fight by proxy, they were kept out of sight of the duel, with a rope round their necks, and the one who was beaten by proxy was immediately hanged in person.

The fight itself took place on a specially selected ground, furnished with seating for the judges, two seats covered with black on which the combatants took the necessary oaths, and a gallows for the execution of the vanquished. On a given signal, the battle began, the accuser or his champion entering the ground from the south and the defendant or his champion from the north. It was understood that 'if the appellee be so far vanquished that he cannot or will not fight any longer, he shall be adjudged to be hanged immediately; and then, as well as if he be killed in battle, Providence is deemed to have determined in favour of the truth, and his blood shall be attainted. But if he kills

the appellant, or can maintain the fight from sun-rising till the stars appear in the evening, he shall be acquitted. So, also, if the appellant becomes recreant, and pronounces the horrible word *craven* (that is, *craves* or begs for his life), he shall lose his *liberam legem* (that is, his right of law), and become infamous; and the appellee shall recover his damages, and also be forever quit, not only of the appeal, but of all indictments likewise for the same offence.'

The first recorded trial by combat after the establishment of the institution by Gundebald took place in 590. In that year, Gontran, another King of Burgundy, was hunting in the royal forest when he came across the remains of a stag which had been killed by some poacher. The gamekeeper accused Cherndon, the king's chamberlain, who denied the charge, and Gontran accordingly ordered a combat. A nephew of the chamberlain acted as his champion, and in the course of the fight wounded the gamekeeper in the foot with his lance, so that he fell to the ground. His adversary was bending over him to dispatch him when the prostrate man drew out a knife and ripped open his belly. Cherndon immediately took flight and tried to seek sanctuary in the church of Saint-Marcel; but Gontron ordered him to be seized and stoned to death.

A few years later, in 626, another noteworthy trial by combat took place. Queen Gundeberge, the consort of Rharvald, King of Lombardy, had expelled from her court a certain Adalulf, who had apparently made an attempt on her virtue. To obtain his revenge, Adalulf went to the king and informed him that the queen had entered into a plot to poison him, and to marry the Duke Tason, whom he alleged to be her lover. Without making any inquiry into the matter, Rharvald banished his consort from his presence and imprisoned her in a castle, ignoring the fact that she was closely related to the Kings of the Franks. He was soon called to order, however, by an emissary from Clotaire, who urged him to order a judicial combat. Rharvald accordingly ordered Adalulf to meet in battle a cousin of the queen's called Pithon, who proved Gundeberge's innocence by the unanswerable expedient of cutting her accuser's throat. It was as a result of this particular trial by combat that Grunvalt, two years later, altered the law so that ladies who found themselves in a similar situation should be able to choose their own champions.

The famous duel between Gontran and Ingelger, which took place in 880, was a similar case. The Count of Gastonois having been found dead one morning in bed with his wife, a cousin of the dead man called Gontran accused the countess of her husband's murder and offered to substantiate the accusation in person. Since Gontran was the most expert swordsman of his time, no one came forward to defend the accused lady until her godson Ingelger, a boy of fifteen, threw himself at the king's feet and asked permission to accept Gontran's challenge. The king and his courtiers did their best to dissuade the boy, pointing to Gontran's frightening reputation – which suggests that they either believed the countess to be guilty or had little faith in the system of trial by combat as an indication of God's judgement. On the appointed day, after attending Mass, distributing alms, and recommending himself to divine protection, Ingelger entered the lists at the Castle of Landon. There, the Countess of Gastonois and Gontran both solemnly swore that what they had said was true, and affirmed that they had not used spells or sorcery of any sort to influence the decision of the coming fight. The combatants then rode headlong at each other, Gontran bending his lance on young Ingelger's shield; but the boy, unperturbed, drove his lance through Gontran's body and felled

1 · *Trial by ordeal: the combat*

2 · *Trial by battle. From a fragment of an assize roll, undated, but belonging to the period of Henry III*

him from his horse. Dismounting, he then cut off his adversary's head, and offered the bleeding trophy to the king. The countess, we are told, in gratitude for this amazing vindication of her innocence, presented her young champion with the manor and castle of Landon.

Ecclesiastics were not always exempt from liability to trial by battle – the clergy of the Abbey of Saint-Maur-des-Fossés, for example, were stated by their charter to possess *bellandi et certificandi licentiam* – and we find several cases of monks and priests engaging in judicial duels. Thus in the annals of St Bertin it is recorded that the Superior of his abbey in the village of Caumont had to defend certain claims in the field, and that his adversary, after being overawed by two white doves which fluttered above the duelling ground, was soundly beaten. Similarly, Geoffroy du Marne, Bishop of Angers, ordered certain of his monks to decide their right to tithes by the same process.

The frequency of these trials by combat led to the publication of a whole series of edicts intended to regulate them. In 1041 the edict known as the Truce of God was issued, prohibiting duels from Wednesday to Monday, these days having been consecrated by Christ's Passion. In 1145, the Provost of Bourges received instructions to call out all persons who failed to obey his orders. In 1167 Louis VII prohibited all duels over claims which did not exceed five sous. In 1256 it was ruled that accusations of adultery should be tried by this method, and in 1324 it was applied to cases of rape and poisoning.

Meanwhile, the practice of trial by battle had spread to England. Here, the duel seems to have been unknown before the Norman Conquest, although there is a tradition that Edmund Ironside and Canute fought a duel for England in 1016 on the Isle of Alney, near Gloucester. One version of this affair states that Edmund, after being told by Canute that he was too fat to fight and panted too much, felled the Dane to the ground and triumphantly remarked that he was not too breathless to lay a mighty king at his feet. Another version quoted the hard-pressed Canute as saying to his adversary: 'Valiant prince, have we not fought long enough to prove our courage? Let us therefore show proof of our moderation; and, since we have equally shared the sun and the honour of this day, let us quit the field of battle and share the kingdom between us.' Probably neither story has any truth in it.

With the Norman accession, however, trial by combat became part of the law of the land, and within a few years it was common practice in both civil and criminal actions.

The first notable case of a judicial duel in England was that between William, Count d'Eu, and Godefroy Baynard, in 1096. Having been accused by Baynard of conspiring against William Rufus, the Count d'Eu engaged him in single combat at Salisbury, before the king and his entire court. Worsted in the fight, the unfortunate count was promptly emasculated and both his eyes were put out, while his squire was whipped and hanged. Another case tried by combat about the same time was settled just as decisively but less cruelly. A certain Ordgar informed William Rufus that Edgar Atheling had claimed that he and his children were the rightful heirs to the crown, and a judicial duel was ordered in which the aged Edgar was represented by Godwine of Winchester. After a fierce struggle, Ordgar was laid low and confessed that his accusation had been false, but Godwine showed him no mercy, stabbing him repeatedly until 'the deep wounds drove out his ungodly soul'.

One of the most famous trials by combat in English history took place in the following century between Baron Henry de Essex and Robert de Montfort. The latter accused Essex, the hereditary standard-bearer of England, of having dropped the standard on the battlefield and taken to flight during Henry II's Welsh campaign of 1157. A trial by combat was decided upon, and the two men met at Reading, fighting on an island in the Thames close to the Abbey. Essex was beaten and left for dead on the field, but when his body was taken to the abbey, the monks found that he was still alive, and nursed him back to health. However, as he was considered to be morally dead, he spent the rest of his days in the abbey, where he was fond of explaining away his defeat by the unnerving intervention of the ghost of St Edward, king and martyr.

From the Norman Conquest until the reign of Henry II, trial by combat was the only honourable means of deciding a matter of right, until the alternative of the grand assizes or trial by jury was instituted by the latter monarch. Even then, judicial duels continued to be fought from time to time, and as late as 1571, during the reign of Queen Elizabeth I, a man called Paramour applied for a trial by combat to decide a civil case concerning the right of some manorial lands in the Isle of Harty in Kent. Paramour's request to maintain his possession by a duel took the Court of Common Pleas by surprise, but it could not refuse, since the petitioners accepted the challenge. Champions were duly appointed by each party, lists of the correct size were prepared in

Tothill Fields in London, and on the appointed day, judges, lawyers and champions appeared at the duelling ground and went through the time-honoured ceremonial. However, the day before, the Queen, anxious to prevent bloodshed, had ordered that the suit should be compounded and that the defendant should remain in possession. Consequently the petitioners failed to appear to acknowledge their champion, with the result that they were non-suited and victory was adjudged to the defendant. And although the petitioners' champion, a fencing-master called Henry Nailer, suggested that he and his adversary should 'show some pastime' to the Lord Chief Justice and the four thousand spectators, not a single blow was struck and the huge crowd went home disappointed.

Astonishingly enough, the right to choose trial by combat, although eventually restricted to cases of treason or murder, lingered on as part of the law of the land until the early part of the last century. The last time it was invoked, after being in abeyance for centuries, was in 1817, when a certain Abraham Thornton was charged with the murder of a girl called Mary Ashford, and, advised by a clever lawyer, claimed the right to 'wage his battel'. After considerable discussion, the Court of Appeal decided in Thornton's favour, Lord

Ellenborough saying: 'The general law of the land is in favour of the wager of battel, and it is our duty to pronounce the law as it is, not as we may wish it to be. Whatever prejudice, therefore, may justly exist against this mode of trial, still, as it is the law of the land, the Court must pronounce judgement for it.' The murdered girl's brother was too young to fight, and no one could be found to 'wage battel' on his behalf, so that after the usual formalities Thornton was discharged. Parliament, however, lost no time in closing this legal loophole, and on March 22, 1819, the right to appeal to the Judgement of God in single combat was finally abolished.

The judicial duel had of course disappeared in England centuries before, as it also had in France. There, the last notable trial by combat, in 1400, was also without any doubt the most curious ever fought, for it took place between a man and a dog. The cause of the combat was the murder of one Aubry de Montdidier in the Forest of Bondy, near Paris, by an envious friend called the Chevalier Maquer. There was no witness to the murder except for Montdidier's greyhound, and, after he had buried the body, Maquer must have thought that his crime would never be discovered. However, when hunger eventually compelled the dog to return to Paris for food, he went to a friend of his master's called the Chevalier Ardilliers, took him back to the place where Montdidier was buried, and scratched the earth until the Chevalier and his servants dug up the corpse.

A little later, meeting his master's murderer, the dog attacked him so savagely that it took several men to pull him off. He repeated his attack on Maquer on subsequent occasions, and as he was generally of a very peaceful disposition this aroused considerable suspicion. It was remembered that Maquer had frequently shown enmity towards Montdidier, and eventually the circumstances were reported to the king, who decided that Maquer's guilt or innocence should be determined by single combat with the dog.

The fight duly took place on the Isle of Notre-Dame, the dog being led into the lists by Ardilliers and then unleashed against Maquer. According to some chroniclers, the latter was armed with a lance, while others relate that he was buried waistdeep in the ground and had only a shield and a stick with which to defend himself. Whatever the truth of the matter, he found it impossible to ward off the dog, which sprang at him and seized him by the throat, so that he screamed that he would confess if only the animal were pulled away.

All was well, indeed, that ended well. As Olivier de La Marche wrote a century later, 'the loyal greyhound, a dog, an animal, had the grace and help of God and proved the truth in this manner. And it seems from this example that God wishes and allows such outrages and treacherous deeds to be proved in order to be punished. For the aforementioned Maquer was hanged and strangled on the gibbet at Montfaucon, and Aubry's body was taken by his friends and given honourable burial as befitted the loyal knight he was. . . .'

2 · The Duel of Chivalry

Springing from the judicial duel, existing concurrently with it for several centuries, and often indistinguishable from it, was the so-called duel of chivalry. This was a meeting in single combat between two knights, generally on horseback and always with great public ceremonial, to settle a difference of law, possession or honour. Since the origins of knighthood itself are shrouded in mystery, it is hard to put a definite date to the institution of the duel of chivalry: thus, although most historians consider that knighthood was instituted in the tenth century, there would appear to have been a chivalric encounter as early as 858, near Strasbourg, between Charles the Bald and his brother Louis of Germany. All that can be stated with any certainty is that knighthood was generally established in France, Spain and England by the twelfth century, and the duel of chivalry with it.

Perhaps a distinction ought to be made at once between the duel of chivalry and the tournament, for the two are often confused – not, it must be admitted, without some justification. Both, after all, took place under the same circumstances: in an enclosed space surrounded by lists and overlooked by crowded stands, with judges to pronounce on the value of the blows exchanged, and heralds at arms to ensure that nothing untoward occurred. Moreover, the tournament, though intended simply as an occasion for knights to display their courage and prowess, was often just as bloody and fatal as a duel, especially in the early years of the institution. Thus it is recorded that a Turkish ambassador who was present at a tournament at the court of Charles VII, seeing several of the combatants killed and wounded, exclaimed: 'If they are in earnest, this is not enough: but if it is only in jest, then we have had too much of it.' It was in fact on account of the frequent deaths caused in tournaments that the Church looked on them with such disfavour; the Council of Reims of 1148 even prohibiting Christian burial for those who fell on such occasions. Nonetheless the tournament and its accompanying bloodshed continued, often under royal patronage: in 1274, Edward I of England, passing through Châlons, joined in a tournament with the French knights to such good effect that the meeting was afterwards known as 'the petty battle of Châlons'; François I once took part in a tournament between Ardres and Guines; and it was in a joust with the captain of his guards that Henri II was killed in 1559.

For our purpose, the close connection between the tournament and the duel of chivalry is important in that the rules governing both institutions were identical. Thus the stringent regulations determining who was qualified to enter the lists also inevitably applied to the participants in a duel of chivalry. These regulations were as follows:

I. Whosoever has done or said anything against the holy Christian faith shall be excluded; and if any such shall presume to intrude himself, on the account of his family and ancient nobility, he shall be beaten and driven back.
II. If any, however nobly descended, have done or said anything against the Roman Empire, or the sacred majesty of the Emperor, he shall not be admitted, but publicly punished before the assembly.
III. If any have betrayed or deserted his lord and master, or have been the occasion of any mutiny, disorder, or shameful flight in an army; or have oppressed and unjustly killed any of his subjects and vassals, or other innocent persons, he shall be publicly punished.
IV. Whosoever has committed violence upon virgins or oppressed widows, or has violated and defamed any woman by word or deed, when he appears at the public tournament, shall be disgraced and punished.
V. Whosoever has been guilty of perjury, or of forging hand or seal, or lies under any other infamy, shall be held unworthy of the honour of a tournament; and, if he enter, he shall not be suffered to go away without some punishment.
VI. Whosoever has secretly or openly made away with his wife, or has advised or assisted the killing of his superior, whose vassal he was, let him be debarred, and let the law of tournament be executed upon him.
VII. Whosoever has been guilty of sacrilege, by robbing churches or detaining what belongs to them, or has wronged widows and children to whom he was left guardian, shall not be admitted, but punished.
VIII. Whosoever keeps up an unreasonable feud with another, and will not refer the difference to law or to a fair battle, but invades his adversary's land, burning and spoiling it, and carrying off his goods, especially if he has destroyed corn, which has caused a dearth or a famine – if he appear at the tournament, let him be put to death.

IX. Whosoever has been the author of any new *gabel* or imposition in any province, city, or other dominion, without the consent of the Emperor, by which means subjects are oppressed, and trade and commerce with strangers are hindered and discouraged, let him be punished.

X. Whosoever is guilty of adultery, let him be punished.

XI. Whosoever doth not live suitably upon his lawful rents and income, but debaseth his dignity by buying and selling, and using mean and sordid arts to the damage of his neighbours and oppression of his tenants, let him be beaten.

XII. Whosoever cannot prove his nobility for four generations at least by both father and mother, shall not have the honour of being admitted into the tournament.

However admirable the ideals of honour, loyalty, service and respect set up by these rules, and however considerable the contribution they made to civilization pending the institution and enforcement of civil law, it may be doubted whether all the knights who engaged in a tournament or a duel of chivalry lived up to such an exalted code – whether each *chevalier sans peur* was also *sans reproche*. Certainly the treatment of the vanquished in a duel ostensibly dedicated to lofty principles or gentle womanhood was generally brutal and pitiless.

A case in point is the duel between Azevedo and Sainte-Croix which is recounted by Brantôme. These two Spanish captains called upon the king's lieutenant in Italy, Monsieur de Nemours, when he was passing through

Ferrara, and asked him for a 'field' in order to settle a difference between them. The Duchess of Ferrara, who was reputed to be the most beautiful lady in Christendom, both in body and mind, and moreover spoke *force belles langues*, asked to be present at the contest; and Monsieur de Nemours, who was naturally deeply enamoured of her, wore her colours of black and grey for the occasion. The combat duly took place, and after a while, Sainte-Croix was so badly wounded that he sank to the ground, weak and helpless from loss of blood. His adversary thereupon put the point of his sword to the fallen man's throat and prepared to kill him, in accordance with the accepted rules of the duel of chivalry. Seeing this, the duchess, who was 'as kind and courteous as she was beautiful and virtuous', clasped her hands and implored Monsieur de Nemours to separate the combatants, a plea to which he replied: 'You cannot doubt, Madam, that there is nothing in the world that I would not do to convince you of my entire devotion to your will; but in this instance I can do nothing, nor offend against the laws of battle, nor can I honestly and unreasonably deprive the conqueror of a prize which he has obtained at the hazard of his life.'

Fortunately for the doomed Sainte-Croix, his second came forward and declared that since his friend, who would undoubtedly die rather than surrender, could obviously fight no more, he would surrender on his behalf. Azevedo was perfectly satisfied with this admission, and left the field with great pomp and glory, to the accompaniment of a flourish of trumpets, while Sainte-Croix's wounds were dressed and he was carried away. But in his triumph, the victor had forgotten to take possession of his adversary's arms as trophies of the battle, and when he belatedly sent for them, they were refused. The case was referred to Monsieur de Nemours, who immediately ordered that Sainte-Croix's arms should be carried to Azevedo, and that if he persisted in his refusal, the dressings of his wounds should be taken off, and he should be carried back to the field and laid in the situation in which he had been lying when his second had intervened on his behalf. Sainte-Croix wisely gave way, and that was the end of the matter for the two combatants, although punctilious commentators went on discussing it for years – some arguing that Azevedo had no right to his adversary's arms once he had forgotten them, while others maintained that Sainte-Croix should have been dispatched, seeing that the duel was to have been mortal and the combatants' arms had been handed to them by the Prior of Messina.

The strict and, to modern minds, horrifying etiquette of the duel of chivalry is also well illustrated by a duel fought at Naples between Monsieur de Bayard, the master of the lists in the Azevedo-Sainte-Croix affair, and a Spanish captain called Don Alonzo de Soto Mayor. The latter had been a prisoner of Bayard's and had afterwards complained so insultingly of the treatment he had received that the Frenchman had offered him the satisfaction of a meeting on foot or on horseback. On the appointed day, Bayard appeared mounted on a charger, dressed in white – 'in token of his humility' we are told – and accompanied by two hundred gentlemen. Don Alonzo, however, decided that they should fight on foot, having heard that the French knight was suffering from a recurrence of a troublesome fever; and although Bayard's seconds urged him to object on the ground of his illness, the Chevalier rejected their plea.

Entering the lists, both combatants knelt down to pray, but Bayard prostrated himself on the ground and kissed the earth before getting up and walking towards his adversary 'as gaily as if he were stepping into a ballroom'. The Spaniard, who was no less confident, advanced in his turn and calmly asked him: '*Señor Bayardo, que me quereys?*' – to which the Chevalier replied: 'To defend my honour.' The two men then started fighting, and for a few minutes several blows were exchanged without any result, until Bayard, instead of parrying one of Don Alonzo's thrusts, let it glance past and promptly drove the point of his own lance four inches into his adversary's throat. The Spaniard closed with his opponent and the two fell to the ground together. Struggling free, Bayard drew his dagger and thrust it into the other man's nostrils, saying: 'Surrender, Señor Alonzo—or you are a dead man!' It was a superfluous threat, for, as the Spaniard's second told him: '*Señor Bayardo, es muerto; vincido haveys!*'

No one, the chronicler records, could have been more distressed than the victor himself, who 'would have given a hundred thousand crowns to have conquered the Spaniard alive'. As it was, he knelt down, kissed the ground three times, and then dragged his enemy's body off the field, saying to Don Alonzo's second: 'Don Diego, have I done enough?' The other sadly replied: 'Too much, Señor Bayardo, for the honour of Spain.'

Finally, Bayard observed to Don Diego that he would make him a present of the corpse, although he was entitled to do what he wished with it – an act of extreme generosity for which the chroniclers vie with one another in praising him. The fact remains that even this paragon of knights was not content to leave his adversary's body on the field, but submitted it to the indignity of being dragged out of the lists – either to emphasize the fact of his victory or simply to assert his rights.

It is scarcely a matter for surprise that the Church, not so much out of principle as because the jurisprudence of the sword interfered with that of the altar, should have condemned the duel of chivalry even more strongly than it condemned the tournament. Prelates such as Gregory of Tours, Avitus and Agobard inveighed against it; anathemas were hurled upon it by the councils of Valence in 855, of Limoges in 994, and of Trent as late as 1563; while several Popes, including Nicholas I, Alexander III, Celestine III and Julius II, excommunicated all sovereigns who allowed duelling to take place in their realms. But all these anathemas and interdicts were in vain; and Charles IX of France for one flouted the authority of the Church in 1564, when he issued an edict expressly reserving to himself the power of authorizing duels when he thought fit. The only restriction placed on duelling by the Church and gradually accepted all over Europe was the *Treuga Dei* or Truce of God mentioned earlier in this work; promulgated by the Council of Toulujes in Roussillon in 1041, it prohibited duelling on all feast-days and from Wednesday evening until Monday morning in each week – a considerable reduction in the fighting-time of irascible knights.

In England, too, the duel of chivalry thrived in spite of the Church's disapproval. Although introduced into this country in the twelfth century, it did not become really established until the reign of Edward III (1327–77), who set the seal of royal approval on the practice by himself challenging the French King Philippe to a duel in 1340. He also instituted a Court of Chivalry which not only decided matters of precedence, coats of arms, and so on, but also had summary jurisdiction in all cases of offences committed by knights. His successor, Richard II (1377–99), followed Edward's example by proposing to fight a duel with Charles VI of France in 1383. Despite his admirably humane motive – 'to stay the effusion of Christian blood and the desolation of the land' – this challenge met with no better response than Edward's; but with Richard's approval the duel of chivalry flourished in England during his reign as never before.

It was fought according to much the same rules as on the Continent, and was usually terminated in the same bloody fashion, with the vanquished being either stabbed with a dagger if it was an ordinary encounter, or hanged and drawn if, as was often the case, it was a duel to decide an accusation of treason. Only rarely was any mercy shown at the conclusion of a duel of chivalry, as it was in the celebrated and otherwise typical encounter between Sir David de Lindsay and John, Lord Welles in 1390.

These two knights fought as the result of an argument at a banquet in Scotland as to the respective courage of the English and the Scots. Since the two countries had concluded a three years' truce in 1389, it was impossible to settle the argument with a full-scale battle, and Lord Welles, the English ambassador to the court of the Scottish king, decided to solve the dilemma by issuing a challenge to fight a mortal combat with any Scottish knight in defence of his national honour – a challenge which was taken up by Sir David de Lindsay.

The duel took place on May 6, 1390, on Old London Bridge, watched by Richard II and his Queen, as well as a huge crowd gathered in the neighbouring houses, on the banks, and in the boats on the river. As the heralds' trumpets sounded for the first course, the two knights rode full-tilt towards each other, breaking their spears as they clashed; but whereas Lord Welles swayed a little at the impact, Sir David sat motionless on his horse, so that the people indignantly accused him of being fastened to his saddle. To prove the contrary, he dismounted, knelt before the King and Queen, and then jumped back into his saddle – a feat which, in view of the tremendous weight of the armour he was wearing, not unnaturally plunged the spectators into astounded silence.

In the second course, the two combatants' spears were once again shattered, but 'without anie great hurt on either part'. The third assault, however, was decisive, for Lord Welles was knocked out of his saddle and fell heavily to the ground. Sir David promptly leapt from his horse, and a groan went up from the crowd, since they imagined that the Scot was going to give their champion the traditional *coup de grâce* with his dagger. But instead, Sir David took off Welles' helmet and held his fallen adversary in a gentle embrace until help arrived and he could be taken home. The Scottish knight even pushed compassion to the extent of visiting the English knight's bedside every day, and when he eventually left London at the end of the month, he took with him the admiration and gratitude of the whole population.

Picturesque and popular though it was, the duel of chivalry was already doomed when this encounter took place, for the mounted knight was steadily losing ground to the unmounted archer. It is difficult to state with any certainty when the last duel of chivalry was fought in England, but it is believed to have been in 1492, when Sir James Parker and Sir Hugh Vaughan met in mortal combat at a tournament at Richmond. In France, the borderline between trial by combat, duel of chivalry and duel of honour was just as hard to draw; but it can be argued that the last French duel of chivalry was the encounter between Jarnac and La Chastaigneraye in 1547, which not only partook of all three institutions but was one of the most famous duels of all time. This duel owes its fame partly to the fact that La Chastaigneraye was the finest swordsman and wrestler in France, revered by his contemporaries and praised to the skies by his nephew Brantôme, but chiefly to the unexpected stroke by which Jarnac cut the ham of each of La Chastaigneraye's legs – a stroke known ever since as the *coup de Jarnac*. Since Brantôme could never bring himself to describe in detail his uncle's humiliating defeat and painful death, we cannot do better than consult Cockburn's vivid description of this classic fight:

> The persons were the Lords of Chastaigneraye and of Jarnac, who were both neighbours and kinsmen. The first had said to Francis I that the other was maintained so plentifully by his mother-in-law, with whom he had unlawful conversation. The

King told this to Jarnac, for whom he had a great affection. Upon which Jarnac said to the King that Chastaigneraye had lied to him: but he not only maintaining what he had said, but adding that Jarnac had divers times owned it to himself, Jarnac did earnestly supplicate the King that the truth might be tried by combat; which Francis I granted, but afterwards recalled.

Upon his death, an earnest supplication was made to his successor, Henry II who, with the advice of his council, not only allowed, but appointed it at Saint-Germain-en-Laye, on July 10, 1547, when the King, the whole court, the constable, admiral, and marshals of France being present, the two parties were brought before the King, attended by their several friends and trumpets, when each took the usual oaths. After this they were led to their several pavilions, where they were dressed for the combat, each having a friend and confidant in the other's pavilion while this was doing. It is said that Jarnac was but newly recovered of a sickness, and that he whispered to a friend, if he did not trust to the goodness of his cause, he should fear the acting of the part of a poltroon. When all the usual preamble of the ceremonies was over, they were called out by the King's trumpet, and by his herald commanded to end their difference by combat. Chastaigneraye was observed to brave it with some insolence; but Jarnac carried it modestly and humbly.

Each attacked the other with great vigour; and, after several strokes and trifling wounds on both sides, while Chastaigneraye was making a pass at Jarnac, he fetched a stroke which cut the ham of Chastaigneraye's left leg, and presently redoubling his stroke, cut also the ham of the right; upon which Chastaigneraye fell to the ground, and the other ran up to him, telling him that now his life was at his discretion, yet he would spare it *if he would restore him his honour, and acknowledge his offence to God and the King*. Chastaigneraye answering nothing, Jarnac turned to the King, and, kneeling down, prayed *that now he might be so happy as to be esteemed by him a man of honour; and, seeing his honour was restored, he would make his majesty a present of the other's life, desiring his offence might be pardoned, and never more imputed to him or his, being the inconsiderate act of youth*: to which the King made no answer. The former returned to his antagonist, and finding him still on the ground, lifted up his face and hands to Heaven, and said: *Lord, I am not worthy: not to me, but unto thy name be thanks!* Having said this, he prayed Chastaigneraye to confess his error: but, instead of this, the latter raised himself on his knee, and, having a sword and buckler in his hand, offered a pass at Jarnac, who told him that if he offered to resist any more he would kill him, and the other bid him to do it; without, however, doing him any harm, Jarnac made a second humble address to the King to accept Chastaigneraye's life, to which the King made no manner of reply.

Whereupon Jarnac coming back to his antagonist, who was lying stretched out upon the ground, his sword out of his hand and his dagger out of its sheath, he accosted him with the fair words of *old friend and companion*, entreated him to remember his Creator, and to let them become friends again. But he attempting to turn himself without the signs of repentance and submission, Jarnac took away his sword and dagger, and laid them at the King's feet, with repeated supplication to interpose for Chastaigneraye's life; which the King at last *was advised to do*, and ordered some of the officers to go to him, and surgeons to take care of his life; but he would not suffer his wounds to be dressed, being wearied of life because of his disgrace, and so died in a little time through the loss of blood. It being told the King that, according to custom, Jarnac should be carried in triumph, Jarnac protested against it, saying that he affected no ostentation or vain glory, that he had been only desirous to have his honour restored, and was contented with that; upon which the King made him this compliment, that he *fought like Caesar and spoke like Aristotle*. Yet the King's inclinations were towards Chastaigneraye. The poor lady, Jarnac's mother-in-law, whose honour was at stake too, was all the while at Saint-Cloud, fasting and praying, and waiting impatiently the issue of this purgation of her innocency.

As can be seen, this remarkable fight was conducted with all the pageantry of the traditional duel of chivalry and all the solemn purposefulness of the ancient trial by combat. Henceforth, however, duels would be fought with less pomp and ceremony, between gentlemen rather than between knights, and as private settlements rather than public battles. The age of the modern duel of honour had arrived.

3 · The Duel of Honour

Probably no better brief account exists of the evolution of the duel of honour than that given in 1610 by John Selden, in his *The Duello, or Single Combat*, where he wrote that 'truth, honor, freedome and curtesie being as incidents to perfit chivalry upon the lye given, fame impeached, body wronged, or curtesie taxed, a custom hath bin among the French, English, Burguignons, Italians, Almans and the Northern people (which as Ptolomey notes are alwaies inclined to liberty) to seek revenge of their wrongs on the body of their accuser and that by private combat *seul à seul*, without judicial lists appointed them.'

However much we may nowadays disapprove of this 'private combat *seul à seul*', the duel of honour in Selden's day, conducted at every stage in accordance with a strict code of rules, was a considerable step in the direction of humanity and law, superseding as it did the murderous assaults so common in the fifteenth century and known in England as 'killing affrays'. But if the fair fight between two men armed with equal weapons was to become an accepted and established institution, the rules governing it had to be generally understood and stringently enforced. Hence the multiplicity of treatises published all over Europe between the sixteenth and nineteenth centuries attempting to regulate every circumstance of the duel, from the cause of the quarrel through the challenge and the choice of weapons to the fight itself.

The causes of duels varied in both nature and seriousness. For the man imbued with a chivalrous respect for the opposite sex, an injury or insult to a woman to whom he was related or attached was the gravest and most obvious reason for a duel. As Bosquett put it, 'I have never known a man whose heart

3 · *Judicial combat. An illumination from the late fifteenth-century 'Chronique d'Angleterre' by Jean de Wavrin*

4 · *Fight between Chevalier Maquer and the dog belonging to Aubry de Montdidier, whom Maquer was thought to have killed. A nineteenth-century engraving*

was in the right place bring an action for damages against another for seducing a beloved wife, a daughter, etc. For these and such like offences the law can make no adequate retribution – in such a state life is a burthen, which cannot be laid down or supported, till death either terminates his own existence or that of the despoiler of his peace and honour.' For another man, the slap or the blow was the mortal, unforgivable offence, while yet another considered a slur on fame or reputation a more serious provocation. But most authorities on the subject, at least in the seventeenth century, agreed that 'giving the lie' was the gravest provocation of all.

'It is reputed so great a shame', wrote Bryskett in 1606, in *A Discourse of Civill Life*, 'to be accounted a lyer, that any other injury is cancelled by giving the lie, and he that receiveth it standeth so charged in his honour and reputation, that he cannot disburden himself of that imputation, but by the striking of him that hath so given it, or by chalenging him the combat.' Small wonder, then, that a contemporary treatise on honour and arms contained a whole chapter on 'the nature and divertise of lies', where they were divided into vain, conditional and certain lies, and subdivided into general and special categories. Or that Touchstone, in *As You Like It*, should have carefully enumerated the seven causes of a quarrel – the retort courteous, the quip modest, the reply churlish, the reproof valiant, the countercheck quarrelsome, the lie with circumstance and the lie direct – before concluding: 'All these you may avoid but the lie direct; and you may avoid that too with an *if*. . . . Your *if* is the only peace-maker; much virtue in an *if*.' These niceties, after all, were all too often matters of life and death.

Once he had recognized that an offence was so heinous that only bloodshed could wipe it out, an offended party had to grapple with the problems of sending a challenge, choosing seconds and selecting weapons before facing up to the actual duel. Here he could turn for help to a variety of Codes of Duelling which provided an answer to every problem of procedure, however delicate or difficult. The most important and comprehensive of these works for the English-speaking world was undoubtedly the Irish *code duello* 'adopted at the Clonmel Summer Assizes, 1777, for the government of duellists, by the gentlemen of Tipperary, Galway, Mayo, Sligo and Roscommon, and prescribed for general adoption throughout Ireland'. This code, though relating particularly to the pistol duel in Ireland towards the end of the eighteenth century, was basically the same as earlier and later codes enforced in England

and on the Continent. The rules which it contained, and which were known in Galway as the twenty-six commandments, were as follows:

I. The first offence requires the first apology, though the retort may have been more offensive than the insult. Example: A tells B he is impertinent, etc. B retorts that he lies; yet A must make the first apology, because he gave the first offence, and (after one fire) B may explain away the retort by subsequent apology.

II. But if the parties would rather fight on, then, after two shots each (but in no case before), B may explain first and A apologize afterwards.

N.B. *The above rules apply to all cases of offences in retort not of a stronger class than the example.*

III. If a doubt exists who gave the first offence, the decision rests with the seconds. If they will not decide or cannot agree, the matter must proceed to two shots, or to a hit if the challenger requires it.

IV. When the lie direct is the first offence, the aggressor must either beg pardon in express terms, exchange two shots previous to apology, or three shots followed by explanation, or fire on till a severe hit be received by one party or the other.

V. As a blow is strictly prohibited under any circumstances among gentlemen, no verbal apology can be received for such an insult. The alternatives, therefore, are:

UNIVERSAL SONGSTER; OR, MUSEUM OF MIRTH.

The Captain missed Pat, for it was not a lucky shot;
Pat Holloway fired next, and a very fine duck he shot.

The offender handing a cane to the injured party to be used on his back, at the same time begging pardon; firing until one or both are disabled; or exchanging three shots and then begging pardon without the proffer of the cane.

N.B. *If swords are used, the parties engage until one is well blooded, disabled, or disarmed, or until, after receiving a wound and blood being drawn, the aggressor begs pardon.*

VI. If A gives B the lie and B retorts by a blow (being the two greatest offences), no reconciliation can take place till after two discharges each or a severe hit, after which B may beg A's pardon for the blow, and then A may explain simply for the lie, because a blow is never allowable, and the offence of the lie, therefore, merges in it. (See preceding rule.)

N.B. *Challenges for undivulged causes may be conciliated on the ground after one shot. An explanation or the slightest hit should be sufficient in such cases, because no personal offence transpired.*

VII. But no apology can be received in any case after the parties have actually taken their ground without exchange of shots.

VIII. In the above case no challenger is obliged to divulge his cause of challenge (if private) unless required by the challenged so to do before their meeting.

IX. All imputations of cheating at play, races, etc., to be considered equivalent to a blow, but may be reconciled after one shot, on admitting their falsehood and begging pardon publicly.

X. Any insult to a lady under a gentleman's care or protection to be considered as by one degree a greater offence than if given to the gentleman personally, and to be regarded accordingly.

XI. Offences originating or accruing from the support of ladies' reputations to be considered as less unjustifiable than any others of the same class, and as admitting of slighter apologies by the aggressor. This is to be determined by the circumstances of the case, but always favourably to the lady.

XII. No dumb firing or firing in the air is admissible in any case. The challenger ought not to have challenged without receiving offence, and the challenged ought, if he gave offence, to have made an apology before he came on the ground; therefore children's play must be dishonourable on one side or the other, and is accordingly prohibited.

XIII. Seconds to be of equal rank in society with the principals they attend, inasmuch as a second may either choose or chance to become a principal and equality is indispensable.

XIV. Challenges are never to be delivered at night, unless the party to be challenged intends leaving the place of offence before morning; for it is desirable to avoid all hot-headed proceedings.

XV. The challenged has the right to choose his own weapons unless the challenger gives his honour he is no swordsman, after which, however, he cannot decline any second species of weapon proposed by the challenged.

XVI. The challenged chooses his ground, the challenger chooses his distance, the seconds fix the time and terms of firing.

XVII. The seconds load in presence of each other, unless they give their mutual honours that they have charged smooth and single, which shall be held sufficient.

XVIII. Firing may be regulated, first, by signal; secondly by word of command; or, thirdly at pleasure, as may be agreeable to the parties. In the latter case, the parties may fire at their reasonable leisure, but second presents and rests are strictly prohibited.

XIX. In all cases a misfire is equivalent to a shot, and a snap or a non-cock is to be considered as a misfire.

XX. Seconds are bound to attempt a reconciliation before the meeting takes place, or after sufficient firing or hits as specified.

XXI. Any wound sufficient to agitate the nerves and necessarily make the hand shake must end the business for that day.

XXII. If the cause of meeting be of such a nature that no apology or explanation can or will be received, the challenged takes his ground and calls on the challenger to proceed as he chooses. In such cases firing at pleasure is the usual practice, but may be varied by agreement.

XXIII. In slight cases the second hands his principal but one pistol, but in gross cases two, holding another case ready charged in reserve.

XXIV. When the seconds disagree and resolve to exchange shots themselves, it must be at the same time and at right angles with their principals. If with swords, side by side, with five paces' interval.

XXV. No party can be allowed to bend his knee or cover his side with his left hand, but may present at any level from the hip to the eye.

XVI. None can either advance or retreat if the ground is measured. If no ground be measured, either party may advance at his pleasure, even to the touch of muzzles, but neither can advance on his adversary after the fire, unless the adversary steps forward on him.

N.B. *The seconds on both sides stand responsible for this last rule being strictly observed, bad cases having occurred from neglecting it.*

N.B. *All matters and doubts not herein mentioned will be explained and cleared up by application to the Committee, who meet alternately at Clonmel and Galway at the quarter sessions for that purpose.*

CROW RYAN, President.
JAMES KEOGH, AMBY BODKIN, Secretaries.

One vital point on which this code failed to give any advice was the wording of the cartel, with the result that more often than not insulting challenges were dispatched which ruled out all possibility of a reconciliation. If our prospective duellist consulted his Shakespeare, all that he found by way of advice was this lesson from Sir Toby Belch: 'Go, write in a martial hand; be curst and brief; it is no matter how witty, so it be eloquent, and full of invention . . . if thou thou'st him some thrice, it shall not be amiss; and as many lies as will lie in thy sheet of paper.' But brevity could be extremely offensive – witness this 'curst and brief' Italian cartel:

> *Signore: S'il suo coraggio è grande come la sua impudenza, m'incontra questa sera nel bosco.* (Sir: if your courage is equal to your impudence, you will meet me tonight in the wood.)

Another challenge which left little scope for peace-making was made in this letter from a fiery young man to a barrister who, he considered, had subjected him to an unfair cross-examination:

> Sir: You are renowned for great activity with your tongue, and justly, as circumstances that have occurred today render evident. I am celebrated for my activity with another weapon, equally annoying and destructive; and if you would oblige me by appointing a time and place, it would afford me the greatest gratification to give you a specimen of my proficiency.
>
> Your most obedient----.

Experienced duellists, however, generally considered cartels of this sort ungentlemanly; and one authority, in a handbook on duelling, observed that 'the most accredited mode is to conduct the whole affair with the greatest possible politeness, expressing the challenge clearly, avoiding all strong language, simply stating, first, the cause of offence; secondly, the reason why it is considered a duty to notice the matter; thirdly, naming a friend; and lastly, requesting the appointing of a time and place'. He added, in a helpful and efficient note, that 'if abroad, it is proper to state at the foot of the letter the length of the challenger's sword-blade; and a correct copy should be kept of all correspondence that takes place'.

Even more important than the wording of the cartel was the choice of a friend to deliver the challenge and act as a second, especially if it was hoped to avoid useless bloodshed. 'There is not one cause in fifty', wrote the peaceable Bosquett, 'where discreet seconds might not settle the difference and reconcile the parties before they came into the field'; while a famous fencing master was often heard to declare that 'it is not the sword or the pistol that kills, but the seconds'. All authorities were agreed that seconds should be men of experience and moral courage, justice and urbanity; and two authorities specifically debarred infidels and Irishmen – the former because, according to Brantôme, 'it is not proper that an unbeliever should witness the shedding of Christian blood, which would delight him,' and the latter because 'nine out of ten Irishmen have such an innate love of fighting that they cannot bring an affair to an amicable adjustment'. While it is unlikely that many infidels were invited to act as seconds in European duels, English travellers in Ireland frequently had to deal with native seconds and were usually extremely critical of them. Thus one English witness of a duel in Ireland later recalled that 'the Irish second was so exacting in the terms of a required apology, that nothing but abject cowardice could account for the acquiescence of the challenged party; and when, upon its being shown to the challenger, the latter pointed out that the word "apology" was misspelt, having two *p*s, the Irishman insisted that he was right, high words ensued, and the principal had the greatest difficulty in appeasing his wrath, which well-nigh rendered a meeting necessary'. And another writer who seconded an English doctor in an encounter outside Dublin has left us this account of the affair, which illustrates not only his opinion of the Irish character but also the difficulties facing any second in any duel:

> We got to the ground at six, the hour appointed, and shortly after the others arrived; the second was the same I expected. After a distant salute I took him aside, and observed that it was rather unfortunate that we had not had an opportunity of talking the affair over before we came there; but that, as it was not of a desperate nature, being a mere war of words, I conceived it might be as much to their honour to make a mutual apology as to fight, when he immediately vociferated that he would not consent that his friend should either give or take any apology, that they came there to fight, and that whilst a ball remained (pulling out a handfull of bullets) or until one or the other fell, they would not quit the field. In this, however, his principal did not second him.
>
> Whilst charging the pistols, our opponent's second addressed himself to my friend in these words: 'Sir, I am glad to meet you here; I have an affair to settle with you the

> moment this is over, if you survive my friend.' I immediately called his principal forward, and told him the unmanly and infamous declaration of his second, whom, as it seemed, he had brought there with a view either to intimidate or to assassinate my friend, but that, as I came there to protect him at all points, he must instantly take the ground with *me*, or immediately withdraw his declaration and apologize; the latter, by the advice of his principal, who disapproved of his conduct, he preferred.
>
> We then proceeded to measure the ground, which he proposed should be seven yards. In this, however, I overruled him, after much resistance, and placed them at twelve yards asunder. By agreement, they fired at the same moment, my friend's ball passing through the hat of his opponent, and his ball grazing the left jaw of my friend, and would certainly have broken both jaws had he not given a full front face. After the first fire, I interfered again, and having made an impression, reconciled them, much to the visible dissatisfaction of my opponent, who had put the second pistol into the hands of his friend, exclaiming that the town would call it a shabby business if they did not proceed. They made, notwithstanding, mutual apologies, shook hands, and ever after lived on a friendly and intimate footing.

After the choice of seconds came the choice of weapons, which on the Continent lay with the offended party or challenger, whereas in the English speaking countries it lay with the offender or challenged party. The duellist with the privilege of deciding the weapons to be used enjoyed a considerable advantage over his opponent, since it enabled him to insist on arms in whose use he had been given special training or which he knew would embarrass his adversary. One knight, for example, in the age of the duel of chivalry, having been taught invariably to strike in the region of the heart, insisted on fighting in a suit of armour with an opening of a hand's-breadth in each cuirass over the heart: the result was naturally fatal to his antagonist. Similarly Jarnac, in his famous duel with La Chastaigneraye, called for the wearing of a cumbersome guard on the left arm, because, according to the admittedly biased Brantôme, he was aware that his adversary, who had recently been wounded in that arm, would find the unaccustomed apparatus both awkward and painful. Brantôme also alleges that Jarnac, like many duellists, used the choice of arms as a subterfuge to gain time and cause trouble and expense, proposing no less than thirty different weapons to be used both on horseback and on foot, and also specifying various horses with different kinds of saddle: if La Chastaigneraye had not been a man of means, and also assisted by his royal master, he could not have afforded to fight the duel, and indeed, on receiving the challenge, he is said to have remarked: 'This man wants to fight both my valour and my purse.'

A duellist with the choice of weapons could also resort to the skill and cunning of armourers to obtain an unfair advantage. It is said, for instance, that an armourer in Milan had brought his method of tempering steel to such a pitch of perfection that the solidity of the sword and dagger depended entirely on the way in which they were handled: on the hands of an inexperienced man the weapons were shivered to pieces, whereas in the grasp of a combatant who was familiar with them they were as trusty as the stoutest Toledo blade.

The sword has, of course, always been the favourite duelling weapon down the centuries, although in the Middle Ages it was closely rivalled by the *hâche d'armes*, or poleaxe, and in the nineteenth century by the pistol. In form and appearance, however, it has changed considerably, as armourers have improved their techniques and as the circumstances of single combat have altered. Thus in the duel of chivalry combatants who rejected the poleaxe were still confined to a choice of heavy, clumsy swords: the two-hander, the 'hand-and-a-half' or bastard sword, and the ordinary one-hand sword, all of which were double-edged, pointed, and provided with a heavy pommel, and the long, stiff estoc, which was usually pointed only and was intended to penetrate strong plate armour. During the second half of the sixteenth century, as the *champ clos* gave way to the *duello alla mazza*, these swords were gradually abandoned in favour of the long Hispano-Italian rapier, used in combination with a dagger or a cloak. This rapier had begun its existence as the plain cross-hilted sword of knightly times, but had been furnished with finger-guards which had developed by way of the so-called 'swept' hilt to the cup. Considerable skill in its use was necessary, since armour had been abandoned, and the art of fencing, taught by Italian masters, was widely cultivated in the seventeenth century. But even the most proficient swordsman found the rapier, which was seldom less than four feet long, so unwieldly that something of a defensive nature had to be carried in the left hand: either a dagger, the most favoured form of defence, or a cloak, which was used to dash aside the opponent's thrusts or to entangle his sword.

Some duellists in this period preferred the dagger to the rapier, and dagger-fighting was practised either 'single', that is to say without any defensive weapon, or 'double', when it was used together with a cloak, a buckler, or a second dagger. The dagger itself had a strong, rather thick blade, about twelve inches long, with two very sharp edges. Early exponents of the single

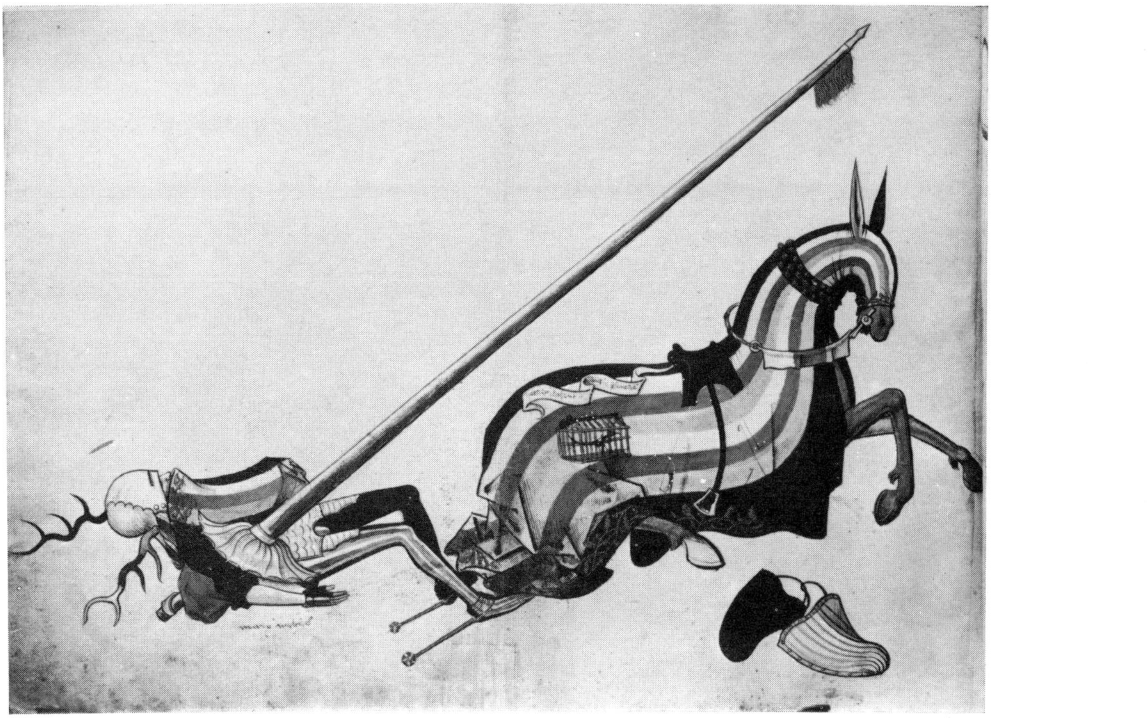

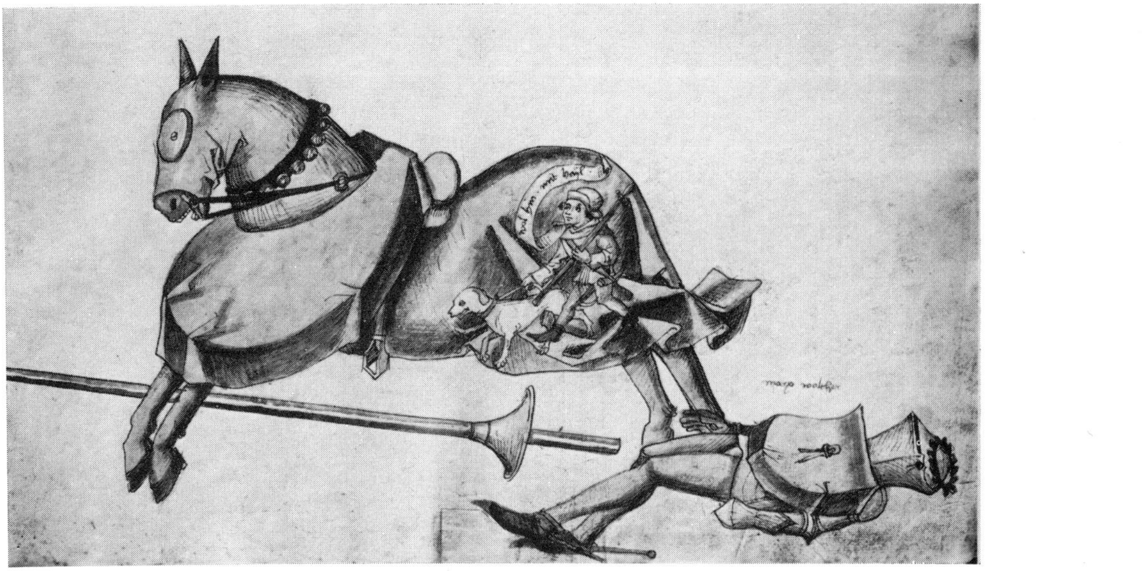

5 · *(a) and (b) 'Unhorsed': drawings by Marx Walther*, 1500

6 · *The duel of Tristan. An illumination from a late fifteenth-century manuscript of the 'Roman de Tristan'*

7 · A fifteenth-cenutry duel and reconciliation
An illumination from Le Grant's 'Livre des Bonnes Moeurs'

8 · *The tourney in which Henri II was mortally wounded in 1559. An early French woodcut*

dagger fight used to grasp the adversary's weapon in a heavily gloved hand, whereupon armourers took to furnishing their daggers with saw-like teeth set backwards like barbs – only to be countered by glove-makers who lined the palms of their gauntlets with fine mail. To keep abreast of these refinements it was essential for the duellist to take lessons from a master of the art of dagger-fighting, or at least to consult a hand-book such as George Silver's *Bref Instructions*, from which these hints are taken:

> *Of the Single Dagger fyght against the lyke weapon.*
>
> 1. First know y^{t} to this weapon ther belongeth no Wards nor gryps, but against such a one as is foolehardy and will suffer himself to have a ful stabb in the face or bodye to hazard the geving of Another, then against him you may use yor left hand in throwing him asyde, or strike up his heeles after you have stab^{d} him.
>
> 2. In this dagg^{r} fyght, yō must use cōtynual motion so shal he not be able to put yō to ye cloze or grype, because yor cōtynuall motion disappointeth him of his true place, and the more ferce he is in runynge in, the soon^{r} he gayneth you the place, wherby he is wounded, and yō not anything the rather endangered.
>
> 3. The mann^{r} of handling yor cōtynuall motion is this, kepe out of distance and strik or thrust at his hand, Arme, face or body, y^{t} shal press upō yō, and yf he defend blow or thrust w^{t} his dagg^{r} make yō blow or thrust at his hand.
>
> 4. If he com in w^{t} his left legg forewards or w^{t} the right, do you strike at y^{t} prte as soone as it shalbe w^{t} in yor reach, remembering y^{t} yō use contynual motion in yor prgression and regressyon according to yor twyfold gov^{r}nors.
>
> Although the dagg^{r} fyght be thought a verye dangerous fyght be reason of ye shortnes and synglenes therof, yet the fyght therof being handled as is aforsaid is as sef and as defencive as is the fight of any other weapon.

The principal drawback of the dagger was, in fact, that it was primarily a defensive weapon, and it was inevitable that once the sword's inadequacies in this respect had been corrected, the dagger would lose favour. This development occurred about the middle of the seventeenth century, when a radical change in the sword took place. The long rapier was considerably shortened and therefore lightened, so that it became possible to effect a few simple parries with the sword itself, and the need to carry something of a defensive nature in the left hand was obviated. The new type of sword, the flamberge, was still quite long, but it soon gave way to the small sword in its earliest form: a weapon about thirty inches in length, with a flat double-edged blade. This flat blade was too supple to be trustworthy, so the section was altered to a diamond shape, a change which made the sword stiffer but at the same time heavier, with the result that some masters taught their pupils to hold it occasionally in both hands.

By the early eighteenth century both flat and diamond-shaped blades had disappeared, and had been replaced by a blade with a triangular section, in the type of small sword known as the colichemarde. Finally, soon after the middle of the eighteenth century, the rather lumpy colichemarde was abandoned in favour of the slender, featherweight small sword *par excellence*, which won enduring popularity as a duelling weapon.

By this time, however, the duelling pistol had begun to supplant the sword, notably in England, as being a means of ensuring a more evenly matched combat. It was thought that if pistols were used, and especially if the two adversaries were obliged to fire without taking aim, neither duellist would enjoy an appreciable advantage over the other. However, during the great era of the duelling pistol – which in England lasted from about 1770 to the middle of the nineteenth century – gunsmiths vied with one another in producing refinements which would give purchasers of their pistols greater fire-power and a better chance of survival. To take only one gunsmith, Joe Manton – admittedly one of the greatest of all makers of duelling pistols – he invented three major aids to victory: a hydraulic barrel tester, a fast-firing recessed breech, and a trigger spring; while he also introduced improvements to the priming-pan and the touch-holes.

Of all these refinements, the best known was probably the hair-trigger, which enabled many a duellist to get in his shot before his opponent. As an early description of this device explained, 'the trigger is cocked against a powerful spring by pressing it forward until it engages with a scear; a very slight pressure, a mere touch on the trigger, now frees it from this engagement and, driven by the spring, it flies up and hits the scear arm, thus discharging the main lock more rapidly and with less disturbance of aim than the ordinary finger-operated trigger'. Another popular device, though one which flouted the duelling code, was the half-rifled barrel: rifling was strictly forbidden, but unscrupulous duellists circumvented the ban by using pistols which were rifled at the breech end but not at the muzzle.

However much skill the gunsmith had lavished on a pistol, all his work could be, and often was, undone before the duel itself by a careless owner or incompetent seconds. 'It frequently occurs', wrote one authority, 'that the flints are so badly adjusted and so bad in themselves, through the ignorance or inattention of the Seconds, and the pistols so much out of order, that the Principal, who is subject to such remissness in his friend, often stands in a very awkward and precarious state. I have known a pistol snapped a dozen times before it went off, though the flint was often chipped; this was putting a man in serious apprehensions of his life, eleven times oftener than he expected. It is no unusual case that a pistol hangs fire, due to the dampness of the powder, or the foulness of the touchhole, by which you always lose your aim, and, of course, your fire, and, it may be, your life.'

In the case of muzzle-loading pistols, the range depended to a considerable degree on the amount of powder used, and it was essential for a second to know the correct amount for his principal's weapon. 'Take a measure,' advised one expert, 'which will hold about six or seven percussion caps full of powder which is about the quantity necessary, and pour its contents into the barrel: the exact proportion of powder will soon be apparent by observing how the balls are flattened when fired at an iron target.' The dire consequences of an error at this stage were emphasized by Abraham Bosquett in this grim warning:

> It has been known, that by injudiciously overloading, the Principal has been killed by his own pistol bursting, a part of the barrel having entered the temple; and it has frequently happened, through the same cause, that the pistol-hand has been shattered to pieces. I was present on an occasion when the Principal shot his own Second through the cheek, knocking in one of his double teeth, not by the ball, but by a part of the pistol barrel, that was blown out near the muzzle. I was also on the ground when a Principal shot himself through his foot, at the instep, which nearly cost him his life, but put an end to farther proceedings at the moment; his Second had given him his pistol at full cock, with a hair trigger, which he held dangling at his side, before the word was given, and in that position it went off. On another occasion the Second had charged his friend's pistol so carelessly, that the ball and powder had fallen out before he presented; when, but not till after receiving the opposite fire, snapping, and burning prime (the matter being then accommodated), he discovered, on making several attempts to discharge his pistol in the air, that it was unloaded.

Even if our duellist's pistols were made by the most highly skilled gunsmith, equipped with all the latest refinements, carefully maintained by himself and accurately loaded by his second, they still suffered – at least until the 1830s – from one apparently ineradicable defect: they did not shoot straight. One writer estimated the 'dispart' as half an inch in a distance of twelve to fifteen yards, but another maintained that he had 'never found any pistol at fourteen yards even when bound in a vice lodge the ball nearer than in inch to the point aimed at, but in general the variation from the right line is three, four, and six times as great'. Bosquett's advice to the duelling man was to find out in advance the exact throw of the ball. In 1817 he wrote:

> It has been almost an invariable maxim with men who are prone to duelling, to ascertain the dispart, or throw, of their pistols, which by repeated trials with the same charge, at a stated distance, a point blank shot, pretty nearly, may be made on every occasion, with a steady hand and quick eye. To come at a precise knowledge of due accuracy in your pistol, it should, in the first instance, be screwed into a vice, or fired repeatedly from a steady hand at the same distance, and with the same quantity of powder; aiming at the center of a circle, of about a foot in diameter, divided by transverse parallel lines, an inch asunder, forming the whole area of the circle in diamonds, or compartments of an inch square; then making your aim precisely at the center, the ball shows its deviation from the right or true visual line, and which being always the same, or very nearly so, with the same quantity of powder, the same ball, at the same distance, the true point blank of your pistol will be found, and by which you will ascertain what angle of the area to level at, when you mean to hit the center – therefore the man who knows his pistols has a deadly advantage against him who does not.

This was certainly the case until the 1830s, when the Dublin firm of William and John Rigby changed the design of their pistol barrels so that the bore was off-centre at the breech end but regular at the muzzle. As John Rigby explained to a meeting of the Royal Dublin Society in 1838, 'by this means we keep the line of sight and the line of bore parallel and our pistols shoot the ball true at all distances, affected only by the parabolic curve common to all projected bodies, and in our shooting gallery he is considered a mere tyro who cannot strike a figure three inches high and one wide'. The result – one which Rigby nobly but rather improbably claimed he had 'calculated on' – was 'that there is not now one hostile meeting for twenty-three there used to be in this country'; and he concluded that 'we are thoroughly convinced that by this means the vicious practice of mortal quarrels from light causes has become most effectually checked'. It is possible that the new-found accuracy of the duelling pistol did something to discourage 'mortal quarrels from light causes' in Ireland, but in some other countries, especially France, pistol-duelling actually gained in popularity and remained in favour until the end of the nineteenth century.

When all the vexed questions of challenge, seconds and weapons had been decided, there remained the duel itself. Here the duellist could no longer derive any benefit from the Code, which in any case it was his second's duty to study. He was more likely to turn for advice to one of the countless manuals of single combat which proliferated during the heyday of the duel. Of all these martial handbooks, probably none was more useful in its time or is more entertaining now than an anonymous manual entitled *The Art of Duelling* published by 'A Traveller' in 1836.

This book naturally dealt at length with such matters as the care and choice of weapons, shooting-practice and so on. But it was when the author came to consider the preparations for an imminent duel that he was most helpful. He insisted that the duellist should not indulge in gloomy thoughts the night before an encounter. 'A man should not allow the idea of becoming a target to make him uneasy; but, treating the matter jocosely, he must summon up all his energy, and declare war against nervous apprehension.' To take his mind off the affair, 'A Traveller' suggested that 'he ought to invite a few friends to dinner, and laugh away the evening over a bottle of port, or, if fond of cards, play a rubber of whist'. And if, when he retired to bed, sleep refused to come, he must 'take some amusing book – one of Sir Walter's novels, if a lover of the romantic; or Byron's *Childe Harold*, if he delights in the sublime; and read until he drops asleep, leaving word with a trusty servant to call him at five, and provide a cup of strong coffee to be taken immediately on rising'. At this point, unfortunately, 'A Traveller' rather spoilt the effect of these encouraging admonitions with a grim afterthought, remarking that 'he should have been careful to secure the services of his medical attendant, who will provide himself with all the necessary apparatus for tying up wounds or arteries, and extracting balls'.

When the fatal morning arrived, the duellist should 'drink his coffee, and take a biscuit with it, directly he rises; then, in washing his face, attend to bathing his eyes well with cold water'. Taking care not to disturb wife or children, if a married man, he should then set out for the *releager* or duelling-ground, preferably in an anonymous postchaise rather than his own carriage, 'in case of molestation by the honourable members of Bow Street'. Before driving off, he should see the pistol-case put into the chaise himself, for 'instances have occurred more than once of pistols being left behind in the confusion of starting, subjecting the parties, of course, to much inconvenience and ridicule'. And on the way, if he should feel the slightest qualms, 'he should stop and take a little soda-water, flavoured with a small wine-glass of brandy, which I can strongly recommend as a most grateful stimulant and corrective'.

Arriving on the ground, preferably in advance of his adversary, 'he should dismount and walk about, coolly puffing his cigar, leaving his second to forward the arrangements and mark out the ground, observing himself, however, that all is correctly done; and when called upon to *leech*, he should step up quietly and firmly, as though he were going to shake hands with an old friend, instead of to shoot one'. The author also advised him to 'cast his eyes closely upon his adversary, and mark if there is any nervous tremulation in his movement', while being careful himself to remain 'as firm and stiff as a statue'.

Once the combatants were in position and had been given their pistols, the others present should go to their respective places, as prescribed by tradition: 'The seconds should retire about eight yards from the line of fire, equidistant from the antagonists; the two surgeons and any friend should be about two yards behind them, and the servants in a line rather further back.' The author admitted that he did not see 'any particular advantage arising from this mode of placing the parties', but conceded that 'it looks better than to see a number of persons straggling round the principals, not infrequently at the risk of their own lives – with hair-triggers in close proximity'. All that now remained for the duellist to do was to adopt his firing stance and await the signal.

any thing but Fair play!

The actual posture adopted by the duellist in a pistol duel was of course of paramount importance. Needless to say, it was customary to stand with the side only turned towards one's antagonist, thus offering him the smallest target-area possible – though one wit suggested that a *bon vivant* should adopt the old method of turning his back to his adversary and firing over his shoulder, 'as only a weapon after the fashion of the Armstrong or Whitworth ordnance could penetrate an alderman's stomach *from behind*', while the portly Charles James Fox is said to have stood full-face to his opponent in one duel, explaining that 'I am as thick one way as the other'. But even standing sideways, a duellist was in serious danger of suffering mortal injury if he had not learnt how to use his arm as a shield to cover himself. As William Douglas wrote in his *Duelling Days in the Army*, 'the method of holding a pistol so that a man's right arm should protect his head or body, or both, was quite an art in the duelling days – one, at the same time, which but a few succeeded in mastering thoroughly. Fighting Fitzgerald, from all accounts, did master it, and to do so he reduced his height five or six inches. His plan was to bend his head over his body until the upper portion of him resembled a bow. His right hand and arm were held in front of his head in such a manner that a ball would have to pan all up his arm before it touched a vulnerable part.'

'A Traveller', in his instructions in the art so thoroughly mastered by Fighting Fitzgerald, wrote that the duellist should 'stand with the right and left shoulder in a line with the object he wishes to hit; his head bent to the right and his eyes fixed on the object. His feet should be almost close together; his left arm hanging down and his right holding the pistol with the muzzle pointing to the ground close at his feet; he should keep his shoulders well back and his stomach drawn in, then stamping his feet twice or thrice on the ground to feel he stands firmly, let him raise his right arm steadily, bending it at the elbow, and drawing the pistol into a line with the object, bring that part of the arm between the shoulder and the elbow close to the side – throw the muscles strongly and let it cover the breast as much as possible.' The duellist, according to his mentor, should single out some point on his target, such as one of the gilt buttons on his adversary's coat. Then, 'A Traveller' continued, 'the arm being closed well into the side and the pistol raised to the proper level, bring the head straight, keeping the eyes turned as much to the right as possible and the pistol directed steadily towards the small object that has been noticed; be cool, collected, and firm, and think of nothing but placing the ball on the proper spot; when the word is given, pull the trigger carefully and endeavour to avoid moving a muscle in the arm or hand – move only the forefinger, and that with just sufficient force to discharge the pistol.'

After that, the result of the encounter was in the lap of the gods. If, despite all the excellent counsel given by 'A Traveller', his reader had the misfortune to be wounded, the author offered him one final word of advice:

> If, upon the discharge, his adversary's ball has taken effect, he must not be alarmed or confused, but quietly submit the part to the examination of his surgeon, who should close round him, with his second, the moment the discharge has taken place.
>
> I cannot impress upon an individual too strongly the propriety of remaining perfectly calm and collected when hit; he must not allow himself to be alarmed or confused; but summoning up all his resolution, treat the matter coolly; and, if he dies, go off with as good a grace as possible.

On this last, all-important point, 'A Traveller', usually so eloquent and helpful, was surprisingly reserved. Yet there were countless examples he could have quoted of duellists who had 'gone off with a good grace'. There were some who had forgiven their opponent before dying, others who had expired without a murmur, and at least one who had courteously asked his unscathed adversary to wear his arm in a sling for a while, so that his own reputation as a shot should not suffer. But the most admirable example of sang-froid in such circumstances was probably that given by Stackpole when mortally wounded in his duel with Cecil. His only observation as he sank to the ground was the faintly surprised comment:

'By George, I've missed him. . . .'

9 · *Fight with axes. A mid-fifteenth-century drawing*

10·(*a*) *The duel between Jarnac and La Chastaigneraye*
A nineteenth-century engraving

10·(*b*) *The 'duel des mignons'*, 1578. *A nineteenth-century engraving*

4 · Duels in France

If it was to Germany that France, like the rest of Europe, was indebted for the trial by combat, it was from Italy that she derived the practice of the duel of honour. During Charles VIII's Italian expeditions at the end of the fifteenth century, and Louis XII's fresh Italian campaigns in the early years of the sixteenth century, the southern vogue for duelling spread to the French army, strongly encouraged, as we have seen, by the Duc de Nemours, and François I did nothing to repress the fashion when he came to the throne. On the contrary, he himself issued a bombastic challenge to Charles V, and in a country as accustomed as France to following any example set by its leader – witness the success enjoyed by the hitherto despised potato once Louis XIV had sported a nosegay of its flowers in his buttonhole – this was enough to incite every French nobleman to draw his sword in defence of his honour on the slightest pretext.

François's successor Henri II, whose reign was ushered in by the famous duel between Jarnac and La Chastaigneraye and concluded by the monarch's own death in a tournament, was too weak a monarch to impose any check on duelling, which obtained greater currency with every year that passed. It was during his reign that a remarkable duel took place between a youth called Châteauneuf and his guardian Lachesnaye, an old gentleman of eighty. The youth, who had challenged his guardian on account of some disrespectful comments he was reported to have made about him, asked Lachesnaye on the duelling-ground whether there was any truth in those reports. The old man asserted on his honour that there was no foundation for them whatever, and his ward accepted his denial; but Lachesnaye would not let the matter rest there.

'You may be satisfied,' he said, 'but I am not; and, since you have given me the trouble of coming here, we must fight. What would all these people who have come here say if they found that we had met here to talk instead of acting? Our honour is at stake, so let us set to.'

They had scarcely begun fighting before Lachesnaye exclaimed: 'Oh, you scoundrel, you are wearing a cuirass! But I'll do for you all the same!' He accordingly started cutting and thrusting at his dishonest opponent's face and throat, but Châteauneuf was in no way disconcerted and within a few minutes ran his old guardian through the body.

Though for ever fighting to defend their honour, the young men of this period were anything but honourable, judging by the incident of Châteauneuf's cuirass and Brantôme's story of another encounter between youth and age, this time during the reign of Henri III. In the course of a royal stag-hunt

in the Bois de Vincennes, the young nephew of Marshal Saint-André picked a quarrel with an elderly gentleman called Matas, and the two of them withdrew to a lonely part of the wood to fight it out. Matas quickly disarmed his opponent, and told him in a fatherly voice: 'In future, young man, learn to handle a sword better, and take care not to attack a man such as me.' However, as he was mounting his horse to ride away, the young man, burning to wipe out the shame of his defeat, stabbed him in the back and killed him. 'Nothing of this deed transpired,' we are told, 'for the young man was the nephew of Marshal Saint-André, whereas the other was only a relation of Madame de Valentinois (the celebrated Diane de Poitiers), who, after the death of Henri II, had lost all her influence at court.' Worse still, the unfortunate Matas was actually blamed for having criticized a proud and honourable youth. 'It is wrong,' declared the chronicler, 'for boastful old fencers to abuse their good fortune, and taunt young men, *car Dieu s'en attriste* – for this grieves God!'

The fighting spirit displayed by the noblemen of the time was quite remarkable. Thus Brantôme tells the story of a duel between a gentleman from Normandy and a chevalier called Refuge, who had taken a boat to cross to the Île du Palais, in order to fight without witnesses. Noticing that some other boats were following them, they jumped ashore, one of them exclaiming: 'For God's sake, let us hurry, for they are coming to separate us!' With these words they set to, and after four lunges they were both dead. The same writer mentions a certain Seigneur de Gensac, who wanted to fight two champion duellists at once; when his friends pointed out that the idea was sheer folly, he merely retorted: 'Why, history is full of such deeds, and, *mon Dieu*, I am determined to have my name recorded.'

The most famous duel, however, which was fought during the reign of Henri III, and the one which distressed the King most of all, was the so-called *duel des mignons*, fought between his favourites Quélus and d'Entragues, who had fallen out over some ladies of the court. With Riberac and Schomberg, who were d'Entragues's seconds, and Maugiron and Livarot, who were Quélus's, they met near the ramparts of the Porte Saint-Antoine, with no one present but 'three or four poor persons, wretched witnesses of the valour of these worthy men'. The principals had scarcely begun fighting before Riberac said to Maugiron: 'I think we ought to reconcile these gentlemen, rather than let them kill each other.' To this unworthy proposal the other replied: 'Sir, I did not come here to tell beads, but to fight.' 'But with whom,' Riberac asked innocently, 'since you are not concerned in this quarrel?' 'Why, with you, to be sure,' replied Maugiron. 'In that case,' said Riberac, 'Let us pray'; and drawing his sword and dagger and crossing their hilts, he fell on his knees. Maugiron was neither a patient, nor, so it seems, a religious man, for before long he told Riberac that 'he had prayed long enough'. At this the two men fell upon each other, and within a few moments Maugiron was dead and Riberac mortally wounded.

Meanwhile, ashamed of standing by while all this slaughter was going on, Schomberg said to Livarot: 'These gentlemen are fighting; what shall we do?' To which Livarot very reasonably replied: 'We cannot do better than fight, to maintain our honour.' Schomberg, who was a German, followed the fighting method of his country and cut off half the left cheek of his opponent, who returned the compliment by running him through the breast, killing him on the spot. Of the two victorious seconds, Riberac died the following day, and Livarot was killed in another duel two years later. As for the principals in the *duel des mignons*, d'Entragues, though severely wounded, made his escape, while Quélus, who had received nineteen cuts, lingered on for over a month. On his deathbed, he complained bitterly that d'Entragues had been armed with a dagger as well as his sword, and that when he had protested that he had no dagger himself, his opponent had retorted: 'So much the worse for you; you ought not to have been such a fool as to have left it at home.' But at least Quélus, when dying and dead, was given all the honour that was his due, and more besides. For although he died continually repeating: 'Oh, my king, my king!' without saying one word of Almighty God, so that a preacher of the time exclaimed in the pulpit that 'the bodies of these blasphemers should be flung into a ditch', the King visited him every day on his deathbed, and gave him and his fellows a princely funeral, a noble monument, and an epitaph peremptorily calling upon God to receive the disrespectful *mignons* into his bosom.

During the next reign, that of Henri IV, despite numerous edicts against duelling, the practice increased enormously, and it was calculated that from his accession to the throne in 1589 until 1607 no fewer than four thousand gentlemen were killed in affairs of honour. Scarcely a day went by without the bloody settlement of some private quarrel, as in the notorious 'duel of the hat' between Lagarde Vallon and Bazanez.

Lagarde was a celebrated duellist of the time whose reputation had attracted the attention and roused the jealousy of another quarrelsome swordsman called Bazanez. The latter decided to have a trial of skill with him, and hit upon the device of sending him a hat adorned with feathers and accompanied by a message stating that he would wear it at the peril of his life. As was only to be expected, Lagarde promptly donned the hat and sallied forth in search of his impudent challenger. The two men had no sooner come together and exchanged the usual civilities before Lagarde inflicted a terrible cut on Bazanez's head, but his opponent's skull was so hard that it deflected the weapon. His second lunge was more successful, and he exclaimed: 'This is for the hat!' as his sword entered Bazanez's body, adding: 'This is for the feathers!' and 'This is for the tassel!' with his following thrusts.

By now Bazanez had lost a great deal of blood, but he made a supreme effort and felled his opponent to the ground. Bending over him, he then stabbed him with his dagger fourteen times between the neck and the navel, remarking: 'I am giving you a scarf to wear with the hat.' In the meantime, as one chronicler of the duel put it, Lagarde was 'not altogether idle', for he bit off part of his opponent's chin and fractured his skull with the pommel of his sword. The two duellists then fainted clean away, and were removed from the battlefield.

Strangely enough, both men recovered from the terrible wounds they had inflicted on each other. Bazanez died a few years later in an ambush, while Lagarde continued to terrorize his contemporaries with bloodthirsty challenges in the following vein:

'I have reduced your house to ashes, ravished your wife, and hanged your children; and I now have the honour to be your mortal enemy, Lagarde.'

The King himself looked favourably upon duelling, at least when there was a serious justification, as can be seen from this characteristic letter he wrote to Duplessis-Mornay when the latter complained of having been insulted by a young nobleman: 'I am deeply grieved to hear of the insult which you have received, in which I share as your sovereign and as your friend. In the first capacity I shall see justice done, both for your sake and mine; and if I bore only the second title, you would find me eager to draw my sword and cheerfully expose my life on your behalf.' Sully, however, the King's minister, used all his influence to check the practice, and it was as a result of his remonstrances that Henri issued a series of edicts declaring duellists to be guilty of *lèse majesté*, and hence liable to the death penalty. The edict of Blois, in 1602, not only condemned both parties in a duel and their seconds to death and the confiscation of their property, but specified that all offended persons should submit their complaint to the governor of their province, for it to be laid before the Constable and Marshals of France. This was the origin of the jurisdiction of the 'point of honour', which would be embodied in an official code during the reign of Louis XIV.

Unfortunately, all these edicts remained without effect, for the King could not bring himself to allow the law to be enforced in all its severity. Bellièvre, the Chancellor of France at this time, maintained that if it were left to him, he would soon put a stop to duelling by refusing a pardon to all offenders, remarking that the most quarrelsome of men would hesitate to fight if they knew that death would be the inevitable consequence of a duel for both parties; but he added that there could be no hope of bringing duelling to a stop so long as the King insisted on meddling with the law. Moreover, the edicts against duelling, though strict enough in their phraseology, contained so many saving clauses as to suggest that they would be unlikely to be put into execution. For example, while duels were denounced as monstrous and criminal, it was specified that an offended party could apply to the sovereign through the Marshals of France for permission to fight; and d'Audiguier, a leading champion of duelling of the time, pertinently remarked 'that as the King never granted permission to fight to any applicant, and had frequently refused it, it was evident that it was useless to make an application, so that the parties came to blows without any reference to authority and were with very few exceptions pardoned by the royal clemency'. Henri IV did in fact grant some seven thousand pardons for duelling in a period of nineteen years, or an average of one a day, so that Sully had good reason to complain 'that the facility with which the King forgave duels tended to multiply them, and hence these fatal examples pervaded the court, the city and the kingdom'.

Matters became even worse during the reign of Louis XIII, which was distinguished by a host of unnecessary duels fought over trifling points of honour. Such a one was the encounter between the eldest of three brothers called Binau and a certain La Faye. The eldest Binau had thrashed his younger brother twice, first for fighting an 'unnatural' duel with the youngest of the family, and then for attacking the inoffensive La Faye; but the latter had refused to accept a reconciliation, and Binau had no option but to fight. They met with pistols on horseback; and while La Faye's shot struck the pommel of Binau's saddle, the latter's ball went through his opponent's body. La Faye's horse galloped off, carrying the wounded man, with Binau calling out: 'La Faye, come back, come back! You are running away!' This futile affair consequently had a bitter ending, for La Faye died the same day, declaring with his last breath that his only grievance was the fact of having been told that he was running away.

The prize for the number of duels fought by a single man at this time, often for the most trivial reasons, probably goes to the Chevalier d'Andrieux. According to Tallemant des Réaux, this worthy had killed seventy-two men in duels by the age of thirty, as he observed one day to a nobleman with whom he was fighting. His opponent had unwisely boasted: 'Chevalier, you will be the tenth man I have killed,' to which d'Andrieux replied: 'And you will be my seventy-second' – suiting the deed to the word. This same d'Andrieux carried his ferocity to supernatural lengths, for he sometimes induced his defeated opponents to deny God, on the promise of their lives, and then cut their throats, in order, so he said, to have the pleasure of killing their souls and bodies together.

Another duellist of this period with a notorious reputation was the Chevalier de Guise, not on account of the number of men he killed, but because he dispatched a father and son in successive encounters. The Chevalier had a violent argument with the Baron de Luz in the Rue Saint-Honoré, one day in January 1613, on the subject of the assassination at Blois of *Le Balafré* or 'Scarface' de Guise in 1588. De Guise dismounted, to place himself on an equal footing with the Baron, and asked de Luz to draw his sword. Although the baron was an old man and had not fought for a great many years, he complied and was promptly run through by his opponent, who calmly wiped his sword, remounted his horse, and rode away in an unconcerned manner.

The dead man had a son of about the same age as the Chevalier, who, as soon as he heard of his father's death, resolved to avenge him. He was well aware that de Guise was of such high rank that, if he killed him, he would be unable to obtain asylum in any part of Europe, but he did not hesitate for a moment. Not daring to approach the great nobleman's house, he sent him the following respectful challenge:

'No one, my lord, can bear witness to the just reason of my sorrow more forcibly than your lordship. I therefore entreat your lordship to forgive my resentment in expressing my desire that you will do me the honour of meeting me, sword in hand, to give me satisfaction for my father's death. The esteem which I entertain for your well-known courage induces me to hope that your lordship will not plead your high rank to avoid a meeting in which your honour is so deeply compromised. The gentleman who bears this will conduct you to the place where I am waiting for your lordship with a good horse and two swords, of which you will have the choice; or, should your lordship prefer it, I shall attend you at any place you may command.'

The meeting took place on horseback, and after a desperate fight the young de Luz had the satisfaction of dying by the same hand which had killed his father. In the meantime, in accordance with the fashion of the day, the seconds had fought a duel of their own, in which they had succeeded in wounding each other. A few voices were raised at court in criticism of de Guise for this dual killing, and particularly for the challenge to the aged and incapable Baron, but on the whole it was accepted as nothing more than an intriguing incident. Certainly d'Audiguier had nothing more disapproving to say of de Guise's second killing than that 'this victory would have been more gratifying to God if the Chevalier had fought for the same cause that took his ancestors to Palestine'.

In view of this remarkable understatement, it is scarcely surprising that d'Audiguier should have been an ardent advocate of duelling. At one point, indeed, he presented a supplication to Louis XIII not only to cancel all edicts against duelling, but to grant explicit permission for the practice. 'A great trial, Sire,' he wrote, 'is in progress between the nobility and the law in Your Majesty's dominions, in which you alone can decide. Your nobility maintain that a gentleman whose honour is impeached should either vindicate it with his sword, or forfeit his life; whereas the law asserts that a gentleman who draws his sword shall lose his life; and surely Your Majesty, who is the chief of the most generous nobility in existence, cannot feel it in your interest thus to blunt their valour, or, under the vain pretence of preserving their honour, behold them reduced to the necessity of losing sight of its dictates, or seek to maintain it with their pen, like the low-bred, disputing the right of arms before menial lawyers.' He concluded by imploring the King to make duels less common by allowing them to take place on certain occasions when the King himself should be present, and when the public, he added, 'instead of being involved in differences and law-suits, which consume both blood and fortune, would be delivered of the two monsters, and would feel proud of displaying their courage in your service, and their valour in your royal presence'.

In spite of these plausible arguments, various edicts against duelling were published during this reign, including one in 1626 which forbade all applications for pardon or pleas in favour of duellists. Like Henri IV, Louis even prohibited any such pleas from the Queen; and he declared before Heaven that he would never under any circumstances grant any exemption from this ordinance. Yet in spite of all these vows and protestations, we find Louis XIII granting a free pardon to duellists 'on account of the earnest entreaties made by his much loved and dear sister, the Queen of England, upon the occasion of her marriage'.

There were, in fact, only very few examples of the law against duelling being rigorously carried out during the reign of Louis XIII. The most famous was undoubtedly the case of François de Montmorency, Comte de Bouteville. This celebrated duellist was in the habit of walking up to any man whose courage he had heard spoken of, and saying: 'I understand, Sir, that you are a brave man; I should like to allow you to prove it – what are your weapons?' He was so impudent in his defiance of the royal edicts against duelling as to compel the Comte de Pont-Gibaut to leave church one Easter Sunday to go and fight him. Finally, in 1627, after a series of notorious duels, he took refuge in Brussels, where the Marquis de Beuvron sought him out in order to avenge one of his victims. Hearing of this, Louis XIII wrote to the Archduchess governing the Low Countries, asking her to prevent the duel. At her request, the Marquis de Spinola invited the two parties to dinner, and made them swear to give up their quarrel; but as they were leaving the house, Beuvron whispered to Bouteville that 'he would never rest satisfied until he had met him sword in hand'. Bouteville, however, refused to fight in Brussels, having given his word to the Archduchess to refrain from any hostile act while on her territory, but he appealed to her to intercede for him with Louis

XIII to allow him to return to France. The King replied 'that all he could do, for the love he bore her, was to allow him to remain in France without further prosecution, but he could not permit him to make his appearance at court'.

After eight challenges from Beuvron, Bouteville finally agreed to meet him in Paris, in the afternoon of May 12, on the Place Royale, one of the most public places in the capital. The fight began with sword and dagger, but after a few minutes the two men threw away the former weapon and set to with their daggers. Finally, when each man was holding his dagger at the other's throat, they mutually asked for quarter, and the duel came to an end. How-

ever, although they both promptly made for the frontier, Bouteville was arrested, condemned to death, and executed on the Place de Grève with considerable military pomp, attended by the Bishop of Nantes. The execution was characterized by a remarkable demonstration of masculine vanity, for it is recorded that Bouteville was as anxious to preserve his mustachios as Sir Thomas More was to keep his beard out of the way of the executioner's axe. Indeed, when the Bishop said to him: 'My son, you must no longer dwell on worldly things. Are you still thinking of life?' the condemned man proudly replied: 'I am thinking only of my mustachios – the very finest in France.'

Even this terrible example did nothing to discourage the vogue of duelling, and it was said that when acquaintances met in the morning at Louis XIII's court, their first inquiry was: 'Do you know who fought yesterday?' Lord Herbert, the English Ambassador at the French Court, observes in his memoirs that during his long residence in France he met scarcely a single Frenchman who had not killed his man in a duel; and, to show the prevalence of duelling in France, and the respect which was felt for duellists, he tells the story of a Monsieur Mennon who, on asking for the hand in marriage of a niece of Monsieur Disancour, was told by the latter: 'My friend, it is not time

yet to marry: I will tell you what you must do if you will be a brave man. You must first kill in single combat two or three men; then marry, and engender two or three children; and the world will neither have gained nor lost by you.' Similarly, in an anecdote illustrating the admiration women had for duellists at this time, Lord Herbert writes:

> All things being ready for the ball, and everyone being in their place, and I myself next to the Queen, expecting when the dancers would come in, one knocked at the door somewhat louder than became, I thought, a very civil person; when he came in, I

remember there was a sudden whisper among the ladies, saying: 'C'est Monsieur Balaguy!' Whereupon I also saw the ladies and gentlemen, one after another, invite him to sit near them; and, what is more, when one lady had his company a while, another would say: 'You have enjoyed him long enough, I must have him now.' At which bold civility of them, though I was astonished, yet it added to my wonder that his person could not be thought at most but ordinary handsome; his hair, which was cut very short, half grey, his doublet, but of sack-cloth, cut to his skin; and his breeches only of plain grey cloth. Informing myself by some standers-by who he was, I was told that he was one of the gallantest men in the world, as having killed eight or nine men in single fight, and that for this reason the ladies made so much of him; it being the manner of all French women to cherish gallant men, as thinking they could not make so much of any else with the safety of their honour.

By the middle of the seventeenth century, duelling had become such an essential part of the life of the French nobility that even Louis XIV was unable to stamp it out, although no fewer than ten edicts restraining the practice were published during his long reign. In the early edicts, considerable blame for the 'monstrous frenzy' affecting the nobility was placed on plebeian subjects who incited their betters to fight; thus the edict of 1651 contained the following stern clause:

Whereas it does appear that there are persons of ignoble birth, and who have never borne arms, yet are insolent enough to call out gentlemen who refuse to give them satisfaction, justly grounding their refusal on the inequality of the conditions; in consequence of which these persons excite and oppose to them other gentlemen of like degree, whence arise not unfrequently murders, the more detestable since they originate from abject sources; we do hereby will and ordain, that in all such cases of challenge and combat, more especially if followed by serious wounds or death, such ignoble and low-born citizens, duly convicted of having caused or promoted such disorders, shall be forthwith, and without any remission, hanged and strangled; all their goods and chattels, etc., confiscated; and we, moreover, do allow our judges to dispose of such part of this confiscated property as they may deem meet, as a reward to all informers who may give due knowledge of such offences; that, in the commission of a crime so deserving of condign punishment, everyone may be induced to make proper revaluation.

These provisions, however, do not seem to have had the intended effect, for in 1679 Louis XIV found it necessary to issue the celebrated *Édit des Duels*, which prescribed the death penalty for all principals, seconds, and thirds, with greater or less confiscation of property; ordained that gentlemen should be deprived of their letters of nobility; and their coats of arms defaced and broken by the public executioner; and ruled that those who fell in a duel should be tried by contumacy, and their bodies deprived of Christian burial, being thrown into 'the common receptacle of nuisances'. The mere sending of a challenge was punished by exile and the confiscation of half the offender's property, while all servants who bore messages or attended their masters on the occasion of a duel were condemned to be whipped and branded with a *fleur de lis*. At the same time a court of honour was set up, composed of the Marshals of France, to decide what satisfaction should be given in a case of provocation, as well as a suitable penalty of imprisonment, fine, or exile.

Theoretically, this edict was bound to bring duelling to a stop, and La Bruyère asserted that 'to cure men of this folly has been one of the most glorious actions of the greatest of monarchs'. But the folly was too deeply rooted in the minds of the French aristocracy to be cured as easily as that; the court of honour, once the novelty of the institution had worn off, lost its popularity; and the King himself was anything but consistent, fulminating against duelling in his official pronouncements, yet issuing patents to fencing-masters to teach his nobles the art of killing one another. What is more, he often turned a blind eye to scandalous duels of which he was fully informed, a fact which led a contemporary journal to remark 'that the King, although jealous of his authority, was not sorry at heart when he saw his nobles punctilious on matters of honour; therefore many of them willingly exposed themselves to the severity of the law, to obtain the secret approbation of their sovereign'. As a result, the reign of the Roi Soleil was marked by a long series of affairs of honour.

There was the duel, for example, in which the Duc de Beaufort killed his brother-in-law the Duc de Nemours, while the seconds followed the fashion by fighting at the same time, the Marquis de Villars shooting his opposite number d'Héricourt, whom he had never met before. There was the famous encounter in which the grandson of Admiral de Coligny, who was murdered in the Massacre of St Bartholomew's Eve on the orders of the Duc de Guise, was killed seventy years later by the duke's grandson. And there was the duel between La Frette and de Chalais, together with their seconds and thirds, to whom fourths were added when Saint-Aignan, sent by the King to stop the affair, agreed to abandon his pacific mission and join in the fight if he could be provided with an opponent.

Only rarely did a note of humour enter into the affairs of honour of the Grand Siècle. One such occasion was when a certain Madaillan sent a challenge to the Marquis de Rivard, who had lost a leg at the siege of Puy Cerda. Since it was considered essential to fight 'on an equal footing', the Marquis sent his opponent a surgeon with a case of instruments, suggesting that he should submit to a similar amputation. Madaillan took the joke in good part and withdrew his challenge.

Another threatened duel was prevented just as amusingly though with far less good humour after the Prince de Conti had accused the Grand Prior of Vendôme of cheating at cards, and called him a coward and a liar into the bargain. The Dauphin, informed of the imminent encounter, jumped out of bed in time to stop it. The next morning the Grand Prior was sent to the Bastille, and was released only on condition that he made a humble apology to the Prince de Conti for having been called by him a cheat, a liar and a coward.

Ironically enough, perhaps the most amusing anecdote of the period concerns one of the very rare cases in which the severe laws against duelling were actually enforced. This was at Toulouse, where the Marquis de la Donze had been condemned to death for killing his brother-in-law in an affair of honour. Whatever effect this severity might have had upon public opinion, it apparently left the offender unmoved, for when, on the scaffold, his confessor exhorted him to pray for forgiveness for his crime, he replied with a typical Gascon oath:

'*Sandis!* Do you call one of the cleverest thrusts in Gascony a crime?'

5 · Duels in Britain

Britain was slower than France to adopt the duel of honour, and during the sixteenth century quarrels still tended to be settled and slights avenged by means of 'killing affrays' or attacks by hired gangs of assassins. Gradually, however, the more honourable method of settlement by means of a fair fight in the presence of seconds was imposed by public opinion; and before long the English gentry had become as sensitive and punctilious about the point of honour as the French aristocracy.

One of the earliest recorded duels of honour which took place in Britain in the seventeenth century was fought in Islington in 1609 between two courtiers and favourites of James I, Sir George Wharton and Sir James Stewart. We have no details of the cause of their quarrel, but are merely told that 'reproachful words passed betwixt them'. However, the letters they exchanged about the duel are still extant, and these reveal on both sides a deep-seated hatred and an implacable determination to fight. In the first, Wharton remarked that Stewart's misconstruction of his message gave him 'cause to think you extreme vainglorious, a humour which the valiant detests'. He went on: 'And whereas you unjustly said I durst not meet you in the field to fight with you, you shall find that you are much mistaken; for I will fight with you with what weapon you shall appoint, and meet you where you will, being contented to give you this advantage, not valuing the worst you can do.' To this proud challenge Stewart replied as follows:

> Sir: Your message either being ill-delivered, or else not accepted, you have since, though ill-advised, retracted, and have repented it; for your messenger willed me from you, that either of us should make choice of a friend to debate

the matter. To which I confess I did but lightly hearken, since I knew some odds which no breath could make even. And now you have to acknowledge no other speeches than you charged me with, which is, that I said you durst not meet me in the field to fight. True it is, your barbarous and uncivil insolence in such a place, and before such a company (for whose respect I am only sorry for what I then did or said), made me do and say that which I now will make good. Wherein, since you find yourself behind, I am ready to do you all the right you can expect. And to that end have I sent you the length of my rapier, which I will use with a dagger, and so meet you at the farther end of Islington (as I understand nearer you than me) at three of the clock in the afternoon; which things I scorn to take as advantages, but as my due, and which I have made indifferent. And in respect I cannot send any of my friends without great hazard of discovery, I have sent my servant, herewith who is only acquainted with this business.

James Stuarte [*sic*].

The only description of the duel which has come down to us is contained in 'a lamentable Ballat of a Combat lately fought near London', in Nichols's *History of Canonbury.* In this work, after laying the scene and recounting the preliminaries, the ballad-monger tells us that

Seven thrusts in turn these gallants had
Before one drop of blood was drawn,
The Scottish Knight then valiant spoke –
'Stout Wharton, still thou hold'st thy own.'
With the next thrust that Wharton thrust
He ran him through the shoulder-bone.
The next was through the thick o' thigh.

After some more fierce thrusts, delivered, so we are told, with 'ruthless hate', the duel came to a mortal and patriotic end, for

They made a deadly desperate close,
And both fell dead upon the ground.
Our English Knight was the first that fell –
The Scotch Knight fell immediately,
Who cried out both to Jesus Christ,
'Receive our Souls, Oh Lord, we die!
God bless our noble King and Queen,
And all the noble progeny!'

The King is said to have been deeply grieved by the news of the death of his two courtiers, and he responded fittingly to their loyal sentiments by

11 · (*a*) *'St. George and the Dragon and Mademoiselle d'Eon "riposting"'*
An eighteenth-century caricature

11 · (*b*) *The trial of the Chevalier d'Eon by a jury of matrons*
An eighteenth-century caricature

12 · *'Living made easy.' A nineteenth-century print*

13 · '*The Fatal Duel between the Duke of Hamilton and Lord Mohun*', 1712. *A contemporary oil-painting*

14 · *'The Duellists'. An eighteenth-century engraving*

ordering them both to be buried in one grave. This was duly done, if we are to judge from the following extract from the Islington register: 'Sir George Wharton, sonne of Lord Wharton, was buried the 10th of November, 1609; James Stewart, Esq., godsonne to King James, was buried the 10th of November, 1609.'

Disturbed by the growing popularity of duelling, which he regarded as 'a vaine that bleeds both incessantly and inwardly', James I condemned the practice in his *Proclamation against Private Challenges and Combats*, published in 1613; while Bacon, when Attorney-General, speaking before the Star Chamber Court, expressed the pious hope that the great of the land would abandon the custom when they found it 'adopted by barber-surgeons and butchers'. Bacon also declared in a letter to Lord Villiers that he was determined to make no distinction between a coronet and a hatband in his efforts to repress the practice, and added: 'I will prosecute if any man appoint the field, though no fight takes place; if any man send a challenge in writing or verbally; if any man accept a challenge, or consent to be a second; if any man depart the realm in order to fight; if any man revive a quarrel after the late proclamation.' However, neither James nor his attorney-general could do much against what the King called 'the bewitching duel'; and there were few prosecutions, even when, as in the case of the famous duel between the Earl of Dorset and Lord Bruce, the participants 'departed the realm in order to fight'.

This duel was said to have been caused by jealousy over a woman, although Lord Bruce had also given the Earl 'two or three good buffets in the face'. On the occasion of the quarrel, the two men had been separated by other noblemen present, and Lord Bruce had gone to France 'to learn to fence'. Now, in 1613, an encounter was arranged at Bergen-op-Zoom, near Antwerp, and, in accordance with the accepted regulations, the Earl of Dorset sent his sword to Lord Bruce so that he could pair it. Instead of doing so, however, the latter brought a sword which was twice as broad, though of the same length. The Earl's second naturally objected to this, and advised him to match his own sword and send Lord Bruce the choice. The swords were delivered by Sir John Heidon, to whom Lord Bruce, according to the Earl of Dorset's account of the affair, declared that 'a little of my blood would not serve his turn, and therefore he was now resolved to have me alone, because he knew (for I will use his own words) "that so worthy a gentleman and my friend could not endure and stand by and see him do that which he must to satisfy himself and his honour". Thereunto Sir John Heidon replied "that such intentions were bloody and butcherly, far unfitting so noble a personage, who

should desire to bleed for reputation and not for life", withal adding, "he thought himself injured, being come thus far, now to be prohibited from executing those honourable offices he came for".' But Lord Bruce was unshakeable in his determination, and the Earl of Dorset therefore agreed to an immediate encounter, witnessed only by their surgeons, both of whom were to be unarmed.

After riding out together for about two miles, the duellists dismounted, stripped off their doublets, and, standing ankle-deep in water, set to. The Earl of Dorset's vivid description of the encounter goes on:

> I made a thrust at my enemy, but was short, and in drawing back my arm I received a great wound thereon, which I interpreted as a reward for my short shooting; but in revenge, I pressed into him, though I then missed him also; and then received a wound in my right pap, which passed level through my body and almost to my back. And there we wrestled for the two greatest and dearest prizes we could ever expect trial for – honour and life; in which struggling, my hand, having but an ordinary glove on it, lost one of her servants, though the meanest, which hung by a skin, and to sight yet remaineth as before, and I am put in hope one day to recover the use of it again. But at last breathless, yet keeping our holds, there past on both sides propositions of quitting each other's swords; but when amity was dead, confidence could not live, and who should quit first was the question, which on neither part either would perform; and restriving afresh, with a kick and a wrench together I freed my long-captive weapon,

> which incontinently levying at his throat, being master still of his, I demanded if he would ask his life or yield his sword? Both which, though in that imminent danger, he bravely denied to do. Myself being wounded, and feeling loss of blood, having three conduits running on me, began to make me faint, and he courageously persisting not to accord to either of my propositions, remembrance of his former bloody desire, and feeling of my present estate, I struck at his heart, but with his avoiding, missed my aim, yet passed through his body, and drawing back my sword, repassed through again, through another place, when he cried: 'Oh! I am slain,' seconding his speech with all the force he had to cast me: but being too weak, after I had defended his assault, I easily became master of him, laying him on his back, when, being upon him, I re-demanded if he would request his life? But it seems he prized it not at so dear a rate to be beholding for it, bravely replying he scorned it, which answer of his was so noble and worthy, as I protest, I could not find in my heart to offer him any more violence, only keeping him down; till at length, his surgeon, afar off, cried out he would immediately die if his wounds were not stopped: whereupon I asked if he desired his surgeon should come? which he accepted of; and so, being drawn away, I never offered to take his sword, accounting it inhumane to rob a dead man, for so I held him to be. This thus ended, I retired to my surgeon, in whose arms after I had remained awhile, for want of blood I lost my sight, and withal, as I then thought, my life also; but strong water and his diligence, quickly recovered me; when I escaped a great danger, for my Lord's surgeon, when nobody dreamt of it, came full at me with my Lord's sword; and had not mine, with my sword, interposed himself, I had been slain by those base hands, although my Lord Bruce, weltering in his blood, and past all expectation of life, conformable to all his former carriage, which was undoubtedly noble, cried out: 'Rascal, hold thy hand!'

Despite all the King's disapproval of duelling, it does not appear that his 'fatal and barbarous affair', as one chronicler called it, resulted in any proceedings against the Earl of Dorset or any diminution in his favour at court.

After thriving during the first decades of the seventeenth century, duelling became an extremely rare occurrence in the Civil War. As Charles Moore explained, 'since it was not a struggle between two powerful factions of the nobility and gentry one against the other, but of the commonalty against whatever was called royal, noble or honourable in rank and fortune, the consequence was that the gentry, and those who had been accustomed to look to their own swords for revenge in personal affronts, would have disdained to have settled points of honour by private duel, with antagonists of such ignoble birth. The general course of their thoughts being also bent on the repulsion of the common enemy of the order of gentry, they became more closely united within themselves, and were less in the habit of paying a scrupulous attention to all the supercilious dictates of a captious honour.'

The same conditions obtained during the Protectorate, yet in 1654 Cromwell thought it necessary to pass an ordinance to prohibit and punish duelling. This ordinance stated that any person sending, carrying, or accepting a challenge was to be imprisoned for six months; and that any person who was challenged and did not report the challenge within twenty-four hours was to be considered as having accepted it. When a duel resulted in death, that death was to be regarded as murder; and any person using provocative words or gestures was to be indicted, and, if convicted, was to be fined, bound over, and compelled to make reparation to the injured party.

Presumably Cromwell's ordinance against duelling was intended to curb the sort of inveterate fighter who would pick a quarrel on the slightest pretext at any period of history. Such a one was Philip Stanhope, the second Earl of

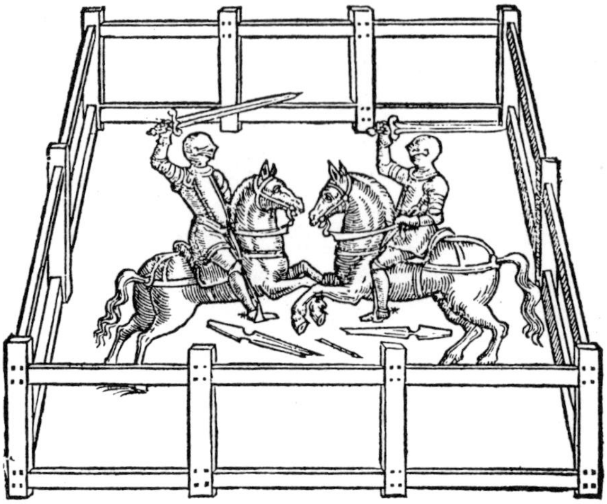

Chesterfield, who was arrested in February 1658 to prevent him from fighting a duel with Lord St John, and then imprisoned in the Tower in June of the same year for wounding John Whalley in an affair of honour. Recounting this last encounter himself, Chesterfield wrote in a letter: 'This year a young lady having drawn me for her Valentine, I presented her with a Purslan Chamber pot and a Looking glass fitted to the bottom of it, with this inscription:

Narcissus se mirent en l'onde
Vit la plus belle chose du monde

which was ill resented, and I had a quarrel with Captain Whaly who in a duel

I wounded and disarmed, for which I went sent Prisoner to the Tower by the Protector Oliver Cromwell.'

After the Restoration, duelling very naturally regained all its previous prestige, and soon ballrooms, coffee-houses and public walks were all scenes of fighting and bloodshed. Covent Garden and Lincoln's Inn Fields were the favourite rendezvous in London for deciding points of honour, and at all hours of the night the clash of swords could be heard by peaceful citizens living in the neighbourhood or returning home. Many duels originated in a quarrel at some theatre, for the young bloods of the day were in the habit of going to a playhouse simply in order to insult some woman and get involved in a dispute which might further their reputation. A typical theatre incident occurred at a performance of *The Scornful Lady*, when the notorious Beau

Fielding insulted a barrister called Fulwood by giving him a push. When Fulwood protested, Fielding put his hand on his sword, but the lawyer drew first and gave his antagonist a serious wound in the body. 'Beau Fielding,' we are told, 'who was then a man of above fifty years of age, came forward, and uncovering his breast, showed his bleeding wound to the public, to excite the compassion of the fair sex; but, to his no small disappointment, a burst of laughter broke forth from the audience.' As for Fulwood, he went triumphantly to Lincoln's Inn Fields Theatre, where he picked another quarrel with a certain Captain Cusack, from whom he demanded satisfaction. But this was pushing his luck too far, and they had scarcely gone out into the fields before the soldier dispatched the lawyer and left him dead on the ground.

All classes, in fact, were now affected by the mania for duelling, and even doctors occasionally settled their professional differences at the point of the sword. Two physicians called Mead and Woodward fought a duel under the gate of Gresham College which is still remembered, not on account of the fight itself, but because of a witty retort made by the defeated duellist. This was Woodward, who slipped and fell to the ground. 'Take your life,' said the magnanimous Dr Mead. To which the prostrate Woodward replied acidly: 'Anything but your physic.'

Pepys deplored the prevalence of duels at this time, which he described as 'a kind of emblem of the general complexion of the whole kingdom'. Fortunately for us, the great diarist's disapproval led him to write this engaging account of a typical duel of the late seventeenth century, that which took place in 1667 between Sir H. Bellasses and Mr Tom Porter:

> They two dined yesterday at Sir Robert Carr's, where, it seems, people do drink high, all that come. It happened that these two, the greatest friends in the world, were talking together, and Sir H. Bellasses talked a little louder than ordinary to Tom Porter, giving him some advice. Some of the company standing by said: 'What! are they quarrelling, that they talk so high?' Sir H. Bellasses hearing it, said: 'No, I would have you know, I never quarrel, but I strike; take that as a rule of mine!' – 'How?' said Tom Porter, 'strike! I would I could see the man in England that durst give me a blow?' With that Sir H. Bellasses did give him a box on the ear; and so they were going out to fight, but were hindered. And by and by Tom Porter went out; and meeting Dryden the poet, told him of the business, and that he was resolved to fight Sir H. Bellasses presently, for he knew, if he did not, they would be friends tomorrow, and then the blow would rest upon him; and he desires Dryden to let him have his boy to bring him notice which way Sir H. Bellasses goes. By and by he is informed, that Sir H. Bellasses's coach was coming; so Tom Porter went down out of the coffee-room, where he stayed for the tidings, and stopped the coach, and bade Sir H. Bellasses come out. 'Why,' said Sir H. Bellasses, 'you will not hurt me coming out, will you?' – 'No,' says Tom Porter. So out he went, and both drew. And Sir H. Bellasses having drawn and flung away the scabbard, Tom Porter asked him whether he was ready. The other answered, he was; and they fell to fight, some of their acquaintances by. They wounded one another; and Sir H. Bellasses so much, that it is feared he will die. And finding himself severely wounded, he called to Tom Porter, and kissed him, and bade him shift for himself; 'for,' says he, 'Tom thou has hurt me; but I will make shift to stand on my legs till thou mayest withdraw, and the world not take notice of thee; for I would not have thee troubled for what thou hast done.' And so, whether he did fly or not, I cannot tell; but Tom Porter showed Sir H. Bellasses that he was wounded too; and they are both ill, but Sir H. Bellasses to the life. And this is fine example! and Sir H. Bellasses a parliament man too; and both of them extraordinary friends!

Bellasses lived for only a few days, and Pepys, noting his death, added as a postscript: 'It is pretty to see how the world talk of them, as a couple of fools, that killed one another out of love. . . .'

Strangely enough, the public made little or no protest at the constant increase in duelling, until its horror and indignation were aroused by the terrible duel between Lord Mohun and the Duke of Hamilton in 1712. Twenty years earlier, in 1692, this same Lord Mohun had been deeply implicated in his friend Captain Hall's attempted abduction of the actress Mrs Bracegirdle and his murder of her colleague William Montford. Hall had made his escape, and Mohun, tried by his peers as an accessory to Montford's murder, had been acquitted. He was to be less fortunate in his encounter with the Duke of Hamilton.

The cause of this duel is not known for certain, but it is believed that the Duke had cast doubts on the truthfulness of a witness for Mohun in some legal proceedings between them, and that Mohun had replied by challenging him. The two men agreed to meet in Hyde Park with their seconds, Colonel Hamilton of the Foot Guards for the Duke, and a certain Maccartney for Lord Mohun. Describing the encounter the same day in a letter to Mrs Dingley, Swift wrote:

> Before this comes to your hands, you will have heard of the most terrible accident that hath almost ever happened. This morning, at eight, my man brought me word that Duke Hamilton had fought with Lord Mohun, and had killed him, and was brought home wounded. I immediately sent him to the Duke's house to know if it was so, but the porter could hardly answer his inquiries, and a great rabble was about the house. In short, they fought at seven this morning. The dog Mohun was killed on the spot, but while the Duke was over him, Mohun shortened his sword, and stabbed him in the shoulder to the heart. The Duke was helped towards the lake-house, by the ring, in Hyde Park (where they fought), and died on the grass, before he could reach his house, and was brought home in his coach by eight, while the poor Duchess was asleep. Maccartney and one Hamilton were the seconds, who fought likewise, and both are fled. I am told that a footman of Lord Mohun's stabbed Duke Hamilton, and some say Maccartney did too. Mohun gave the affront, and yet sent the challenge. I am infinitely concerned for the poor Duke, who was a frank, honest, and good natured man. They carried the poor Duchess to a lodging in the neighbourhood where I have been with her two hours, and am just come away. I never saw so melancholy a scene, for indeed all reasons for real grief belong to her; nor is it possible for anyone to be a greater loser in all regards – she has moved my very soul. The lodging was inconvenient, and they would have moved her to another, but I would not suffer it, because it had no room backwards, and she must have been tortured with the noise of the Grub Street screamers dinging her husband's murder in her ears.

Judging by the number of wounds that each of the two duellists received, this was one of the most savage sword fights ever recorded. The Duke of Hamilton had a wound about seven inches long in the right leg, another in the right arm, a third in the upper part of the right breast, running down into the body, and a fourth on the outside of the left leg; while Lord Mohun had a large wound in the groin, another in the right side through the body and up to the hilt of the sword, and a third in one arm.

As for the seconds, Colonel Hamilton was found guilty of manslaughter but 'prayed the benefit of the statute'. Maccartney fled to Holland, but was tried for murder in the Court of King's Bench in 1716 and likewise found guilty of manslaughter. The only amusing incident in the whole grim story occurred while he was still at liberty. A reward had been offered for his capture, and a gentleman who was attacked by highwaymen one night hit upon the idea of posing as the wanted Maccartney. Tempted by the reward, the robbers took him before a justice of the peace, and were dumbfounded when their victim gave them in charge for attempted highway robbery.

As a consequence of the terrible Mohun-Hamilton fight, a bill was introduced into the House of Commons for the suppression of duelling, but after two readings it was lost. However, a few year later, a more effective curb than any Act of Parliament was put on the practice by the death sentence passed on Major Oneby in 1726 for the murder of Mr Gower. The two men in question had been gambling in a tavern with three other people, and had exchanged first words and then blows, Oneby throwing a bottle at Gower and the latter retaliating with a candle stick. They had then gone to fetch their swords, but had been prevented by the others from fighting, and had sat down again for an hour. At the end of that time, Gower had offered his hand to Oneby, but the latter had spurned it, saying: 'No, damn you, I will have your blood.' A little later, when the company had been dispersing, Oneby had called to Gower: 'Young man, come back, I have something to say to you.' And when the others had eventually been readmitted after hearing the sound of clashing swords, they had found the young man mortally wounded.

The judges were unanimous in finding Oneby guilty of murder, arguing that he had acted with premeditation and not out of sudden passion. The main point on which the judgment turned was the evidence of 'express malice' in the remark 'I will have your blood' and the contemptuous appellation of 'young man'; and the Court held that the full hour during which the two men had sat together after their quarrel had given the accused 'reasonable time for cooling'. Oneby was accordingly sentenced to death, but cheated the executioner and public curiosity by committing suicide.

A somewhat similar duel, though fought on a higher social level, was the famous encounter in 1765 between Lord Byron, the great-uncle of the poet, and his neighbour Mr Chaworth. This affair was the result of a quarrel between the two men at the Star and Garter Tavern in Pall Mall, at what was called the Nottinghamshire Club. The rest of the company thought that the quarrel had been mended, but as they were leaving the tavern, Lord Byron called out Mr Chaworth, or Mr Chaworth called out Lord Byron – there is no certainty as to who challenged whom – and the two of them went into an empty room lit only by a tallow candle, and closed the door behind them. A few minutes later, one of them rang the bell, and the waiter opened the door to find them clasped in each other's arms, each holding his sword and Mr Chaworth dying.

The account which Chaworth gave to his friends, when they were admitted to see him, was that 'he could not live many hours; that he forgave Lord Byron, and hoped the world would forgive him; that the affair had passed in the dark, only a tallow candle burning in the room; that Lord Byron asked him if he meant the conversation on the game to be referred to Sir Charles Sedley or to him? to which he replied: "If you have anything to say, we had better shut the door": that while he was doing this, Lord Byron bid him draw, and in turning, he saw his lordship's sword half drawn, on which he whipped out his own, and *made the first pass*; that the sword going through his lordship's waistcoat he thought he had killed him, and asking whether he was mortally wounded, Lord Byron, while he was speaking, shortened his sword, and stabbed him in the belly.'

Though the details of this fight were and still are extremely confused, the circumstances argued strongly in Lord Byron's favour, especially the fact that Mr Chaworth had not only provoked or insulted him, but, by his own admission, had managed to get the first thrust at him. It was therefore no matter for surprise that the House of Lords should have found him 'not guilty of the felony of murder, but of manslaughter' – a verdict which meant that, under a statute of Edward VI in favour of peers of the realm, he was immediately discharged on payment of his fees. Authorities on duelling, however, were extremely critical of the whole incident, declaring it to be 'only one of the many instances that show the impropriety of fighting without seconds, since no positive evidence can be produced to prove that the foulest treachery may not have been perpetrated.'

This duel was one of the last important encounters to be fought with swords in this country, for the wearing of side-arms had ceased to be customary, and

the pistol duel was now considered to lend itself better to both formality and fairness. Even so, the early pistol duels of which we have some record show little more punctilio than the hastiest brawl between two swashbuckling bloods or bucks. Such an affair was the famous encounter between John Wilkes and Lord Talbot on October 5, 1762, arising from an offensive anonymous article about Lord Talbot which Wilkes had published in August in the *North Briton*. The duel had been arranged for the morning of Wednesday, October 6, at Bagshot, where indeed Wilkes had invited his antagonist and the two seconds to join him for supper on the Tuesday evening. On his arrival, however, Lord Talbot flew into a fury and insisted on fighting immediately. In an account of the whole affair which he gave late that night in a letter to Earl Temple, Wilkes wrote:

> Soon after he grew a little cooler, and in a soothing tone of voice said: 'I have never, I believe, offended Mr Wilkes, why had he attacked me? He must be sorry to see me unhappy.' I asked him upon what grounds his Lordship imputed the paper to me? that Mr Wilkes would justify any paper to which he had put his name, and would equally assert the privilege of not giving any answer whatever about a paper to which

he had not; that was my undoubted right, which I was ready to seal with my blood.

He then said he admired me exceedingly, really loved me, but I was an unaccountable animal – such parts! But would I kill him who had never offended me? etc., etc. We had after this a good deal of conversation about the Bucks Militia and the day his Lordship came to see me on Wycombe Heath, before I was Colonel. He soon after flamed out again, and said to me: 'You are a murderer, you want to kill me, but I am sure I shall kill you, I know I shall, by God! If you will fight, if you will kill me, I hope you will be *hanged*. I know you will.' I asked if I was first to be *killed* and afterwards to be *hanged*? That I knew his Lordship fought with the King's pardon in his pocket, and I fought him with a halter about my neck. That I would fight him for all that, and if he fell I should not tarry here a moment for the tender mercies of such a ministry; but would directly proceed to the next stage, where my valet waited for me, from thence I would make the best of my way to France, as men of honour were sure of protection in that country. He then told me that I was an *unbeliever* and wished to be killed. I could not help smiling at this, and observed that we did not meet at Bagshot to settle articles of faith, but points of honour; that indeed, I had no fear of dying, but I enjoyed life as much as any man; that I am as little subject to be gloomy or even peevish, as any Englishman whatever; that I valued life and the fair enjoyments of it so much, I would never quit it with my own consent, except on a call of honour.

I then wrote a letter to your Lordship, respecting the education of Miss Wilkes, and gave you my poor thanks for the steady friendship with which you have so many years honoured me. Colonel Berkeley took the care of the letter, and I have since desired him to send it to Stowe; for the sentiments of the head at such a moment are beyond all politics, and indeed everything else, except such virtue as Lord Temple's.

When I had sealed my letter, I told his Lordship I was entirely at his service, and I again desired that we might decide the affair in the room, because there could not be a possibility of interruption; but he was quite inexorable. He then asked me how many times we should fire. I said, that I left it to his choice. I had brought a flask of powder and a bag of bullets. Our seconds then charged the pistols which my Adjutant had brought. They were large horse-pistols. It was agreed that we should fire at the word of command, to be given by one of our seconds. They tossed up, and it fell to my Adjutant to give the word.

We then left the room, and walked to a garden at some distance from the house. It was near seven, and the moon shone brightly. We stood about eight yards distant, and agreed not to turn round before we fired, but to continue facing each other. Harris gave the word. Both our fires were in very exact time, but neither took effect.

I walked up immediately to his Lordship, and told him, that I now avowed the paper. His Lordship paid me the highest encomiums on my courage, and said, he would declare everywhere that I am the noblest fellow God had ever made. He then desired that we might now be good friends, and retire to the inn to drink a bottle of claret together, which we did with great good humour and much laugh.

Rarely have the experts on duelling found so much to criticize in an affair of honour as they have in this encounter between the earl and the journalist.

They have raised shocked hands at Wilkes's 'improper' invitation to his antagonist to supper before the duel, an invitation which suggested 'that he contemplated the possibility of a reconciliation'. They have criticized Talbot for bullying Wilkes, Wilkes for refusing to admit authorship of the offensive article, and both men for talking of killing in an effort to terrify each other. They have expressed horror at the barbarism of using 'large horse-pistols' in a duel; surprise at Wilkes's precipitation in promptly advancing towards Talbot before ascertaining, as the challenged party, whether his opponent was 'satisfied'; and astonishment at Talbot's readiness to end the affair once Wilkes had 'avowed the paper', in spite of the fact that the journalist had made no apology.

Altogether, in fact, this was considered an ill-conducted affair. Or, as the stern Dr Millingen put it, 'the frequency of the duels that occurred in those days does not appear to have given them, generally speaking, a character of much delicacy or punctilious honour; and they seem to have been the result of fashion more than of feeling'.

6 · More Duels in France

The institution of duelling, which Louis XIV had failed to destroy, took on a new lease of life under the Regency of Philippe d'Orléans, since no attempt was made to enforce the law on this point. Six weeks after the King's death, two officers of the Guards fought on the Quai des Tuileries in broad daylight; but since the young men came from families of the 'long robe', the Regent, out of respect for the Parlement, simply suspended them from the corps and sentenced them to a fortnight's imprisonment. This duel had been fought over an Angora cat; and the duke, when reprimanding the young men, remarked that a matter of that sort should have been settled with claws instead of swords. The feeble wit and lenient punishment dispensed in this case offer a blatant contrast with, say, the death sentence carried out on Bouteville early in the previous reign.

Soon other duellists followed the example of the two officers, scorning any effort at concealment. Thus a duel took place between Contades and Brissac, in which both were wounded, in the palace itself, without any proceedings being taken against the two parties. Another duel, fought in broad daylight in the centre of Paris between two noblemen, Jonzac and Villette, also went unpunished; and Duclos, in his secret memoirs, asserts that the Regent openly stated that duelling had gone too much out of fashion.

With no curb on duelling, offended parties did not need to resort to the Court of Honour, and its services were called for even more rarely than under Louis XIV. Even so, it restricted its labours still further by refusing to intervene when one of the parties was not of high birth or distinguished rank. A case of this sort which caused something of a scandal in Paris concerned an abbé called d'Aydie who had fought with a clerk, allegedly at an opera-dancer's house, and wounded him. The Duchesse de Berry, the Regent's daughter, immediately had the Abbé d'Aydie deprived of his preferment, and compelled to become a knight of Malta. This did not prevent the clerk, once he had recovered from his wound, from repeatedly seeking out his antagonist and forcing him to fight four duels, until at last the duchess brought both parties before the Court of Honour. Here, however, her efforts to make peace were thwarted by the President of the Court, Marshal de Chamilly, who, on hearing of the social rank of one of the parties, exclaimed: 'What the devil has he come here for? Does a fellow who calls himself *Bouton* presume to think that we can be *his* judges? Does he take us for bishops or keepers of the seals? And the fellow dares to call us *my lords*!'

It should perhaps be explained, with regard to this last point, that the Marshals of France were only called *my lords* by the aristocracy, and regarded the same appellation from a commoner as an insult. It should also be added that d'Aydie was the lover of the Duchesse de Berry, who was not unnaturally afraid that the clerk might deprive her of him in a duel. The Court recommended the Regent to imprison his daughter's lover as a punishment for having fought the low-born Bouton, whom they ignored as being beneath their notice. This, of course, was not at all what the duchess wanted; so, after obtaining d'Aydie's release, she persecuted the unfortunate clerk with such relentless spite that she finally had him hanged, thus arousing, according to Madame de Créqui, 'the horror and the animadversion of all Paris'. Morality, however, was saved: the vindictive duchess died a month to the day after the execution of her victim.

Matters did not improve when Louis XV took over the government of France, receiving from the Regent, as one historian put it, 'a sceptre stained by corruption and a crown dimmed by depravity'. True, in the first year of his personal rule he resolved to check the practice of duelling, and issued an edict to the effect that any gentleman who struck another should be degraded from his rank and forfeit his arms; and he solemnly declared that he would religiously observe the coronation oath, by which he had bound himself to enforce the law. But under the influence of his libertine court, his coronation oath was soon forgotten; and when a counsellor at the High Court of Grenoble was condemned to be broken on the wheel for having killed an army captain in a duel, it was only an effigy which was executed, the man himself having made his escape.

The greatest duellist of this time was undoubtedly the celebrated Duc de Richelieu, who was forever engaged in affairs of honour, and even killed one of his own relations, the Prince de Lixen, in 1734. The two men were at supper at the Prince de Conti's during the siege of Philippsbourg. Richelieu, who had exerted himself considerably during the day, was hot and tired, and beads of sweat broke out on his forehead. The Prince de Lixen, offended by some of the duke's witticisms, remarked 'that it was surprising that he did not appear in a more suitable state, after having been purified by admission into his family'. The suggestion that Richelieu had bettered himself by his marriage was all the more intolerable in that it was true; and at midnight the two men met in the trenches, where the Prince fell a victim to the duke's sword, which, as contemporary wits observed, was only poetic justice, since Lixen had himself killed one of his relations, his wife's uncle the Marquis de Ligneville.

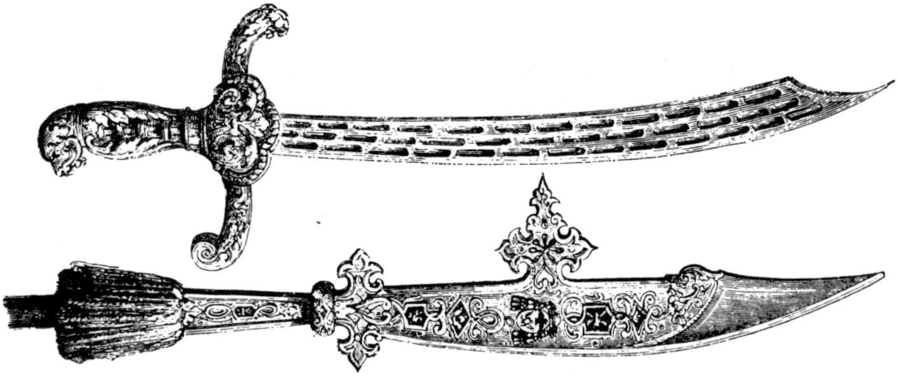

Another well-known duellist of the day was Du Vighan, who was so handsome that hackney coachmen are said to have driven him without a fare, simply for the pleasure of serving such a *joli garçon*. The King granted him letters of nobility on the ground of his appearance, for he was only of 'middling birth'; the Archbishop of Paris called him 'the serpent of the terrestrial paradise'; and he was known to the ladies of the court by the name of *Le Charmant*. His charms, alas, proved his undoing, and he died as the result of a duel which they had provoked. He had the presumption to pay court to a beautiful princess, Mademoiselle de Soissons, who was so attracted to him that her aunt was obliged to shut her up in a convent at Montmartre. This, of course, was not enough to discourage a determined lover, and after a letter and a rope-ladder had been discovered, the princess's family appealed to the Baron d'Ugeon, one of their number and an expert swordsman, to punish the young man. A challenge was sent and accepted, but the duel was postponed as a result of the illness and death of Louis XV. When it finally took place, d'Ugeon defeated his antagonist, inflicting two dangerous wounds in his right side. In spite of his injuries, the incorrigible Du Vighan managed to scale the walls of the Abbey of Montmartre to see his princess; but he was obliged to spend the night in the cloisters, since Mademoiselle de Soissons had been locked up. During this cold and painful vigil, his wounds opened again, and they bled so profusely that he was found dead the following morning. The body was surreptitiously taken home, and it was given out that he had died from smallpox, caught from the King while he was attending him during his last illness. As for the princess, after a period of utter prostration, she consoled herself by marrying the Prince de Cobourg.

Saint-Évremont was another famous duellist of this period; he enjoyed the special distinction of having his name given to a thrust which he had devised, and which was called *la botte de Saint-Évremont*. His great rival was Poulain de Saint-Foix, a writer who condemned duelling but was always to be found sword in hand. A man with a strict sense of honour, he never hesitated to refuse a challenge when he knew that he was far superior to his challenger; but on the other hand, he could never resist teasing or provoking a man who seemed likely to be able to give him a good fight. One day, for example, at the Café Procope, an officer of the King's Guards came in and called for a *café au lait* with a roll, adding: 'That will do for my dinner.' Saint-Foix promptly remarked: 'Pon my soul, that's a sorry dinner!' – an observation which so infuriated the officer that he called out the writer on the spot and wounded him in the arm. But Saint-Foix had the last word. 'That still doesn't prevent a *café au lait* and a roll,' he said, 'from being a very sorry dinner.'

On another occasion, meeting a lawyer whose face displeased him, Saint-Foix walked up to him and whispered in his ear: 'Sir, I have some business with you.' The attorney, showing remarkable calm for a man whose life was in mortal danger, quietly named a time when he would find him in his office. Both men were astonished when they met at the appointed hour, the lawyer at seeing his supposed client arrive accompanied by a second and ready for battle, and Saint-Foix at finding his supposed antagonist armed with nothing more lethal than a quill. The misunderstanding was, of course, due to the

Rev. de Paris ÉVÉNEMENT DU 12. 9bre. 1790. No. -o Page 248 I at.

Duel entre M.M. Charles de Lameth et de Castries.

15 · *The duel between Charles de Lameth and de Castries,* 1790
A contemporary engraving

16 · *A late nineteenth-century French duel*

expression which Saint-Foix had used, to the effect that 'he wanted to have an *affaire* with the lawyer', the term *affaire* being equally applicable to a duel and a legal transaction.

One of the first affairs of honour in the following reign, that of Louis XVI, was the famous duel between the Comte d'Artois, the future Charles X, and the Duc de Bourbon. At a ball held at the Opera on Shrove Tuesday in the year 1778, the Comte d'Artois appeared, giving his arm to Madame de Carrillac. The couple were masked, but the Duchesse de Bourbon recognized them and followed them, insulting them with a venom which a chronicler attributed to two potent motives – that 'Madame de Carrillac had been the mistress of her husband, whom she had quitted for the Comte d'Artois, to whom the duchess herself was not indifferent'. Madame de Carrillac contrived to slip away and mingle with the crowd, whereupon the duchess tried to tear off the mask from the count, who, 'forgetting at the moment his usual gallantry and the privileges of the fair sex', crushed the duchess's mask on her face and rushed out of the ballroom. A few days later, the duchess stated in the presence of all the guests at her supper table that the conduct of the Comte d'Artois had been that of a scoundrel, and it was generally agreed that the Duc de Bourbon was under a moral obligation to call out the offender, who himself could not decently avail himself of his rank to refuse the satisfaction which such a public insult to a woman demanded. However, the duchess's desire for vengeance was nearly thwarted when the King summoned the Duc and Duchesse de Bourbon and the Comte d'Artois to his presence and forbade any of them to take any notice of what had happened. This decision did not satisfy the duchess and the ladies of the court, and the Queen instructed the Baron de Besenval to consult with de Crussel, the Captain of the Prince's guards, and decide what should be done. At this meeting, which took place at the Comte Jules de Polignac's, it was decided that a duel should take place, but de Crussel and de Polignac proposed that as soon as swords were drawn and crossed, the former should produce an order from the King to separate the combatants. Besenval indignantly refused to comply with this proposal, remarking: 'Pray, gentlemen, are you going to make the prince play in a farce? I will never agree to such an arrangement.' To this de Crussel retorted 'that it was quite sufficient for the prince to go to the ground, and that the sovereign had then the right to prevent bloodshed'.

When the duel actually took place, no order to stop the fight was in fact produced. But a certain doubt remains as to the seriousness of the encounter, judging by this description of it which has come down to us:

> The following day the count went to the Bois de Boulogne, attended by de Crussel, who had placed the prince's best sword in the carriage. Arrived at the wood, they perceived the Duc de Bourbon surrounded by several gentlemen: upon seeing him the count alighted, and stepping towards him said: 'I understand, sir, that the public say that we are seeking each other?' To which the duke replied, taking off his hat: 'I am here, sir, to receive your commands,' to which polite reply the count answered: 'I am here, sir, to fulfil yours.'
>
> After this courteous preamble both parties drew their swords; when the duke observed: 'You are not aware, sir, that the sun shines full upon you.' 'You are right,' answered the count; 'we had better proceed to that wall, where we shall find more shade than under these leafless trees.'
>
> The parties then placed their drawn swords under their arms, and proceeded, conversing with each other, to the appointed spot, followed by their two seconds, all other persons keeping at a distance. Monsieur de Vibraye, the second of the duke, observing that they had both kept on their spurs, which might prove inconvenient, the seconds immediately proceeded to unbuckle them; and, while doing so, de Vibraye had an eye nearly put out by the point of the duke's sword. The spurs being off, the duke asked the prince's permission to take off his coat; to which proposal the Comte d'Artois not only acceded, but threw off his own.
>
> Several lunges had passed between the parties, and d'Artois was evidently becoming impatient and flushed, when the duke was observed to stagger; and the seconds, thinking that he had been wounded, interfered, and begged the parties to suspend all further hostility. The count replied: 'It is not for me to offer any opinion; it is for Monsieur le Duc de Bourbon to express his wishes, I am here at his orders.' The duke

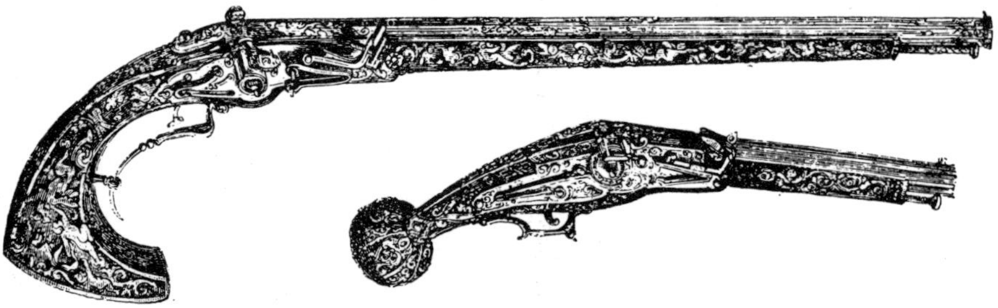

> immediately lowered his sword, and replied: 'I feel penetrated with gratitude at your kindness, and shall never forget the honour that you have conferred on me.' The Comte d'Artois then opened his arms, and the duke flew into his embrace.
>
> After this harmless meeting, at the suggestion of the Queen and the Baron de Besenval, the count repaired to the Palais Bourbon, and made an ample apology to the insulted duchess. The punishment awarded to the combatants was an exile for a week; the count at Choisy, and the duke at Chantilly.

Nineteenth-century commentators tended to consider this duel as an illustration of the moral corruption of the period. 'A woman of the highest rank', wrote one scandalized historian, 'insults another woman who had been her husband's mistress; not on that account, but for having become the mistress of another man, to whom she herself was attached: and the foolish husband is made to peril life and liberty by fighting the real object of the dispute, who had so far lost sight of all gentlemanly deportment as to insult a female by actually inflicting a blow!' To our age, less easily shocked by such commonplace incidents, it is of greater interest as bearing a suspicious resemblance to those spurious duels of this century arranged to deceive and satisfy public opinion.

It certainly contrasts sharply with a duel fought by this Duc de Bourbon's father, the Prince de Condé, with just as much courtesy and far more courage and determination. The prince's antagonist, a captain in the Guards called the Vicomte d'Agout, had been paying court to a young widow in the household of the Princesse de Condé, and had promised to marry her; discovering, however, that she 'had bestowed her favours' on the prince, he broke off the engagement. The lady complained to her protector, who ordered d'Agout to resign his situation in the Guards. D'Agout complied with this order, but asked if he might know the reason for his disgrace, and was told by the prince 'that he would not keep in his service liars and slanderers'. To this d'Agout replied: 'Your Highness is aware that when I took the liberty of putting this question, I was no longer in Your Highness's service, and will be pleased also to recollect that I am a gentleman.' 'I understand you, Sir,' answered the prince; 'and I am ready to maintain what I have asserted, in whatever manner you may think proper.'

An encounter was arranged for nine o'clock on the following day in the Bois de Boulogne. D'Agout arrived first, accompanied by his brother. The prince appeared shortly afterwards, and handed his opponent a declaration admitting that he was the aggressor, together with letters of recommendation to foreign powers, for use in case d'Agout killed him and found it necessary to leave the country. After thanking the prince for this chivalrous gesture, d'Agout took off his coat, whereupon the prince observed: 'No doubt, Sir, by taking off your coat, you expect that I should do the same.' With unfailing courtesy, d'Agout replied: 'I have no right to demand anything from Your Highness, as I trust implicitly in your honour, and was only anxious to afford Your Highness a proof of mine.' The prince promptly took off his own coat, and the duel began.

The captain, we are told, 'fought with that desperate determination which his critical position inspired', and the prince was soon slightly wounded. The seconds then intervened and parted the combatants. Shortly after this encounter, the prince gave a further proof of his chivalry by promoting d'Agout to the rank of major in the Guards.

People regarded this duel between a prince of the blood and an individual of humble rank as a sign of the times, an indication of the collapse of the barriers dividing the various castes of society. It might be supposed that this process, and the consequent vulgarization of duelling, would have led to an increase in the practice. In point of fact, however, duelling decreased slightly under Louis XVI, largely because, as in Britain, the sword had ceased to be worn as a mark of distinction in society; as a result, this weapon of the 'gentleman' was no longer at hand when a quarrel occurred, so that duels took place with premeditation and were not fought on the spur of the moment. Even so, the French remained firmly attached to the duel as a means of settling affairs of honour, and an inveterate duellist still found no lack of opportunities for a fight. As de Tilly, a famous character of the period, stated in his memoirs:

> France is the birthplace of duelling. I have roved over a great part of Europe, and travelled in the New World; I have lived with soldiers and courtiers; and nowhere else have I met with this fatal *susceptibility*, which is incessantly creating affronts, injuries, and provocations. Whence arises this disposition, so peculiar to the French, whose character is too noble to become vindictive, and which induces them to fight a duel in matters that are chiefly frivolous? It is education, and that only.
>
> You have had a discussion with a close friend; although it may not have exceeded the limits of an excusable warmth, women have observed in it *injurious shades*; and you would rather expose yourself to kill your friend or be killed by him, than to the mere suspicion, on the part of woman, of being deficient in courage.
>
> At a gambling table a misunderstanding arises; a by-stander has smiled ironically; he has whispered to his sister, who has whispered something to her cousin: get yourself killed by all means, for you may have been suspected of cheating at play; and nothing can set such a question in a proper light but the thrust of a sword!
>
> Your wife is an acknowledged coquette; get yourself run through the body by her lover, and her honour will be restored. You yourself may have seduced the wife of an honest man, who dares to suspect you, and receives you with ill-humour; kill him; for, having deprived him of happiness and peace, you need not be punctilious in ridding him of life!

One of the most quarrelsome duellists of the time was the Breton Marquis de Tenteniac, who was celebrated for having once challenged the whole pit of a theatre. Watching a play one day from the wings, he moved so far forward on to the stage that the audience rebuked him. He immediately stepped up to the footlights and announced: 'Ladies and gentlemen, with your permission a piece will be performed tomorrow, called *The Insolence of the Pit Chastised*, in as many acts as may be desired, by the Marquis de Tenteniac!' This impudent declaration was received, astonishingly enough, with considerable applause, and no individual playgoer thought fit to take up the collective challenge.

Another celebrated duellist of this reign, as also of the reign of Louis XV, was the Chevalier d'Éon, who owed his fame partly to his remarkable skill with the sword and partly to the mystery surrounding his sex. For a long period, in fact, he wore female dress, possibly out of choice or for reasons of diplomacy to begin with, but later on in obedience to an order from the French Foreign Minister prohibiting his appearance in France except in female costume. Not unnaturally, it began to be rumoured that he was really a woman, especially as one of his breasts was extirpated, though his friends maintained that what was extirpated was a mammary tumour caused by a thrust in the breast from a foil. Whatever the truth of the matter, the

Chevalier found his dress an insurmountable obstacle to the fulfilment of his obligations as a duellist; and there exists a pathetic letter which he wrote to the Minister Maurepas, begging him to revoke the order obliging him to wear female attire, so that he might give satisfaction to the son of a man he had once offended, the late Comte de Guerchy.

'I am under the necessity', he wrote, 'of humbly submitting to your lordship that the period of my female novitiate is expired, and that it is impossible for me to become a professed nun. I have been able, in obedience to the orders of the late King and his ministers, to remain in petticoats during peacetime; but that is quite out of the question in time of war. It is necessary for the honour of the illustrious house of de Guerchy that I should be allowed to continue my military services; such, at least, is the opinion of the whole army and society. I have always thought and acted like Achilles; I never wage war with the dead; and I only kill the living when they attack me.'

Unfortunately for the honour of both the Chevalier d'Éon and 'the illustrious house of de Guerchy', the young count's mother, justly alarmed at the prospect of a duel between her son and the most experienced swordsman in France, begged the minister to reject this application. The injunction to wear female dress was accordingly renewed, and the pension of five hundred pounds per annum granted to the Chevalier by Louis XV was continued on this express condition. This situation inevitably exposed d'Éon to repeated insults and humiliations, but after 1789, when he finally installed himself in England, he was able to resume male attire and exercise his skill as a swordsman without let or hindrance. He gave lessons in the art, and occasionally fenced in public, several times with the Prince of Wales and once with the no less celebrated Chevalier de Saint-Georges. He died in London in 1810, at the age of eighty-one, and the post-mortem finally settled the question of his sex, on the anatomical if not the biological or psychological level, by stating him to be a man.

The Chevalier de Saint-Georges, d'Éon's great rival in swordsmanship, popularity and notoriety, was a mulatto, being the son of a Monsieur de Boulogne, a receiver-general on the Island of Guadeloupe, and a negress. His skill as a swordsman, demonstrated in countless duels, together with his swarthy good looks, made him a great favourite with the ladies. He also had considerable talent as a musician, and in 1776 he tried to become manager of the Opera; but the dancers and actresses begged the Queen not to degrade the Royal Academy of Music by placing it under the direction of a mulatto, and the Queen yielded to their entreaties, thus arousing a hatred in Saint-Georges which he vented on the Royal Family during the Revolution. Though he fought in a great many duels, he was generally the insulted party, and was never known to take advantage of his skill to insult a less gifted swordsman. On the other hand, he often gave a salutary lesson to quarrelsome or bumptious young men, as in the incident described a few years later in the following account:

> At Dunkirk he met in the company of several ladies a young officer of Hussars, who, not knowing him, was boasting of his skill as a swordsman, and asserting that no fencer in France was a match for him. 'Did you ever meet the famous Saint-Georges?' asked one of the ladies. 'Saint-Georges? Many a time; he could not stand a moment before me!' answered the Hussar, twirling his mustachios. 'That is strange,' observed Saint-Georges, 'and I should much like to have a trial of skill with you, young man. Possibly the ladies could procure us foils, and an *assaut d'armes* might entertain them.' The young officer assented to the proposal with a smile of contempt: foils belonging to the brother of the lady of the house were produced, and without hesitation the Hussar was preparing to shame his aged antagonist, who, politely addressing the ladies, asked them to name the buttons he should touch on his adversary's doliman. The delighted women, glad to see a coxcomb corrected, named the number of the buttons; which Saint-Georges touched one after the other, and then whipped the foil out of the hand of the inexperienced hand of the boaster, who, infuriated by rage and shame, wanted immediate satisfaction; when Saint-Georges quietly observed: 'Young man, your time is not yet come, you may still live to serve your country; but recollect you have met Saint-Georges, for I am that very person who could not at any time prove a match for you.' The lesson was a severe one; the young officer, confused and concealing his offended vanity, withdrew, and never after visited at the house.

Another example of a boastful young man being corrected by a master swordsman was given about this time by a colonel of the Guards. The latter remarked one day in company that he enjoyed the good fortune of never having been obliged to fight a duel. A young officer present immediately cast doubt upon the colonel's courage, asking: 'How could you avoid fighting when insulted?' The colonel replied that he had never given offence, and that no one had ever presumed to insult him, adding that if anyone should insult him, he would consider the person's character before demanding satisfaction. He had no sooner finished talking than the other struck him in the face with his glove, saying: 'Perhaps, Sir, you will not consider this an insult!' The colonel calmly put on his hat and walked out of the room, but the next morning he sent a challenge to his aggressor. When they arrived on the ground, the colonel was seen to be wearing a patch of sticking-plaster, the size of a crown piece, on the cheek which had received the blow. At the very first lunge he wounded his adversary in the sword-arm; then, taking off the plaster, he cut off part of it with a pair of scissors, and, replacing it on his cheek, took his leave of his antagonist, politely asking him to be good enough to let him know when he had recovered from his wound. As soon as he heard that the man was able to hold a sword, he called him out and wounded him a second time, after which he cut off another piece of his sticking-plaster. As the weeks went by, he called him out, fought him and wounded him, until the plaster had been reduced to the size of a shilling. When they next met, the colonel ran him through the body, and then, calmly contemplating the corpse, remarked with macabre satisfaction: 'Now I can take off my plaster.'

While duelling was on the decrease among the civil population, it still remained a serious problem in the army, where discipline was compromised by the frivolous quarrels which occurred every day among the officers. The Duc de Brissac, when he was appointed colonel of the King's Regiment, adopted a ruthless but very effective method of curbing the practice. On the day he joined the regiment, he invited all the officers to dinner, and informed them at dessert that he would be obliged if they would come and tell him of their intentions if any two of them decided to fight a duel. He had scarcely returned to his quarters when his orderly announced two young captains, a viscount and a chevalier. They informed that they were going to fight over a dispute as to whether a gentleman could appear at Versailles in undress coat and unpowdered, and the colonel agreed that this was a serious matter which could only be settled on the duelling ground. However, he added an ominous warning as he dismissed them: 'Remember this, gentlemen – a duel is only a ridiculous joke if neither of the parties is killed.'

The next day, on parade, he noticed the two captains at the head of their respective companies, and expressed his displeasure that the duel should have had no result. The chevalier showed him his arm in a sling, but the colonel dismissed the wound as a mere scratch, and insisted that the two officers should 'set to work again'. They accordingly fought once more, and this time the viscount received a wound which kept him in bed three months. During this time several officers of the regiment applied for permission to fight, but were asked to wait until the quarrel of the two friends had been terminated.

One morning, the colonel met the viscount taking an airing, leaning on the chevalier's arm, and observed with an air of satisfaction that now they could continue their battle. 'And this time,' he added, 'do let us have an end of it. I don't like protracted quarrels.'

The end of it came at last, when the two friends ran each other through and fell dead on the spot. The Duc de Brissac thereupon assembled the officers who were waiting for his permission to fight, and told them that they were now at liberty to terminate their quarrels. 'But as I do not wish the service to suffer by this sort of affair,' he said, 'I intend to grant only one permission at a time. And it must be understood that each quarrel shall be pursued to the last extremity – like the one which has just been concluded.' The result was as the colonel had foreseen: from that day the King's Regiment became a model regiment, with not a single duel to mar its discipline.

When the Revolution broke out, duelling fell into immediate disfavour, being regarded as a relic of the *ancien régime*. Consequently when a duel was fought between Charles de Lameth and Castries, in which Lameth was seriously wounded, a mob sacked Castries's house in the Rue de Varennes, while numerous deputations called on his adversary to express their disapproval of duelling. Referring to this event in one of his eloquent speeches, Mirabeau drew a comparison between the honour of the people and the honour which aristocratic duellists were so proud to defend. 'Are you not aware,' he asked his listeners, 'that this people, in the midst of their excitement, showed their respect for age and misfortune, by their delicate attention to Madame de Castries? Are you not aware that the people, on leaving those premises, which they destroyed, it must be said in a calm and orderly manner, insisted that the pockets of every individual should be searched, so that no base action might tarnish a just revenge? Such is true honour, which the prejudices and atrocity of gladiators can never display.'

Since Lameth was a revolutionary and Castries a representative of the old order, the suspicion arose that the partisans of privilege, defeated in the National Assembly, had decided to win the struggle by killing their opponents in single combat. Patriotic soldiers and citizens accordingly came forward to defend the Revolution with their own swords and bodies. Thus the chasseurs of the Battalion of Sainte-Marguerite passed a resolution to the effect that 'every chasseur will attend in turn the meetings of the National Assembly, will consider as personal every quarrel provoked with the patriot-deputies, and will defend them to the last drop of his blood'. Similarly, a certain Citizen Boyer hit upon the idea of taking upon himself all affairs of honour brought about by the 'blacks', as the enemies of the people were called, and issued the following manifesto: 'I swear that the entire earth will not be big enough to permit the escape of a man who wounds a deputy. I have weapons that the hands of patriotism have been pleased to make for me; all are familiar to me; I am not particular as to any of them; all of them will suit me, provided the result be *death.*' Boyer opened a special office to receive challenges from counter-revolutionaries, and so many came in that he was obliged to accept the aid of fifty other patriotic swordsmen, whom he formed into a sort of bodyguard under the name of the Battalion of Spadassinicides. However, the news of the formation of this body chilled the ardour of Boyer's challengers, who had imagined that they would have only one man to deal with, with the result that the Spadassinicides waited in vain for an opportunity to draw their swords.

Other patriots decided that a better method of dealing with the problem was to prohibit duelling entirely. The Mayor of Paris, for example, presented a petition to the National Assembly calling for 'a law against the practice of duelling, which would recall the citizens to a sense of their moral obligations, and warn them against the suggestions of sentiments incompatible with the character of a free and benevolent people'. Another petition called for a decree making duelling a crime against the nation, and begged the Assembly to 'wield the sword of justice in punishing the perverse individual who had shed the blood of one of the representatives of the people, and whose crime the capital had justly avenged'. This address was received with applause from both the deputies and the public, and when the member for Angoulême, a certain Monsieur Roy, exclaimed that 'none but scoundrels could applaud such a proposal', he was sentenced to three days' imprisonment.

On this occasion, the deputy Barnave made an eloquent speech against duelling, but only three months later he himself was involved in an encounter of the kind he had condemned so fiercely. During a debate in August 1790, the Royalist deputy Cazalès insulted all the members of the Left, and glanced so pointedly at Barnave that the latter rightly assumed that he was being singled out for attack. Ironically enough, the duel which the two men fought the next morning in the Bois de Boulogne, without any result save a bruise on Cazalès's forehead where Barnave's ball struck his hat, was characterized by exactly the sort of pleasant courtesy which marked some of the greatest duels under the *ancien régime*. Thus Cazalès told his antagonist: 'It would grieve me to kill you, but you are really very much in my way. However, I only want to keep you from the tribune for a while.' To which Barnave replied: 'I am more generous; I scarcely wish to touch you, for you are the only orator on your side, whereas on mine, my absence would go unnoticed.'

Possibly the only great orator of the Revolution who not only spoke against duelling but practised what he preached was Camille Desmoulins. Insulted at the Théâtre-Français by two actors, he replied to the double provocation with a mere gesture of contempt; and he justified his behaviour in the following eloquent passage:

'One may brave death in the cause of liberty for one's country, and I feel that I could stretch my neck out of my litter, and hold forth my throat to the sword of Anthony. I feel that I could possess sufficient fortitude to mount the scaffold with a mingled sentiment of pleasure. Such is the courage which I have received, not from nature – which shudders at the aspect of death – but from philosophy. To be assassinated by the bravo who provokes me is to be stung by a tarantula. I should have to spend all my days in the Bois de Boulogne were I to give satisfaction to all those whom my frankness offends. I may be accused of cowardice; but I feel that the times are not far distant when we shall have ample opportunities of dying in a more glorious and useful manner. Then the love of my country will inspire me again with that courage which enabled me to mount a table at the Palais Royale, and be the first to assume the national cockade.'

Unfortunately, Desmoulins's restraint was poorly rewarded, for he died in 1794, not 'in a more glorious and useful manner' than on a duelling-ground, but on the scaffold to which the Robespierre Terror had condemned him.

Under the Directory, with the counter-revolutionary movement in full force, duelling naturally returned to favour, especially among the upper classes and the *nouveaux riches*, while in the army both officers and soldiers were in the habit of settling their quarrels by force of arms. Pistols were now used by civilians when they fought a duel, and the military for their part adopted the sabre as their weapon.

The vogue for duelling inevitably continued during the Empire, although Napoleon disapproved strongly of the practice. However, there was little he could do to discourage duelling when the superior officers of his army were often fanatical duellists themselves. In 1802, for example, when he was First Consul, Generals Destaing and Regnier quarrelled about the Egyptian Campaign and fought a pistol duel in which Destaing was killed. On that and subsequent occasions, Napoleon visited his displeasure on the survivor; and he was often heard to say that he could never place any reliance on a duellist in battle, or to cite Latour-Maubourg, the bravest of the brave, as a man who had never drawn his sword in a private quarrel. But duelling went from strength to strength, and Napoleon's last period of power, the Hundred Days, was marked, like the first, by a duel between two generals.

This encounter took place between General Ornano, subsequently Governor of the Invalides, and General Bonnet, who later became a Senator. An appointment had been given to the former which the latter had hoped to receive, and General Bonnet showed his disappointment in various ways, culminating in a refusal to return General Ornano's salute one day at the Tuileries. A duel was arranged for the following day, but it rained so hard that the pistols failed to go off. When the two men met again the next day, Bonnet had the first fire, and missed. Ornano, who prided himself on his skill with the pistol, fired in his turn and was surprised to find that his shot had had no apparent effect. 'What, sir, you are not dead?' he asked. 'No, sir,' said Bonnet. 'That's very odd,' observed Ornano; 'when I fire at a man I generally kill him.' Going up to his antagonist, he discovered the explanation in a five-franc piece in Bonnet's pocket which had stopped the ball in its progress. '*Morbleu!*' he remarked sardonically. 'You have invested your money very luckily.'

The Allied occupation of Paris resulted in countless duels between officers of the foreign armies and those of the disbanded French army, and these encounters generally proved fatal to the foreigners. Rumour had it that the French spent their days and nights fencing in preparation for these conflicts, and it was even alleged that their *provosts* or fencing-masters donned the uniform of officers in order to meet any young foreigner who was rash enough to accept their challenges. Similar scenes occurred in the South of France, where the British army was quartered, but although the French had the choice of weapons, and invariably picked their favourite small-sword, the English fared better than the Austrians and Prussians in these so-called 'Waterloo duels'. This was because, knowing nothing of the niceties of swordsmanship, they rushed headlong at their opponents and spitted them straight away. It was in vain that the French protested at this 'brutal', 'unchivalrous' behaviour, for the English seconds stood by with loaded pistols, and threatened to shoot anybody who attempted to intervene. As a contemporary English commentator remarked, 'this system gradually produced a more wholesome state of feeling'.

When the occupying troops left France, the French inevitably turned to fighting amongst themselves, and for several years duels were fought almost every day between officers on half-pay and officers of the Royal Guards. As the nineteenth century wore on, these political duels became more frequent in the civil population, opposing Royalists and Bonapartists under the Restoration, Republicans and Legitimists under the bourgeois monarchy of Louis-Philippe, Bonapartists and Republicans under the Second Empire, and the supporters or opponents of Boulanger or Dreyfus under the Third Republic.

Occasionally a leading figure of some faction or other would take part in a duel himself. Thus there was the famous duel between the editors of two Paris newspapers, Armand Carrel of the Republican *National*, and Roux Laborie of the Legitimist *Revenant*; Carrel was seriously wounded and the mob vented its fury on the offices of the Royalist paper. Then there was the encounter in 1870 between the journalist Victor Noir and Prince Bonaparte; Noir's death in this duel resulted in a wave of violent feeling against the Second Empire which contributed to its overthrow later that year. Or again there was the grotesque affair of honour between the popular General Boulanger and the aged lawyer Floquet, in which the latter ran his sword into the soldier's neck; it was later explained that the *brave général* had no experience of fencing, but the ridicule which the duel brought upon him was a foretaste of what he would suffer when he neglected the opportunity to stage a *coup d'état* in order to go to bed with his mistress.

With few exceptions, the duel in nineteenth-century France – though not yet the farce it was to become in this century – was as drab and uninteresting as the manner and dress of the participants. One affair of honour, however, deserves to be quoted here, not on account of the eminence of the combatants, nor on account of the duel itself, but because its aftermath was observed and recorded by one of the most brilliant writers of the age, Edmond de Goncourt.

Early in 1886, the young journalist and novelist Robert Caze refused to fight Félicien Champsaur, whom he accused of having libelled him in a newspaper article, and took legal action against him instead. Taunted with cowardice by a certain Charles Vignier, he fought a duel with the latter on February 15 and spitted himself on Vignier's sword. Goncourt went to see him the next day in the little fourth-floor flat where he lived with his wife and children, and returned, with a vulture-like flair, on March 23, the very day that Caze died. After his second and last visit, he wrote down this brief but harrowing impression of a duellist's last hours:

> I had set off to go and call on Robert Caze, who Daudet had told me was getting better, and I had practically got to the station when a young man came up to me, raised his hat and asked me if I was Monsieur de Goncourt. When I answered that I was, he said: 'Here is *Grand'mère*, the book by Robert Caze which he has dedicated to you . . . He has asked me to apologise to you for not having written anything in the book, but he is too weak to write.' And he told me that the poor fellow was regarded as done for.
>
> Filled with gloom, I continued on my way, trying like a coward to put off my visit, dawdling in the streets, dropping into La Narde's and Bing's, and hesitating in the Rue Condorcet as to whether I should not just leave my card with the concierge. I finally decided to go upstairs, where poor Madame Caze told me that her husband was desperately ill and that he had had a dreadful fever for a good five hours.
>
> I sat down in the little study, where Huysmans, Vidal, and an Impressionist painter were waiting. Through the open door I could hear the *glug-glug* of all sorts of drinks the wounded man kept tossing down one after the other, in his unquenchable thirst; I could hear the incessant coughing of his consumptive wife; I could hear the scolding

voice of the maid, as she told one of the children: 'You're taking advantage of your father's illness to do no work.' The surgeon was expected, but he didn't come. After waiting for half an hour, Huysmans and I got up and left, talking about the dying man and his preoccupation with his book and with the dispatch of the copies printed on superior paper. Huysmans saw him today for a moment, and the only thing he had to say was: 'Have you read my book?'

7 · More Duels in Britain

The first half of the nineteenth century, which was to witness the virtual end of duelling in Britain, began with a spate of affairs of honour. Quite apart from the personal disputes common to all times and the martial atmosphere produced by the war with France, there was a host of internal political troubles, ranging from the incorporation of Ireland to the refusal of Catholic Emancipation, all of which contributed to bring tempers to boiling point.

One of the first noteworthy duels of the century took place in Hyde Park in March 1803 between two officers known to us simply as Lieutenant W– of the Navy and Captain I– of the Army. This murderous affair, which was as it were a repetition with pistols of the famous sword-duel between Mohun and Hamilton a hundred years before, was described by a contemporary in the following record:

> The antagonists arrived at the appointed place within a few minutes of each other. Some dispute arose respecting the distance, which the friends of Lieutenant W– insisted should not exceed six paces; while the seconds of Captain I– urged strongly the rashness of so short a distance, and insisted on its being extended. At length the proposal of Lieutenant W–'s friends was agreed to, and the parties fired per signal; when Lieutenant W– received the shot of his adversary on the guard of his pistol, which tore away the third and fourth fingers of his right hand. The seconds then interfered to no purpose. The son of Neptune, apparently callous to pain, wrapped his handkerchief round his hand, and swore he had another, which never failed him. Captain I– called his friend aside, and told him it was in vain to urge a reconciliation. They again took their ground. On Lieutenant W– receiving the pistol in his left hand, he looked steadfastly at Captain I– for some time, then cast his eyes to Heaven, and said: 'Forgive me.' The parties fired as before, and both fell. Captain I– received the shot through his head, and instantly expired. Lieutenant W– received the ball in his

> left breast, and immediately inquired of his friend if Captain I–'s wound was mortal? Being answered in the affirmative, he thanked Heaven he had lived thus long. He requested that a mourning ring, which was on his finger, might be given to his sister; and that she might be assured it was the happiest moment he ever knew. He had scarcely finished the word when a quantity of blood burst from his wound, and he expired almost without a struggle.

It was supposed at the time that it was on his sister's account that the Lieutenant had fought this duel, in order to avenge her dishonour, and his conduct was generally approved. But the next fatal duel which took place in London, on April 6, 1803, although between two older officers, was fought over a far less important matter. The two men involved, Lieutenant-Colonel Montgomery of the 9th Regiment of Foot and Captain Macnamara of the Royal Navy, were riding that morning in Hyde Park, each followed by a Newfoundland dog, when the dogs started fighting. Colonel Montgomery, who failed to see Captain Macnamara, separated the animals, exclaiming: 'Whose dog is that? I will knock him down!' To this Captain Macnamara is said to have replied: 'Have you the impudence to say that you will knock my dog down? You must first knock me down.' High words ensued, followed by an exchange of cards and an agreement to meet at seven o'clock that evening near Primrose Hill.

Both men were excellent shots, and both were wounded, the Colonel mortally. His ball went through Captain Macnamara's body, entering on the right side just above the hip and taking part of the waistcoat in with it. As for Captain Macnamara's ball, it entered the right side of Colonel Montgomery's chest, and he fell groaning to the ground; he was carried into Chalk Farm, the house which subsequently gave its name to the surrounding district, and died about five minutes later.

Captain Macnamara recovered from his wound, and was tried for murder. At the trial he made an eloquent statement in his defence, asserting the absolute necessity for a gentleman to defend his honour at all costs, even when – though he did not say this – the matter at dispute was something as trivial as a dog.

'I am a Captain of the British Navy,' he said. 'My character you can hear only from others. But to maintain my character in that situation I must be respected. When called upon to lead others into honourable danger, I must not be supposed to be a man who sought safety by submitting to what custom has taught others to consider as a disgrace. I am not presuming to urge anything against the law of God, or of this land. I know, that in the eyes of beauty and reason, obedience to the law, though against the feelings of the world, is the first duty, and ought to be the rule of action; but upon putting a construction upon my motives, so as to ascertain the quality of my actions, you will make allowance for my situation. It is impossible to define in terms the proper feelings of a gentleman; but their existence has supported this country for many ages, and she might perish if they were lost.'

The jury were impressed by this moving plea, together with the excellent character given to Captain Macnamara by Lords Hood, Nelson, Hotham and Minto, as well as 'a great number of highly respectable gentlemen'. The result was that, although the judge insisted that on all the evidence and the prisoner's own admission they were bound to find the accused guilty of manslaughter, they obstinately returned a verdict of 'Not guilty'. The honour of Captain Macnamara, and also presumably that of his Newfoundland dog, was triumphantly vindicated.

A duellist who killed his adversary could not, however, always count on a favourable verdict from a British jury, as Major Alexander Campbell of the 21st Regiment discovered to his cost in 1808. On June 23 of the previous year, in Armagh, Ireland, he had quarrelled with a Captain Alexander Boyd of the same regiment over the correct way of giving a word of command; and in a pistol duel which the two men had fought later that night, without seconds, Boyd had been mortally wounded. In the presence of two brother officers, the dying man had accused Campbell of being 'a bad man', and had complained: 'You know I wanted you to wait, and have friends.' But when the Major had replied that he was 'an unfortunate man, but I hope not a bad one', and had begged his adversary's forgiveness, Boyd had stretched out his hand and said: 'I forgive you; I feel for you, and I am sure you do for me.'

Campbell had then fled to England, where he had lived for several months at Chelsea under a fictitious name; but remorse had affected him so deeply that he had finally decided to surrender himself, whatever the result might be. He was put on trial for murder at Armagh in August 1808; and despite the excellent character given him by a host of senior officers, 'for humanity, peaceable conduct and proper behaviour', the jury found him 'Guilty of murder', though they added a recommendation to mercy.

The Major was sentenced to be hanged on the following Monday, but the execution was postponed to 'Wednesday s'ennight' to allow his wife to apply for a Royal pardon. There then began a race against time and the elements, in the finest tradition of nineteenth-century melodrama, which a contemporary chronicler recorded as follows:

Mrs Campbell, who was tenderly attached to her husband, having resolved to proceed to London and solicit the Royal mercy, hastened to the sea-coast, but found that unexpected circumstances threatened to frustrate her fondest hopes. It blew a perfect hurricane, and no reward could tempt the captain of any vessel to venture to sea. While she was running up and down the shore in a distracted state, she met a few humble fishermen; and these poor fellows no sooner heard the cause of her agony than they offered her their service and their boat, in which she actually crossed the channel. Her noble companions not only refused to receive any reward, but attended her to the coach-office, and followed her several miles on the road, praying God to bless her, and grant her success.

On arriving at Windsor with her petition it was past eight o'clock, and the King had retired to his apartment; but the Queen, compassionating the afflicted wife, presented the memorial that night, and Mrs Campbell received the kindest attention from the whole of the Royal family.

The case was anxiously debated in the council, but, after a full review of the circumstances, it was finally resolved that the law should take its course. Mrs Campbell in the meantime proceeded to Scotland, cheered with the hope of obtaining at least another respite. She reached Ayr, her paternal home, and on the very morning that her husband's corpse was brought thither to be interred.

When Major Campbell heard that his fate was decided, he prepared to meet death with the fortitude of the soldier and the resignation of the Christian. A change had come over the public mind, and universal sorrow for his fate had taken place of the prejudices which inaccurate reports of the duel had produced. By a strange concurrence of circumstances, his own regiment mounted guard round the scaffold. A vast multitude occupied every spot from which a view of the place of execution could be obtained. The crowd displayed the unusual show of all the gentry from the neighbouring country, assembled in deep mourning.

Precisely at noon Major Campbell appeared on the platform, supported by his father-in-law. Instantly the brave highlanders took off their military bonnets; and with streaming eyes, joined in prayer for the spirit about to be parted from its mortal tenement. The vast crowd stood uncovered in solemn silence, so that the grating of the falling drop was heard to the remotest extremity. One groan from the thousands of spectators for an instant broke the profound silence and proclaimed that all was over! His body, after having been suspended for the usual time, was put into a hearse in waiting, which left the town immediately, escorted by Doctor Bowie, for Ayr in Scotland, to be interred in the family vault.

Major Campbell, in his conversation with his intimate friends, previously to surrendering himself, had always said, that if he were convicted of murder, he should suffer, as an example to duellists in Ireland; but it was always his opinion that a jury would not convict him of murder.

It was widely believed that his rash declaration that he was sure that the verdict could only be manslaughter turned the jury against him. His contrite behaviour at the trial and the good character which his superior officers gave him did something to modify their opinion of him, but it appears that one of the witnesses for the defence assumed a dictatorial air which damned the accused in their eyes. The only consolation which could be drawn from the whole sorry affair was, as a writer of the time observed, that 'the unfortunate catastrophe, which produced such an awful result to Major Campbell, it is hoped will not fail to leave a lesson to mankind of salutary influence'.

Whatever influence the execution of Major Campbell may have had on mankind, at least in Britain, was nullified in September of the following year, when Lord Castlereagh, the Secretary of War, sent a challenge to Canning, the Secretary of State for Foreign Affairs. Castlereagh's complaint was that Canning had secretly intrigued to have his fellow member of the cabinet removed from office, so that the Marquis of Wellesley could be installed in his place, and had indeed obtained a promise to that effect from the Duke of Portland. 'Notwithstanding this promise,' Castlereagh wrote in the letter accompanying his challenge, 'by which I consider you presumed it unfit that I should remain charged with the conduct of the war, and by which my situation as a Minister of the Crown was made dependent on your will and pleasure, you continued to sit in the same Cabinet with me and left me not only in the persuasion that I possessed your confidence and support as a colleague, but allowed me, in breach of every principle of good faith, both public and private, to originate and proceed in a new enterprise of the most arduous and important nature (the Walcheren expedition), with your apparent concurrence and ostensible approbation. You are fully aware that, if my situation in the Government had been disclosed to me, I could not have submitted to remain one moment in office, without the entire abandonment of private honour and public duty. You knew I *was* deceived, and you *continued* to deceive me.'

The duel was fought at Putney Heath, where the two men fired by signal at a distance of ten yards. The first fire missed, and as no 'explanation' took place, the combatants fired again. This time Canning was wounded in the left thigh, and the encounter was terminated.

An amusing anecdote was later told by Cunningham in connection with this duel. Lord Castlereagh had promised to make Sir Alexander Johnston Chief Justice and President of Ceylon, but his cousin Mrs Damer, a confirmed Whig, had warned the latter: 'The fellow will cheat you; he is a Tory.' Shortly afterwards, Castlereagh summoned Sir Alexander urgently, saw the great seal affixed to his commission, and offered him his congratulations. This was late at night, and the next morning he fought the duel with Canning. Calling on the victor later in the day, Sir Alexander expressed astonishment at his self-possession in doing official business on the eve of a duel. 'Oh, I had a reason for it,' said Castlereagh. 'Had I fallen before the great seal was set to your commission, you would have lost the appointment, and my cousin would have said: "The fellow, sir, was a cheat; he was a Tory." ' This confidence procured an additional satisfaction for Lord Castlereagh, for when it was repeated to Mrs Damer, tears came into her eyes and she declared: 'Go to my cousin, and say I have wronged him; that I love his manliness, and his regard for honour, and that I wish to renew our intercourse of friendship.'

Meanwhile, in spite of Major Campbell's pious hope that his death would prove an example to Irish duellists, duelling had continued to flourish in Ireland. It could, of course, be argued that this was only to be expected, since the judicial duel had lasted longer there, and the duel of honour was held in greater regard, than in England. 'A duel', wrote a noted Irish duellist in the last century, 'was indeed considered a necessary part of a young man's education, but by no means a ground for future animosity with his opponent. When men had a glowing ambition to excel in all manner of feats and exercises they naturally conceived that manslaughter, in an *honest* way (that is, not knowing *which* would be slaughtered), was the most chivalrous and gentlemanly of all their accomplishments. No young fellow could finish his education till he had exchanged shots with some of his acquaintances. The two first questions always asked as to a young man's respectability and qualifications, particularly when he proposed for a lady wife, were: "What family is he of?" and "Did he ever blaze?" Tipperary and Galway were the ablest schools of the duelling science: Galway was most scientific at the sword, and Tipperary most practical and prized at the pistol; Mayo not amiss at either, while Roscommon and Sligo had many professors and a high reputation in the leaden branch of the pastime. . . .'

It was inevitable that the rumbustious Daniel O'Connell should have been constantly involved in duels, and in 1815 he took part in one of the most celebrated encounters in Irish history. The affair began with a reference O'Connell made in Capel Street to 'the beggarly Corporation of Dublin', a remark to which a certain Mr d'Esterre who was a member of that Corporation took exception. He wrote to O'Connell and was assured by the latter that 'no expression which language could furnish was sufficient to convey the sentiments of contempt he had for that body'. After further letters from d'Esterre, but no challenge, a meeting was at last arranged at a place twelve miles outside Dublin. A local journal gave this account of the duel itself in its issue of February 2:

> The hour appointed was half-past three o'clock. At three precisely (we can speak confidently, for we now speak from personal knowledge), Mr O'Connell, attended by his second, Surgeon Macklin, and a number of friends, was on the ground. About four, Mr d'Esterre, attended only by Surgeon Peel, Sir Edward Stanley (his second), and a Mr d'Esterre of Limerick, appeared. There was some conversation between the seconds as to position, mode of fire, etc.; which, added to other sources of delay, occupied forty minutes. During this interval Mr d'Esterre took occasion to say that his quarrel with Mr O'Connell was not of a religious nature. To the Catholics, or their leaders, he said he had no animosity whatever.
>
> At forty minutes past four the combatants were on the ground; they both displayed the greatest coolness and courage. The friends of both parties retired, and the combatants, having a pistol in each hand, with directions to discharge them at their discretion, prepared to fire. They levelled, and before the lapse of a second, both shots were heard. Mr d'Esterre's was first, and missed. Mr O'Connell's followed instantaneously, and took effect in the thigh of his antagonist, about an inch below the hip. Mr d'Esterre of course fell, and both the surgeons hastened to him. They found that the ball had 'traversed the hip', and could not be found. There was an immense effusion of blood. All parties prepared to move towards home, and arrived in town before eight o'clock.
>
> It is said that Mr d'Esterre's wound is very dangerous; we sincerely hope, however, that it will not prove mortal. The ball passed through both thighs. There was a violent haemorrhage of the bladder last night, but it had ceased before morning.
>
> We need not describe the emotions which burst forth all along the road, when it was ascertained that Mr O'Connell was safe.

D'Esterre died at five o'clock in the afternoon of February 3, and was mourned as 'a young man of great respectability and high spirit'. It was believed in Dublin that his natural indignation at O'Connell's attack on the Corporation had been fanned by his colleagues, who knew him to be a crack shot and hoped that he would rid them of their formidable opponent.

As for O'Connell, he heaped coals of fire on the Corporation's collective head by offering d'Esterre's widow a pension equal to the amount her husband had been earning; but the City Fathers rejected the offer and voted the promised sum themselves. O'Connell also made a solemn vow never to fight another duel, a promise which – since he failed to bridle his notoriously quick tongue – meant that his son Morgan was kept busy taking on all comers on behalf of 'the governor'.

If O'Connell's fatal duel with d'Esterre caused considerable excitement in Ireland, it was nothing compared to the sensation caused in England by the innocuous, bloodless but highly publicized encounter which took place in London in 1829 between the Duke of Wellington and the Earl of Winchilsea.

The fundamental cause of their quarrel was the part the Duke of Wellington had played in bringing in the Roman Catholic Relief Bill, a measure which had aroused the fanatical wrath of the Earl of Winchilsea. When the Duke gave his patronage to the establishment of the King's College, London, the Earl saw his opportunity to damage the great man's reputation, and he wrote to the secretary of the committee, stating his conviction that 'the whole transaction was intended as a blind to the Protestant and high-church party; that the noble Duke, who had, for some time previous to that period, determined upon "breaking in upon the constitution of 1688", might more effectually, under the cloak of some outward show of zeal for the Protestant religion, carry on his insidious designs for the infringement of our liberties, and the introduction of Popery into every department of the state'.

This letter was also communicated to the Press, and gave rise to a voluminous correspondence between the two peers. Having established that Winchilsea was in fact the author of the letter in question, the Duke wrote to the culprit declaring that 'it does not appear necessary to impute to me, in no measured terms, disgraceful and criminal motives for my conduct in the part which I took in the establishment of the college', and adding that he was sure that 'your Lordship will, upon reflection, be anxious to relieve yourself from the pain of having thus insulted a man who never injured or offended you'. After Winchilsea, through the Earl of Falmouth, had expressed a desire to know the extent of the reparation the Duke expected, and had been told that he should write a letter of withdrawal and apology to either the secretary of the King's College or the Duke himself, he stated his own terms.

'I am ready,' he announced, 'to allow that I was mistaken in my view of the noble Duke's conduct, as expressed in my letter to Mr Coleridge, on the 14th instant, and to state my regret at having so expressed it, provided the noble Duke will state on his part, that at the time he came forward to preside at the meeting for the establishment of the King's College, London, he did not contemplate the measures which are now in progress for Roman Catholic

17·(*a*) *'The Duel in Tothill Fields.' A drawing in an edition of Ainsworth's 'The Miser's Daughter' by George Cruikshank*

17·(*b*) *A duel. A drawing by George Cruikshank*, 1825

18·(*a*) *'Patriots Deciding a Point of Honour.' A drawing by James Gillray*, 1807

18·(*b*) *'Och, my Canning, my Canning.' A drawing by George Cruikshank*, 1809

19·(*a*) *'Peter Sham Love's Duel.' A drawing by James Marks*, 1821

19·(*b*) *'The Point of Honour.' One of a series of drawings by Edwin Landseer on contemporary life*, 1827

20·(*a*) *The duel between Lord Lennox and Lord Glengall*, 1826
A drawing by George Cruikshank

20·(*b*) *The duel between the Duke of Wellington and Lord Winchilsea*, 1829
A drawing by W. Heath

emancipation; or, to use Mr Peel's words, "for breaking in upon the constitution of 1688", but without some statement to that effect from the noble Duke, I cannot withdraw the expressions contained in the above letter.'

This condition was of course totally unacceptable, and the Duke of Wellington continued to press for 'reparation', by which he now clearly meant 'satisfaction'. The Earl, however, pretended not to understand the drift of the Duke's demands, and Falmouth wrote on his behalf to Sir Henry Hardinge, who was acting for the Duke, that 'if by the word "reparation", any withdrawal of Lord Winchilsea's public letter, or expression of regret for its contents, be expected, he does not feel himself in a situation to comply with such expectation'. Finally, tiring of this word-play, Hardinge fixed on a meeting place and curtly informed Falmouth on March 20 that 'the Duke of Wellington will be at the place appointed at eight o'clock tomorrow morning'. To put the matter beyond question, the Duke himself wrote to the Earl: 'I now call upon your lordship to give me that satisfaction for your conduct which a gentleman has a right to require, and which a gentleman never refuses to give.' After this, Winchilsea could no longer keep silent, and he at last replied, literally at the eleventh hour, that 'the satisfaction which your Grace has demanded, it is of course impossible for me to decline'.

The two peers met at Battersea Fields on the following morning, but were disturbed by 'the presence of some common people' and moved to another spot to settle their quarrel. At the word 'Fire', the Duke raised his pistol, but hesitated for a moment, as he saw that Lord Winchilsea had kept his pistol pointing to the ground, and clearly had no intention of firing. The Duke accordingly fired at random, and the Earl followed his example. Falmouth then handed Hardinge a memorandum expressing Lord Winchilsea's regret for publishing the letter in question, and after the word 'apology' had been added in pencil at the Duke's request, the latter declared himself satisfied.

The parties then separated, but not before an onlooker had expressed his indignant astonishment to Lord Falmouth that the Duke of Wellington should have been put in such a perilous situation. Falmouth answered him that he had only agreed to act as second to the Earl of Winchilsea on the condition that the latter should not fire at the Duke. He explained this astonishing arrangement by saying that the Earl of Winchilsea thought that the injury he had done the Duke was too great for a mere apology, and that he ought to receive his fire.

As for the impression which the duel made on the public at large, some idea of it may be gained from the following account of the affair given in the *Morning Herald* on the 23rd:

> The City was thrown into a great ferment this morning by a report which seemed so utterly improbable, that at first few people believed it, except those whose mental swallows are so outrageously capacious as to take down everything in the shape of news that is presented to them. For our part we were amongst the incredulous, considering the story as only fit to amuse male and female old ladies – the gossipers in and out of petticoats. Notwithstanding our unbelief, however, we were seriously told by every third person we met how his Grace the Duke of Wellington had taken offence at his lordship's, the Earl of Winchilsea's letter, about the King's College; how the aforesaid noble Duke had challenged the aforesaid noble Earl; how the said noble belligerents had agreed, through their seconds, the Earl of Falmouth and Sir Henry Hardinge, to meet, stand up, and fire at one another, at the distance of twelve paces, like sage legislators and true Christians; how they accordingly did meet this morning in Battersea Fields, among the cabbages; how his Grace, the premier, the champion of emancipation, shot at his lordship, the Earl of Winchilsea, the champion of Protestantism; how the above-mentioned Duke was near settling emancipation, and the above-mentioned Earl to boot, by shooting him through the body; how, notwithstanding, the ball hit the lappel of his lordship's coat only; how thereupon the noble Earl fired his pistol in the air; how the seconds then interfered; how the lord presented to Sir Henry Hardinge, the Duke's second, a written apology; how it was accepted; and lastly, how the affair was thus amicably arranged; the Duke luckily being left at liberty to defend the Emancipation Bill instead of being called upon to defend himself from a charge of murder; while the Earl may, if he chooses, again take his place at the head of the 'No Popery' boys instead of being quietly laid up in the narrow house, to decay among the bones of his buried ancestors. Strange as this story appears, it turned out in all its principal features to be literally true. Yes, reader, the Duke of Wellington, the conqueror of a greater conqueror than either Alexander or Caesar, the first warrior of his day, the victor of a hundred battles, the Prime Minister of Great Britain, and the author of a measure which, he says, is necessary, absolutely necessary, for the welfare of the Empire, setting all these things at nought, placed himself in a situation where it was probable that he might have become a murderer; might have committed a deadly crime, which would have brought him to the bar of his country to plead for his life as a felon of the blackest dye. And all this risk was run, forsooth – all this wickedness was to be perpetrated – merely because a noble lord, in a fit of anger, wrote a pettish letter, which even his best friends and warmest admirers laughed at. Truly it is no wonder that the multitude should break the laws when we thus see the law-makers themselves, the great, the powerful, and the renowned, setting them at open defiance.
>
> The Duke wished Lord Winchilsea good morning, and, the compliment being returned, the parties left the ground and returned to town. About fourteen or fifteen gardeners and labouring men, who were on the spot during the transaction, advised the noble combatants to settle the matter in dispute with their fists.

Première position pour tirer L'Epée

Position pour la garde en quatre

Première position du Salut

Du coupe sur pointe de quatre sur les Armes

Seconde position du Salut

Quatrième position du Salut

Cinquième position du Salut

At this period of the nineteenth century, with peers of the realm flouting the law against duelling, the Bow Street runners were hard put to it to keep track of the countless duels which were arranged in and around London. One of the runners, Henry Goddard, has left us this vivid account of a typical early morning's work, 'frustrating' a duel:

> In the middle of the following night I was woke up from my slumbers by hearing a loud single knock at the street door, and a ringing of the bell. Before I could get up to answer it there was another knock which rather alarmed me and it took me some time before I could find the door to let myself out. In the middle of my fright at length having found it, I made my way along the passage and opened the street door, when to my astonishment there stood like a statue Tom Clements, one of my brother officers, who said it was now past two o'clock in the morning, that Sam Plank our chief had just called him up and we had to meet him at Tyburn Gate without delay, as he had only just received information that there was going to be a duel between two gentlemen at Wormwood Scrubs. (I was residing at this time at No. 12 Robert Street, Hampstead Road.)
>
> My wife in the mean time struck a light, and I got myself dressed in less than five minutes, telling her at the same time the business I was going upon, which rather alarmed her; but there being no time for parley I bade her good morning and away I went with Tom Clements, running and walking till we reached Tyburn Gate, where we found Sam Plank, who had just arrived in a Post-Chaise belonging to Robert Newman of Regent Street. We got in and the post-boy was instructed to proceed down the Uxbridge Road and turn down the Lane leading to Wormwood Scrubs.
>
> On arriving at the Lane we went down it for some distance, turned round a bend in an out of the way place and concealed ourselves behind a very high hedge. (It was about four in the morning.)
>
> We had not been there more than half an hour before we heard in the distance the sound of Carriage wheels and heavy trotting of Horses, which became louder and louder, and as they advanced we distinctly heard voices till the noise of the carriage ceased. I being the youngest of the party climbed upon a high bank and then on to a tree commanding a distant view. I then saw the tops of three carriages, and climbing higher, I counted eight Gentlemen, which I reported to my brother officers.
>
> We then lost no time in approaching the spot, walking in a stooping position to prevent observation, advancing nearer by degrees; but seeing their hasty preparation, we sallied out upon them to their very great astonishment, so suddenly that they were completely taken off their guard. Mr Plank our chief informed them who we were and said from all appearances at this early time in the morning and at this retired spot it was evident there was about to be committed a breach of the Peace and therefore they must all consider themselves in custody. While he was thus engaged, Clements and I took possession of three pistol-cases containing two duelling pistols in each, with flasks of gunpowder, percussion caps, bullets, etc.
>
> Among the party there were two surgeons who had brought three cases of Instruments, wadding, lint, etc., and these gentlemen seeing how matters stood and the

predicament they were in, very quietly and with great civility returned to their carriages with the seconds, I in one, Clements and Plank in the two others, and being all quietly seated, Plank took the lead bidding myself and Clements to follow. We drove rapidly to Marlborough Street office, arriving about five in the morning, having then to knock, ring and wake up the office-keeper, Bill Waistcott, who in about ten minutes opened the door and was bewildered at seeing four carriages containing eight gentlemen and ourselves making up the number to eleven, getting out and walking into the office. The next thing to be done was to call and wake up the resident Magistrate, Mr Conant, who was very soon woke up, but he wanted to know what all this stir was about at so early an hour, and the reason of so many carriages at hand. Mr Plank having made him acquainted of the circumstances, he came downstairs into the private room, and after hearing the case the whole party, eight in number, were held to bail.

Thus ended an affair which in all probability, if it had not been interrupted, might have concluded seriously if not fatally.

No account of the above circumstances that I am aware of ever reached the Press and consequently was not made known, so many years having now passed away very likely all the parties are dead.

The names of the Duellists were Capt Burton and William Ford, Esq.

Another duel arranged at Wormwood Scrubs, but which did not receive the attention of the Bow Street runners, was the encounter on June 16, 1838, between the young Lord Castlereagh and Monsieur Gérard de Melcy. This somewhat melodramatic affair was the result of the young peer's infatuation for the famous singer Guilia Grisi, who was then married to de Melcy. Not content with applauding the lady with frenzied enthusiasm every night during the Italian Opera's season in London, and going back-stage in the intervals to offer her his admiration, Lord Castlereagh wrote her a letter, 'conceived in the warmest terms', which fell into de Melcy's hands. The outraged husband promptly demanded satisfaction from the young Englishman, and, when the latter 'expressed his great regret for the error, promising to renounce the insane delusion', replied that he could not be satisfied with verbal excuses. A duel was accordingly arranged for half-past four the following morning at Wormwood Scrubs, with Mr Bentinck acting as Castlereagh's second and another Frenchman, Monsieur Cottreau, attending de Melcy.

When the principals arrived on the ground, bringing their own pistols, an objection was raised to allowing them to use the weapons with which they had been accustomed to practise, and it was decided to send to a gunsmith's for a new pair. This, of course, caused considerable delay, and it was not until ten o'clock that the husband and the supposed lover were able to take up their positions. At the last moment, Mr Bentinck gave Monsieur Cottreau a letter from Lord Castlereagh, with permission to read it where and as he wished.

At last the signal to fire was given, and both shots went off together. De Melcy's ball entered Castlereagh's wrist, furrowed his arm, and grazed his chest, causing a substantial loss of blood. Bentinck naturally declared that the affair should not go any further, but de Melcy interposed: 'For the present.'

It was then that Lord Castlereagh's letter was read to the offended husband. In this letter the young Englishman solemnly stated that 'having, perhaps, in a few minutes to appear before his Maker, he declared that Madame de Melcy's honour was utterly untainted, and that the lady had never even written to him, nor authorized him to write to her'. With this letter the punctilious de Melcy conceded that his honour was satisfied, and he agreed to terminate the affair.

This romantic, aristocratic affair, in which there was nothing commonplace except the name of Wormwood Scrubs, was followed on August 22 of the same year by an encounter in which everything was irremediably plebeian. This duel was fought between Mr Mirfin, a sometime linen-draper from the Tottenham Court Road, and Mr Eliot, the nephew of an inn-keeper at Taunton, not over the love or honour of a lady, but apparently for a bet of one hundred pounds. It took place on Wimbledon Common, the two parties firing at a distance of twelve paces. At the first shot Eliot's ball went through Mirfin's hat. The seconds promptly intervened, but Mirfin objected and insisted on having a second shot, with dire consequences to himself, for he fell to Eliot's next ball. He was immediately attended by a surgeon called Scot, but died within a few minutes.

The spirit and circumstances of this ungentlemanly affair are well indicated by the evidence given at the inquest by Thomas Dunn, the owner of a near-by mill. He testified as follows:

> The first thing I saw, when the parties arrived in the ravine, was a carpet-bag, from which was taken a box containing some pistols. Five persons were standing together, and another alone on my left, and a second about two hundred yards more to the left on the hill. While the pistols were loading, the one on my left, who was the person who shot the deceased, came up to me and said: 'Good morning!' I said: 'It appears to me those gentlemen have some difference to decide.' He answered: 'Oh! damned nonsense, it's only a bet for a hundred pounds.' I replied: 'That will not do for me'; on which he passed on whistling. In a minute or two he again passed me, on which I remarked, it was a pity gentlemen could not settle their differences in a better way; when he said: 'Oh! damned nonsense, I am used to it, and am one who is going to

> fight.' A half-penny or penny-piece was then tossed up, as I suppose, for the choice of pistols, or the ground. As the man who shot the other was going to the place, one of the party went up to him and said: 'You are all right: you have nothing to fear.' I saw both parties present their pistols, and heard reports. Shortly after, I again heard the pistols discharged. Directly after, the gentleman who had spoken to me came towards me, and said: 'I have done for the —' I at that moment saw the deceased falling. I went to him and saw him stripped; when I saw a wound resembling that from a ball. All except one, who was engaged in pinching up the wound, left the ground. I said to him: 'I fear he is a dead man.' The carriages all left, except the hired cab. The deceased was dead when I left the spot.

The jury at the inquest returned a verdict of 'Wilful murder' against Francis Lionel Eliot, as principal, and John Young, Henry Webber, Edward

Broughton and two other persons unknown, as principals in the second degree. Warrants were immediately issued for their arrest, but only Young and Webber could be found. They were put on trial in September 1838, found guilty, and sentenced to death, this sentence subsequently being commuted to twelve months' imprisonment, the last month to be passed in solitary confinement.

A curious note of class prejudice entered into both the judge's summing-up at the trial and the comments of the Press on the whole affair. The judge, Mr Justice Vaughan, admitted that no unfair advantage appeared to have been taken by either party, and that 'as far as he knew anything of such matters, the affair appeared to have been managed with a strict regard to the practice usually followed on such occasions'; but he complained that there were some peculiarities in the case which were not to be found in any other case of duelling with which he was acquainted, notably the large number of persons involved.

The newspapers were franker in their comments, and openly jeered at the ludicrous, not to say, unseemly, pretension of a linen-draper to fight a duel, and of a brickmaker's son – John Young – to act as a second. As a distinguished contemporary duellist sadly observed, 'the disgusting exhibition at Wimbledon in this case is believed to have done much to bring the practice of duelling into ridicule and detestation'.

No doubt to his great relief, the institution of duelling recovered something of its ancient prestige, and Wimbledon Common was so to speak reconsecrated, as the result of an encounter which took place there on September 12, 1840, between the Earl of Cardigan and Captain Tuckett. This affair began at a party given by Lord Cardigan at Brighton, at which he made certain disobliging remarks about a certain Captain Reynolds. These remarks were reported to the Captain, who demanded an explanation, and, when no explanation was forthcoming, sent a challenge to Lord Cardigan. The latter ignored the challenge, on the ground that army regulations prohibited a duel between a superior and an inferior officer, and eventually sent the whole voluminous Reynolds correspondence to his Colonel, Prince Albert, who in turn passed the letters to the Commander-in-Chief, Lord Hill. He for his part, instead of calling a court martial, took it upon himself to place Captain Reynolds under arrest. At this stage in the story, Captain Tuckett took up the cause of his comrade Reynolds, and inserted in the *Morning Chronicle* a letter signed 'An Old Soldier' which Lord Cardigan considered offensive to his honour. This time the noble earl disregarded the difference in rank, and sent a challenge to Captain Tuckett which the latter accepted.

The first shot in the duel was ineffectual on both sides; but on the second, Captain Tuckett was wounded in the back part of the lower ribs. As Lord Cardigan and his second, Captain Douglas, were leaving the duelling ground they were taken into custody; and they were released only on payment of heavy recognizances. On September 28, the two men and Captain Tuckett's second were brought before the bench of magistrates at Wandsworth, and were committed for trial at the Central Criminal Court. There, however, the judges referred the case of the Earl of Cardigan to the House of Lords, and decided that the trial of Captain Douglas and Captain Wainwright should wait until after that of Lord Cardigan.

The earl was tried by his peers in the House of Lords on February 16, 1841, with all the pomp and circumstance of law. The issue was a foregone conclusion, the Lord High Steward shutting the mouth of each witness in turn with a reminder that he was not bound to incriminate himself, and the Attorney General himself insisting that 'the charge against the noble prisoner at the bar does not imply any degree of moral turpitude, and, if he should be found guilty, his conviction will reflect no discredit on the illustrious order to which he belongs'. The peers duly pronounced the earl 'Not guilty', the Lord High Steward ceremonially broke the white staff and declared the commission to be dissolved, and Cardigan left the House of Lords a free man.

It should perhaps be added that Captain Douglas and Captain Wainwright were similarly acquitted when they were brought for trial, while Captain Reynolds was deprived of his commission by court martial for having committed the heinous crime of challenging his superior officer.

The impunity with which Cardigan and the two seconds had flouted the law inevitably resulted in a certain recrudescence of duelling in Britain. But public opinion remained highly critical of the institution, and *The Times* sternly observed that 'Lord Cardigan's acquittal was "honourable", no doubt, in the eyes of those who would have thought it equally honourable to be convicted, and of those alone'.

There was further criticism of duelling later in that same year of 1841, when Colonel Paterson of the East India Service was seriously wounded in a duel with a gentleman called Marsden. Several peers, including Lord Eldon, Lord Melbourne and the Bishop of London, took the opportunity to denounce 'the barbarous, wicked, and unchristian practice of duelling'. And *The Times*, hitting out once more at the Cardigan verdict, declared in a long leading article: 'What the effect upon society in general must be of letting it be understood, that there is a crime which must not, or cannot, be restrained or punished, because peers and "gentlemen" think proper to commit it, while the law declares it to be a felony, we leave those to judge who know the power of example, and the aptness of the lower orders to learn evil from their betters. We are firmly convinced that no more pernicious or anarchical principle than that of the defenders of duelling was ever broached by Chartism, or even Socialism itself.'

The last straw was probably provided by a duel fought on July 1, 1843, between Lieutenant-Colonel David Fawcett of the 55th Regiment and his brother-in-law Lieutenant Alexander Munroe of the Royal Horse Guards, in which the colonel was mortally wounded. There was a considerable public outcry at this fresh killing, and an Anti-Duelling Association was formed, whose members denounced duelling as contrary to the laws of God and man, and pledged themselves to discourage by their influence and example the practice they condemned.

The Queen and her Government were also disturbed at the prevalence of duelling, especially in the army, and consulted together to see what steps could be taken to curb the practice. Thus an entry in Queen Victoria's journal for March 11, 1844, reads: 'After luncheon saw Sir Robert Peel. Amongst other things we talked of the law, or arrangement, restricting as far as possible duels in the Army, by repealing an article of the Mutiny Act, which cashiered officers for not redeeming their honour by duel.' The chief result of this consultation was the publication by the War Office, later that year, of the following amended articles relating to duelling:

1. Every officer who shall send a challenge, or who shall accept a challenge to fight a duel with another officer, or who, being privy to an intention to fight a duel, shall not

take active measures to prevent such duel, or who shall upbraid another for refusing or not giving a challenge, or who shall reject or advise the rejection of a reasonable proposition made for the honourable adjustment of a difference, shall be liable, if convicted before a general court-martial, to be cashiered, or suffer such other punishment as the court may award.

2. In the event of an officer being brought to a court-martial for having acted as a second in a duel, if it appear that such officer exerted himself strenuously to bring about an honourable adjustment of the difference, but failed through the unwillingness of the adverse parties, then such officer is to suffer such punishment as the court shall award.

3. Approbation is expressed of the conduct of those who, having had the misfortune to give offence to, or injure or insult others, shall frankly explain, apologize, or offer redress for the same, or who, having received offence, shall cordially accept frank explanations or apologies for the same; or, if such apologies are refused to be made or accepted, shall submit the matter to the commanding officer; and, lastly, all officers and soldiers are acquitted of disgrace or disadvantage who, being willing to make or accept such redress, refuse to accept challenges, as they will only have acted as is suitable to the character of honourable men, and have done their duty as good soldiers who subject themselves to discipline.

With surprising suddenness, these articles, which were recognized as constituting a British 'Code of Honour', combined with the obvious determination of judges and juries to convict duellists of murder, the sarcasm of the Press, and the sheer pressure of public opinion, succeeded in suppressing duelling in Britain. True, a fatal duel took place in 1845 at Southsea between a naval Lieutenant and an officer of the 11th Hussars, the survivor fleeing to France; in 1852, two Frenchmen called Cournet and Barthélemy fought a duel at Egham in which Cournet was killed; and to this day, undergraduates have continued to engage in affairs of honour, generally with swords rather than pistols. But the duel as a thriving, honoured and respected institution to all intents and purposes ceased to exist in Britain in the middle of the nineteenth century.

8 · Duels in America

Alexis de Tocqueville, commenting in 1831 on the state of duelling in America, observed that 'the duel based on extreme susceptibility to points of honour, the monarchic duel, is almost unknown in America; the laws which *oblige* a man to fight in some parts of Europe in certain defined cases do not exist at all'. He conceded that duels did take place in the New World, but described them as no more than a means outside the law of satisfying violent passions. 'In Europe', he wrote, 'one hardly ever fights a duel except in order to be able to say that one has done so; the offence is generally a sort of moral stain which one wants to wash away, and which most often is washed away at little expense. In America one only fights to kill; one fights because one sees no hope of getting one's adversary condemned to death. There are very few duels, but they almost always end fatally.'

When he made these observations, duelling in America was almost exactly two hundred years old. The first recorded duel fought in America took place at Plymouth, Massachusetts, on June 18, 1621, between Edward Doty and Edward Leicester, who, although they engaged in single combat with the gentlemanly arms of sword and dagger, were not gentlemen but the servants of a certain Mr Hopkins. Both men were wounded, one in the hand and the other in the thigh, but immediate punishment was none the less inflicted on them for the double outrage they had committed against the law and social convention. 'As it was deemed expedient', wrote one chronicler, 'to repress such affairs, the parties were condemned to have their hands and feet tied together, and to lie in that condition for twenty-four hours, without either meat or drink. This punishment was begun to be inflicted, but in an hour the pain they endured was so severe that, at their own supplication and their master's request, Governor Bradford liberated them on their promise of future good behaviour.'

At first it was thought that this example would be sufficient to nip this European evil in the bud, but in 1719 the same state of Massachusetts found it necessary to enact a law by which any person fighting a duel was deprived of

political rights and rendered ineligible for any public office for twenty years, while if the encounter proved fatal, the body of the dead duellist was 'appropriated to anatomical demonstration'.

It was only at the beginning of the nineteenth century, however, that duelling assumed serious proportions in America, becoming a positive scourge in certain states of the Union. Strangely enough, whereas in Europe the practice often enjoyed popular favour, while governments and rulers employed the harshest methods to suppress it, in the United States it was generally regarded with disapproval, but few states instituted measures to restrain it. Thus it was not until 1838 that the District of Columbia passed a bill prohibiting the sending and accepting of challenges; and even then, Thomas Clayton, the Senator from Delaware, maintained that while he believed duelling to be illegal and immoral, he thought 'that it was not of that class of crimes which should subject offenders to the cells of a penitentiary and make them the associates of felons'. Similarly, Senator Linn from Missouri declared that 'from what I have seen, fighting is like marrying: the more barriers that are erected against it, the surer are the interested parties to come together'. In the end, it was the great Clay of Kentucky who swayed the vote. 'The man with a high sense of honour,' he said, 'and nice sensibility, when the question is whether he shall fight or have the finger of scorn pointed at him, is unable to resist; and few, very few, are found willing to adopt such an alternative. When public opinion is renovated and chastened by reason, religion and humanity, the practice of duelling will be discountenanced. It is the office of legislation, however, to do all it can to bring about this healthful state of the public mind; and, although it might not altogether effect so desirable a result, I have no doubt it will do much towards it.'

There are few states in the Union in which duelling has never been known, but there have been far fewer encounters in the North than in the South. Only one duelling society is known to have existed in the United States – in Charleston, South Carolina, in the early nineteenth century – and that was disbanded through the intervention of an Englishman. This man, a retired naval officer, arrived at Charleston to look after some property he had come into, and was challenged to fight by the president of the duelling club, a crack shot who owed his position to the fact that he had killed or wounded more opponents than any other member. The Englishman was warned by several of the townspeople not to engage in such a hopeless fight, and assured that he would incur no contempt if he refused to meet a professional duellist; but he replied that he had accepted the challenge in good faith and proposed to meet his man. The duel was accordingly fought, and at the first fire the Englishman mortally wounded his opponent, who called the members of the club to his bedside and 'requested them to disorganize, and to do all in their power to suppress the further encouragement of an atrocious custom, the practice of which had at last brought him to his grave'. This pressing if unexpected plea convinced his hearers, and the club was disbanded the day after its president's funeral.

No purely American Code of Honour has ever existed, and most of the duels which have taken place in the United States have been fought in accordance with rules adapted from the duelling codes of European countries. One feature of American duelling, however, was peculiar to the United States, and that was 'posting'. It is said to have originated in 1807 with General James Wilkinson, whose challenge to a Virginian member of Congress called John Randolph was rejected by the latter on the ground that 'I cannot descend to your level'. To this contemptuous rebuff Wilkinson replied: 'You cannot *descend* to my level! – vain, equivocal thing! And you believe this dastardly subterfuge will avail you, or that your lion's skin will longer conceal your true character? Embrace the alternative, still in your reach, and *ascend* to the level of a gentleman, if possible; act like a man, if you can, and spare me the pain of publishing you to the world for an insolent, slanderous, prevaricating poltroon.' Randolph giving no further sign of life, the next time that Congress assembled, General Wilkinson stuck up or *posted* in all the taverns and on all the street corners in Washington, notices reading as follows:

'HECTOR UNMASKED: In justice to my character, I denounce to the world John Randolph, a member of Congress, as a prevaricating, base, calumniating scoundrel, poltroon and coward.'

After this episode, posting became a regular practice in the United States, and it was soon a common thing to see a notice in a newspaper or some public place declaring that some person or other was 'an unprincipled villain and a coward'. Sometimes this printed denunciation would be backed up by a personal appearance, as when a young gentleman of Los Angeles, who had sent a former friend a challenge he had ignored, posted him as 'a cur and a coward', and sat under the notice with a double-barrelled shotgun for seventeen hours.

The first fatal duel in what later became the United States was fought on the Common in Boston, Massachusetts, between Benjamin Woodbridge and Henry Phillips in the evening of July 3, 1728. These two young men, described as 'both of good social position', had quarrelled over cards at the Royal Exchange Tavern, and had agreed to settle their difference with swords. Woodbridge was mortally wounded in the fight, and his body was found on the Common the following morning. He was buried in the Old Granary Burying Ground, under a plain slate slab with a simple inscription giving no indication that his was a historic death.

This duel was followed by countless others, particularly between Army officers and notably in the early nineteenth century. Most of them were undistinguished by any unusual features, but occasionally a remarkable fight occurred, such as the encounter between the Hon. De Witt Clinton and the Hon. John Swartwout in New York in 1802. This fight, which was one of the most determined duels recorded in America, was later described as follows by N. S. Smith, Swartwout's second:

> The gentlemen took positions and fired without effect. At Mr Riker's request, I asked Mr Swartwout if he were satisfied. He answering in the negative, the second shot was fired without effect. I again asked Mr Swartwout if he was satisfied. He replied: 'I am not,' and the third shot was exchanged without injury. I then asked Mr Swartwout: 'Are you satisfied, sir?' He replied: 'I am not, neither shall I be until the apology is made which I have demanded. Until then we must proceed.' I then presented a paper to Mr Riker for Mr Clinton's signature, containing the apology demanded, observing that this paper must be signed or we would proceed. Mr Clinton declared he would sign no paper on the subject, that he had no animosity to Mr Swartwout, and would willingly shake hands and agree to meet on the score of former friendship. Mr Swartwout insisted on the signature to the apology, and Mr Clinton declining, they stood at their posts and fired a fourth shot. Mr Swartwout was wounded in the left leg, about five inches below the knee. Being asked if he was satisfied, Mr Swartwout replied: 'It is useless to repeat the question. My determination is fixed, and I beg we may proceed.' Mr Clinton repeated that he had no animosity against Mr Swartwout; was sorry for what had passed; proposed to advance, shake hands and bury the past in oblivion. During the conversation, the surgeon, kneeling at his side, extracted the ball from Mr Swartwout's leg. The fifth shot being fired, Mr Swartwout received a ball in the left leg, about five inches above the ankle, still, however, standing at his post perfectly composed. At the request of Mr Riker I asked: 'Are you satisfied?' He forcibly answered: 'No, sir; I am not. Proceed.' Mr Clinton then quit his post, declining the combat, and declared that he would fire no more. Mr Swartwout expressed himself surprised that Mr Clinton would neither apologize nor give the satisfaction required, and addressing me, said: 'What shall I do, my friend?' I answered: 'Mr Clinton declines making the apology required, refuses taking his position, and positively declares he will fight no more. His second appearing to acquiesce in the disposition of his principal, there is nothing further for you to do now but to have your wounds dressed.' The surgeons attending dressed his wounds, and the gentlemen returned in their respective barges to the city.

The next duel of note to take place in the United States – an encounter described by one American as 'the most famous duel known in history' – owes its fame less to the character of the fight itself than to the names of the two antagonists. They were Alexander Hamilton, Washington's close friend and the leading figure among the Federalists, and Aaron Burr, the Vice-President of the United States and the head of the Democrats; both were men of considerable eminence and both aspired to the Presidency, but in other respects they were completly different. The origin of their quarrel lay in a letter published by a certain Dr Cooper which alleged that Hamilton had declared that he 'looked upon Mr Burr as a dangerous man, and one who ought not to be trusted with the reins of government'. When Burr demanded 'a prompt and unqualified acknowledgement or denial of the expression', Hamilton admitted the statement, the language of which he claimed 'came fairly within the bounds prescribed in cases of political animosity', and rejected Burr's demand 'as calling on him to retrace every conversation which he had held, either publicly or confidentially, in the course of fifteen years' opposition; and to contradict that which, very possibly, had escaped his memory'. After a lengthy correspondence, Burr demanded a duel, and an encounter was arranged to take place at Weehawken, New Jersey, on July 11, 1804.

On the eve of the duel, Hamilton prepared a paper containing his views on duelling, and expressing the 'reluctance with which he obeyed a custom so repugnant to his feelings'. In this paper he explained his reluctance to fight on the following grounds:

> *First:* My religious and moral principles are strongly opposed to the practice of duelling; and it would ever give me pain to shed the blood of a fellow creature in private combat forbidden by the laws.
>
> *Secondly:* My wife and children are extremely dear to me, and my life is of the utmost importance to them in various views.
>
> *Thirdly:* I feel a sense of obligation toward my creditors, who, in case of accident to me, by the forced sale of my property, may be in some degree sufferers. I did not think myself at liberty, as a man of probity, lightly to expose them to hazard.
>
> *Fourthly:* I am conscious of no ill-will to Colonel Burr distinct from political opposition, which, as I trust, has proceeded from pure and upright motives.
>
> *Lastly:* I shall hazard much, and can possibly gain nothing, by the issue of the interview.

However, despite these cogent reasons, Hamilton felt that 'my *relative* situation, as well in public as in private, enforcing all the considerations which constitute what men of the world denominate honor, imposed on me a peculiar necessity not to decline the call'.

The duel duly took place on July 11, on a little ledge beneath the heights of Weehawken, just above the Hudson, on the very spot where Hamilton's eldest son Philip had fallen in a duel about three years before. On the given signal, Hamilton fell forward on his face, his pistol going off involuntarily. Burr was hurried away to his boat by his friends, while the doctor and Hamilton's second attended the mortally wounded general. Later in the day, Hamilton declared that he had met Burr with the determination to do him no harm, and that he forgave him for what had happened. He lingered on for the remainder of the day and the following night, but died at two o'clock in the afternoon of the next day.

With the exception of the death of Washington and the assassinations of Lincoln and Kennedy, probably no death in the history of the United States has caused such widespread sorrow as the killing of Alexander Hamilton. It immediately produced a revulsion against duelling throughout the Northern States, and the president of the Society of the Cincinnati proposed that it should 'resolutely set its face against the practice'. As for Burr, he was disfranchized by the laws of New York for having fought a duel, and was charged with murder in New Jersey. 'The city', wrote one of Hamilton's admirers, 'was not a safe place for Burr. He fled for his life, and his terrified myrmidons hastened to avail themselves of the protection of obscurity. Never again could that blood-stained man redeem his reputation before mankind, so infinitely more fatal was that duel to the survivor than the victim.' A virtual outcast from the circles he had once dominated, Burr spent the rest of his life in growing poverty with an ever diminishing legal practice, and died destitute on Staten Island in September 1836.

A duel almost as famous as the Hamilton-Burr affair was fought two years later, on May 30, 1806, between General Andrew Jackson and Charles Dickinson, who were not only men of great distinction, but two of the best shots in the country. Dickinson had been challenged by Jackson for having slandered his wife, and while each man undoubtedly expected to be hit by the other's bullet, he hoped at the same time that he would be able to kill his opponent or at least inflict a dangerous wound. Both were experts with the pistol, and Dickinson amused his friends on the way to the rendezvous by giving a display of his skill. Once, at a distance of twenty-four feet, he fired four bullets into a space no bigger than a silver dollar, and several times he cut a string with a bullet from the same distance. It is said that he left one severed cord hanging near a tavern, and said to the landlord as he rode off: 'If General Jackson comes along this road, be kind enough to show him that.'

If Jackson saw this proof of his enemy's deadly skill, he showed no sign of it, for when the two parties met in the morning they seemed perfectly calm. The arrangements agreed on by the seconds were that the pistols were to be held pointing downwards until the signal to fire was given, and then each man was to fire when he pleased. As soon as the signal was given Dickinson raised his pistol and fired. A puff of dust flew from the breast of Jackson's coat, and his second saw him raise his left arm and press it tightly across his chest. But the General stood firm, and Dickinson cried out in astonishment: 'Great God, have I missed him?' The next moment, Jackson took careful aim and pulled the trigger, but his pistol stopped at half-cock. Correcting it, he took aim a second time, and fired. Dickinson staggered, his face turned white, and he fell to the ground, mortally wounded. It was only then that it was noticed that one of Jackson's shoes was full of blood, and it was found that Dickinson's bullet had hit him in the breast, breaking two ribs and making a painful but not dangerous wound. He shrugged off his friends' expressions of amazed admiration at his courage, however, remarking that even if he had been shot through the heart he would have lived long enough to have killed his opponent.

This very determination to kill his adversary at all costs did not win universal commendation. In later years an authority on duelling wrote of this encounter:

> There is one feature about this duel with Dickinson that seems a little peculiar, and that is that General Jackson, who was a very spare man in his person, should have been dressed in a loose-fitting gown or coat, so that his antagonist could not readily tell the location of his body. Dickinson aimed right; and if Jackson's body had been where Dickinson supposed it was, and where, perhaps the *code duello* would say it ought to have been, there is no just reason to doubt that General Jackson would at that time have 'passed in his checks'; for the ball from Dickinson's pistol would have struck his heart beyond any doubt, according to the account of the duel. Now, the criticism and point I make in the character of 'Old Hickory', in respect to this duel, is this: Having dressed in a manner to deceive Dickinson as to the precise location of his (Jackson's) body, and having received Dickinson's bullet without any serious injury, it was not a just and fair thing in Jackson afterwards to take deliberate aim at Dickinson and kill him. No matter what the provocation was on the part of Dickinson which led to the duel, it seems to me that, having resorted to what was then considered an honourable method of settling the difficulty, they were each bound to give the other fair play; and the only excuse or justification I can find for General Jackson for his deliberate and premeditated killing of Dickinson is the fact that, perhaps, upon general principles, Dickinson ought to have been killed for slandering so upright and honourable a woman as the wife of General Jackson.

It was undoubtedly Jackson's great love for his wife – whom he worshipped, according to one contemporary, 'with a romantic tenderness and strength surpassing the dream of fiction' – which was responsible for the ferocious determination he showed in his duel with Dickinson. When Rachel Jackson died in December 1828, just after her husband had been elected President of the United States, he had her tomb inscribed with the words: 'A being so gentle and yet so virtuous, vile slander might wound but could not dishonor.' And as he stood by the graveside at her burial, Andrew Jackson declared in a slow, bitter voice: 'In the presence of this dear saint I can and do forgive all my enemies. But those vile wretches who have slandered her must look to God for mercy.'

One of the most mysterious duels fought in the United States during the early nineteenth century took place in Illinois in 1819. A young lawyer of the town of Belleville called Alonzo Stuart had quarrelled several times with a farmer called William Bennett over the habit the latter's horse had of cropping the lawyer's cornfield. Two of Bennett's friends, Jacob Short and Nat Fike, urged him to demand satisfaction from Stuart, and then went to see the lawyer, to whom they suggested an amusing prank. This was a mock duel, in which the guns would be loaded with powder only, though Bennett would not know this until later. The plan was successful, Bennett agreed to a duel, and the two opponents met one morning in the presence of an excited crowd, Stuart perfectly calm and Bennett pale and trembling.

When the signal was given, Bennett fired and the lawyer fell to the ground with a bullet near the heart. In the excitement that followed, one of the seconds fired Stuart's gun into the air, and the two seconds then accused Bennett of having tampered with the gun and put in a real bullet, an accusation which Bennett fiercely denied. He and the two others were charged with murder, and while they awaited trial speculation about the truth of the matter ran rife in Illinois. Some believed that Bennett had learned of the trick and had retaliated by putting the bullet in the gun; others pointed to the suspicious way in which one of the seconds had fired off Stuart's pistol, making it impossible to tell whether it had been loaded too; and yet others thought that one of the seconds, out of spite or perhaps merely intoxication, had put bullets into both pistols.

Then rumours spread that Short and Fike were going to stand together and 'make it look bad' for Bennett; and the latter, thoroughly scared, broke out of the primitive log-cabin jail and escaped to Arkansas. When the seconds came up for trial, they produced a witness, the ten-year-old daughter of the local tavern-keeper, who testified that before the duel she had seen Bennett put something in his gun. Her story saved the lives of the two men.

As for Bennett, nothing was seen or heard of him for some time, but a year later he was trapped and arrested at St Genevieve, Missouri. His defence was taken by the great Thomas Hart Benton, who argued eloquently for him but lost the case. After repeated appeals to the Governor had been rejected, Bennett was hanged in the autumn of 1821, still crying out on the scaffold that he had not put the bullet in the pistol, that he was innocent of murder. Whatever the truth of the matter, the whole affair had aroused such horror and bitterness as to turn the local people violently against duelling. Illinois had never known a duel before, and the circumstances of the Bennett-Stuart encounter prevented any repetition.

In the South, of course, it was a different matter, and duels were fought there with increasing frequency, especially in New Orleans. Any excuse for a fight was good enough, and the aged Lafayette's triumphant visit to the city in 1825 nearly gave rise to a whole spate of duels. There was a quarrel between the French and the American elements in the welcoming party over the question of precedence in greeting the general, and several duels were arranged for the following day. Hearing of this, Lafayette expressed dismay at the thought that he should have brought discord to New Orleans, and urged his hosts to settle their differences peacefully. One after another, the local officers came forward and agreed to place their honour in Lafayette's hands, so that 'he had the pleasure of seeing all embrace each other, who, but a few minutes before, were ready to renounce the title of brothers in arms'.

It was a rare thing, however, for quarrelsome Southerners to have a distinguished peacemaker among them to advise them to 'renounce all animosity and seal their declarations in a glass of wine', and the wine of Louisiana more often than not inflamed tempers and led to murderous combats. The duels fought in New Orleans alone are too numerous to recount even briefly, but one fight – that between Hippolyte Trouett and Paulin Prué in June 1840 – deserves more than a passing mention.

Prué had called Trouett out with a challenge cunningly worded to avoid any legal penalty; it asked Trouett to 'a luncheon across the lake', adding: 'You will find there an acquaintance who wishes greatly to see you. I shall have two friends with me; please bring along two of yours. Choose whatever dishes you like.'

The duel was arranged to take place early in the morning at Bayou St John, and it was agreed that the two men should stand back to back, a pistol in each hand, should step forward five paces at the given signal, and should then wheel about and fire. If they survived, each would drop the first pistol and use the second; a misfire would count as a shot.

The two parties duly met and took their places, ominously enough under the grim eye of the local recorder of births and deaths, a certain Monsieur Crozat, who was one of Trouett's seconds. The first exchange of shots had no effect, and the duellists accordingly transferred their second pistols to their right hands. While Prué was doing this, his pistol went off accidentally, and since this was technically a shot, Trouett was now at liberty to take careful aim at him with complete immunity. Either out of a Gallic sense of drama or in the hope of influencing his opponent, Prué bared his chest and called on Trouett to fire, while some of the onlookers protested at what they described as murder. Recorder Crozat sternly rebuked them, offering to shoot it out with anyone who disputed Trouett's right to a second shot, and then told his principal: 'You may fire.'

After hesitating for a few moments which must have seemed hours to the white-faced Prué, Trouett, 'grinning ferociously' accordingly to one account, pulled the trigger and his opponent fell dead. Whereupon Crozat, pausing briefly before going off to record the victim's death, told the indignant crowd: 'Messieurs, the blood is on your hands. Had you appealed to us to be merciful, we would have let him go. But you provoked us.'

There was such violent feeling at what was generally regarded as this cold-blooded murder that Trouett went to trial. There were eloquent speeches by two leading barristers, and the jury stayed out for hours; but – this being the South – the verdict was 'Innocent'.

Duels in the middle of the nineteenth century became so frequent in New Orleans that the most professional and proficient duellist of that city took the eminently reasonable step of buying and operating his own graveyard. This man, a Spaniard called Don José Llulla and familiarly known as Pepe, had been a whaler and a slaver before coming to New Orleans, where he had added to his proficiency with a knife and fists by mastering the arts of the sabre, the broadsword and the pistol. Before long, his skill was so great that friends would confidently hold silver dollars between finger and thumb for him to shoot out, and he would occasionally knock an egg off his little son's head at thirty paces. As for his proficiency with the sword, he bested his fencing-master in a public demonstration; and he punished a Frenchman who excluded him from a *grand assaut d'armes* on the ground that he held no European diploma by 'opening the master's flank in two places' in a broad-sword duel, and then apologizing for doing so much to him without the proper qualifications.

He was a quick fighter, who liked to finish with a duel as speedily as possible; and there were opponents who felt the steel enter their bodies before they even saw Pepe's blade. Like most of the great masters of duelling, he was always calm, never shouting or gesticulating, but killing coldly and efficiently when the need arose. He has been credited with thirty full-scale duels, but the actual figure may well have been much higher, for he kept no records and was not a boastful man. It was rumoured that nearly all the resting-places in his private graveyard – the St Vincent de Paul Cemetery on Louisa Street – were occupied by his victims, and punsters said that he would run you through with his sword and then bury you at a cut rate. On the other hand, his friends maintained that he never accepted the body of a man he had killed, and all that Pepe himself would say was that if he looked hard he might just possibly find a few of his victims in his graveyard.

The last duel fought by this mild-mannered, soft-spoken killer was in the 1870s, by which time he had moved to Grande Terre, one of the former Barataria pirate islands in the Gulf. He quarrelled with the lighthouse keeper, and when a friend suggested that they should meet and discuss their disagreement, Pepe agreed, provided that the discussion should be conducted with pistols. No seconds were required: the two men would simply exchange shots in a civilized, gentlemanly way. The next day, Pepe emerged from the lighthouse alone.

This remarkable duellist died in March 1883 at the age of seventy-three, and was buried, suitably enough, in his own cemetery. For a while, New Orleans recalled his countless exploits – the sword-duel in which he had run his opponent precisely through the coat-button as he had promised, or the pistol-duel in which he had remained standing with his head half turned away long after the signal had been given, only to kill his puzzled adversary in a flash as soon as the man had raised his gun. And they remembered how, with characteristic modesty, he had always refused to attribute his long survival to his skill as a duellist, explaining simply: 'It was just that I never drank.'

Almost every duel, whether in the North or South, was of course attended by a doctor; but sometimes, especially in hot-blooded New Orleans, the doctor packed a pistol in his bag and played one of the leading parts in a fight. Occasionally the duel would be between the doctor and a layman, but more often it was between two medical practitioners who had fallen out over a diagnosis or a method of treatment. No accusation was too outrageous to be hurled at a hated professional rival, and one doctor went so far as to allege that a colleague who had been victorious in several duels used the corpses of charity patients as targets for pistol practice, 'suspending the bodies at the hospital in order to improve his skill as a marksman'.

One of the most ferocious medical vendettas in the South was that between two doctors at the Charity Hospital in New Orleans, the house surgeon Dr Samuel Chopin and his successor and rival Dr John Foster. Their hatred, which was revealed in a thousand little insults and slights, came to a head during the Carnival season. A law student injured in a knifing brawl with an intern was admitted to the hospital, where he was attended by both Chopin and Foster, though at different times. What one doctor prescribed in the morning, the other threw out of the window in the afternoon, but somehow the patient survived this erratic treatment. He even lived through the terrible scene which occurred when his doctors accidentally called to see him at the same time and came to blows at his bedside. But when the inevitable gunfight took place and Chopin fell, his jugular vein severed, the unfortunate law student found himself abandoned to Foster's undisturbed attentions. The wounded doctor recovered, but the patient died.

An even bloodier medical encounter took place in the North, near Philadelphia, between a Dr Smith and a Dr Jeffries. The distance agreed upon was only eight paces, at which they exchanged shots without effect. After an unsuccessful attempt had been made to reconcile the two men, they were handed pistols for a second time, and at this fire Smith's right arm was broken. He refused to give in, however, and declared that as he was wounded he was ready to die. The pistols were accordingly given to the duellists again, Smith using his left hand, and this time Jeffries was wounded in the thigh. He fainted away, but recovered consciousness after a few minutes, and both men than asked for the distance between them to be reduced. They now stood facing each other for the fourth time, covered with blood, and only six feet apart. Two shots rang out, and both combatants fell to the ground, Smith dead and Jeffries mortally wounded. 'When Dr Jeffries saw that his antagonist had fallen,' wrote a contemporary chronicler, 'he asked if he was dead; and being assured that he was, he declared his own willingness to die. Before he expired, he said he had been schoolmate with Dr Smith, and that they had been on terms of great intimacy and friendship for fifteen years; and he bore honourable testimony to his character as a man of science and a gentleman.'

This murderous duel was regarded in the North as one of the most horrifying examples of the practice; but it was a modest, innocuous affair compared with the notorious encounter in the South which gave its name to that classic

21 · (*a*) *Mexican duel in a bedroom, as depicted by one of the protagonists*
Samuel Chamberlain, 1846
21 · (*b*) *John Gump's gun-fight with his wife*, *Idaho*, 1886
A contemporary American engraving

22 · *The duel between Burr and Hamilton*

American weapon, the bowie-knife. This encounter was the culmination of a feud which had existed for several years between two groups in the Red River parish of Rapides, in Louisiana. The principals were Dr Maddox, Major Wright and the Blanchards on the one hand, and the Curreys, the Wellses and the Bowies on the other; and when a challenge passed between Dr Maddox and Samuel Wells, a duel was arranged to take place opposite Natchez, Missouri, in August 1827. The duelling-ground was a large sand-bar, and the friends of each party were stationed on the opposite side of this bar. A deadly feud had existed for a long time between Colonel Crane, Maddox's second, and James Bowie and General Currey, and a few months before this duel General Currey had shot Colonel Crane on Bayou Rapids, disabling one of his arms. If anything, therefore, there was a greater enmity between the friends of the two principals in this new encounter than between Maddox and Wells themselves.

Various accounts of the duel or duels of August 1827 have been given, differing slightly in detail or emphasis. Possibly the fairest and fullest is this version written by a local chronicler some forty years later:

> The parties to the duel approached the spot selected for the combat from different directions. The preliminaries were soon arranged. The combatants took their positions and exchanged two shots without effect, and the difficulty was amicably adjusted. Bowie was just in the edge of the woods with Generals Wells and Currey, armed with pistols, Bowie carrying a huge knife. As the duelling party started to leave the grounds Bowie and his party advanced to meet them. The friends of Maddox and Crane on the opposite side of the sand-bar, seeing this, and being furthest from the party, started to run to meet them as soon as they should reach the retiring combatants. General Currey was the first on the ground, closely followed by Bowie. Currey immediately advanced upon Colonel Crane and remarked: 'Colonel Crane, this is a good time to settle our difficulty,' and commenced drawing his pistol. Bowie did the same. Crane was armed with a brace of duelling pistols, and awaited the attack of Currey. At this moment Currey was seized by his brother and begged to desist. Bowie and Crane fired at each other, it is said, without effect. There were those who said Bowie was wounded. The latter statement I think most probable, for Bowie stopped, felt his hip, and then, drawing his knife, limped towards Crane, who was watching General Currey. Released from the hold of his brother, Currey was advancing. At this moment Crane leaped across a small ravine cut through the sand by the rain water flowing from the acclivities above, and, resting his pistol upon his crippled arm, fired at Currey, wounding him fatally, from the effects of which he fell. Crane was now disarmed, and Bowie advanced cautiously upon him. Clubbing his pistol he struck Bowie over the head as he avoided his knife adroitly, and felled him to the ground. Crane retreated a step as his friend,

> Major Wright, advanced upon him, and with a long, slender spear, drawn from a walking-cane which he carried, attacked Bowie, who made a pass to parry the spear with his knife, in which he failed. The spear was of cold iron, and striking the breast-bone bent and went round upon the rib. Bowie at this moment seized Wright and fell, pulling Wright down with and on top of him, and holding him strongly to his person. Wright was slender, and by no means a strong man, and was powerless in the hands of Bowie, who coolly said to him: 'Now Major, you die,' and plunging the knife into his heart, killed him instantly. This knife was made by Resin P. Bowie out of a blacksmith's rasp or large file, and was the original of the famous bowie-knife. When James Bowie received it from his brother, he was told by him that it was 'strong, and of admirable temper. It is more trustworthy in the hands of a strong man than a pistol, for it will not snap; Crane and Wright are both your enemies; they are from Maryland, the birthplace of our ancestors, and are as brave as you are, but not so cool. They are both inferior in strength to yourself, and therefore not your equal in a close fight. They are both dangerous, but Wright the most so. Keep this knife always with you. It will be your friend in a last resort, and may save your life.' After this conflict Resin P. Bowie carried this knife to Philadelphia, where it was fashioned by a cutler into the form of a model made by him, and I presume the knife is yet in the possession of some member of the family. There was no reconciliation between Crane and Bowie after the conflict, though Crane aided personally in carrying Bowie from the ground, and Bowie thanked him and said: 'Colonel Crane, I do not think, under the circumstances, you ought to have shot me.' Almost immediately after the attack of Currey upon Crane, the fight between their friends became general, in which there were fifteen wounded and at least six killed, among whom were Currey and Wright. All the men engaged in this terrible affair were men of wealth and high social position, and the two parties included almost every man of fortune in the extensive and wealthy parish of Rapides. All are gone save Maddox and Wells, both very old, and still residing in the same parish.

Bowie's name soon became synonymous with courage and generosity, and stories about his exploits were told all over the South. One of the most typical is about a duel which was fought on a wheel-house roof on a Mississippi steamer in the autumn of 1832. Joining the steamer *Orleans* at Vicksburg on his way to Natchez, Bowie saw a young man, married that summer and carrying a large amount of money entrusted to him by some fellow planters, fleeced of over sixty thousand dollars by three professional gamblers in a game of 20-card poker. After preventing the young man from throwing himself in the river, Bowie confided him to his wife, telling her that everything would be all right if she would keep her husband in their cabin until his return. He then flourished a bulging wallet under the noses of the gamblers, who invited him to join them in a game of poker, and embarked on the same technique which had proved so successful with the young bridegroom.

Waiting until the total amount on the table was some $100,000, of which he had contributed a third, Bowie seized the dealer with one hand as he was slipping a card to an associate, and produced a murderous-looking knife with the other. An old steamboatman later gave this account of what ensued:

> The baffled gambler, livid with rage and disappointment, swore that the stranger should fight him, demanding, with an oath, to know who he was anyway. Quietly, and as if in the presence of ladies, the stranger answered, 'James Bowie'. At the sound of that name two of the gamblers quailed, for they knew that the man who bore that name was a terror to even the bravest; but the third, who had never heard of 'James Bowie', demanded a duel at once. This was acceded to at once by Bowie, with a smile; pistols – derringers – were the weapons selected, the hurricane-roof the place, and the time at once. Sweeping the whole of the money into his hat, Bowie went to the room where the unhappy wife sat guarding her husband's uneasy slumbers, and, rapping on the door, he handed her, when she had opened it, the hat and its contents, telling her that if he did not come back, two-thirds of the money was her husband's and the balance his own. Ascending to the hurricane-roof, the principals were placed one upon the top of each wheel-house. This brought them about twelve yards apart, and each was exposed to the other from the knee up. The pistols were handed to them and the gambler's second gave the word, 'One, two, three, fire, stop', uttered at intervals of one second each, and they were allowed to fire at any time between the utterance of the words one and stop. As 'one' rang out in the clear morning air both raised their weapons, as 'three' was heard the gambler's pistol rang out and before the sound had ceased and while the word 'fire' was being uttered, Bowie's pistol sounded, and simultaneous with this sound the gambler fell, and giving a convulsive struggle rolled off the wheel-house into the river. Bowie coolly blew the smoke out of his pistol, shut down the pan (the flint-lock was in use at the time), and going down into the ladies' cabin, obtained his hat and divided the money which it contained into three portions. Two of these he gave to the young wife and the other he kept, as it was his own money. Having awakened her husband, the fond wife showed him the money, and told him all she knew about the affair, not having heard of the duel. When the husband became acquainted with all the facts, his gratitude to his benefactor was deep and lasting. Not desiring to be made a hero of, Bowie, when the boat reached Rodney, determined to go ashore; and as he was leaving the boat both the husband and wife clung to him as though he was a father leaving them. It was afterwards ascertained that the amount which Bowie returned to the wife was within less than $100 of the sum which the gamblers had won from her husband.

James Bowie was undoubtedly the most attractive personality among the duellists of the South, but he was not the most flamboyant, the most proficient or the most feared. That was Alexander Keith McClung of Kentucky and Mississippi, the so-called 'Black Knight of the South', a handsome, red-haired, dark-eyed killer with a taste for dramatic attitudes, picturesque clothes, poetry and the bottle. A nephew of Chief Justice Marshall of Virginia, McClung left home at an early age and, after a brief but tempestuous career as a midshipman in the United States Navy, studied law, eventually setting up a practice in Mississippi in 1834. He had been in the state only a few months when he quarrelled with one of the most distinguished and honoured men in Mississippi, Colonel Allen, and insisted on bringing the affair to a duel. The terms agreed upon were so unusual that traditionalists would probably not

have recognized the encounter as a legitimate duel, for the two opponents were to stand forty paces apart, armed with bowie-knife and pistol, and were to advance on each other, firing at discretion. To the astonishment of the onlookers, McClung raised his pistol when he was over one hundred feet from his antagonist and fired, shooting Allen through the mouth and mortally wounding him. The distance from which McClung fired was a much longer range than that for which duelling pistols were intended, and his mortal shot created a sinister record, at the same time establishing his reputation as one of the most dangerous men in the South.

Before long, as the number of his victims increased, the mere mention of his name was enough to unnerve the bravest of men. Thus when another guest in a hotel complained to the waiter because he had stuck his knife in the butter, and McClung retaliated by slapping the butter on to the stranger's face, calling out: 'Waiter, remove the butter – this man has stuck his nose in it,' the man fled as soon as he discovered his assailant's identity. Again, a man who found McClung's manner offensive and thrust his card at him by way of a challenge, turned white when he recognized the name on McClung's card, and stammered in terror: 'Just let me have my card back, that's all I ask.'

The last notable duel that McClung fought, and possibly the last of any sort in his murderous career, was with John Menefee, a planter-merchant of Vicksburg, shortly before the outbreak of the Mexican War. The antagonists on this occasion were well matched, for if McClung had never missed his man, Menefee was the leader of the Vicksburg Rifles and 'the gamecock of the river'. The duel, which was fought with Mississippi rifles, was described as follows by a correspondent:

> Sixty yards was the distance chosen, and when the seconds went to measure off the ground it was with great difficulty that the crowd could be forced back so as to allow the fight to go on. The positions were taken and the rifles were placed in the combatants' hands. 'Are you ready?' 'Ready', both firmly responded. 'Fire; one, two' – Here Menefee's rifle exploded, and the bullet whistled by the head of McClung and lodged in a tree that appeared to be on an exact line with the body of the latter. To the surprise of everybody, instead of firing his piece, McClung attempted to break it in half, and with a fierce oath hurled it a distance of twenty feet away, where it alighted upon a pile of sand and stuck, muzzle down, several feet in it. The seconds soon learned the cause of this strange action – the gun had hung fire. It was rescued, the sand removed from the muzzle, and reloaded. After an interval of ten minutes the combatants resumed their positions, and the crowd gathered around them again. During the interval many bets had been wagered on the result of the duel, the odds being generally in favour of Menefee, who was a popular favorite, and who, moreover, was generally supposed to be more proficient with the rifle. The word was again given. This time McClung's piece was more faithful. Before Menefee's finger had pressed the trigger of the rifle, that of McClung had been discharged, and the ball, striking the cock of Menefee's gun, hurled a piece of it deep into the brain of the unfortunate young man, who fell, and died before he could be removed from the field.

McClung, who had already given a furious display of temper during the duel, behaved even more strangely after Menefee had fallen. Rising to his full height, he peered through the smoke to make sure that his antagonist was dead, and then, dropping to his knees and pressing his rifle to his chest, he kissed it tenderly. He also gave a prayer of thanks to God 'for having directed the bullet so well' – a piece of arrogance which provoked resentful comments from the onlookers. After this encounter, he found it difficult to find anyone willing to risk his life in a fight with him, and on his return from distinguished service in the Mexican War he became morose and melancholy, resorting more and more to the bottle. It was rumoured that this was because at nightfall, wherever he went, he saw a file of grey men – the shades of those he had killed in duels – and this rumour gained greater credence when, in 1855, Alexander Keith McClung pinned an *Ode to Death* to his shirtfront and blew out his brains with his pistol.

During the 'thirties and 'forties the South witnessed most of the duels fought in the United States, but with the discovery of gold in the Sacramento Valley in 1848, duelling moved westwards, together with the tens of thousands of Americans, often Southerners, infected with 'California fever'. Duels were fought in towns and camps over the gold itself, over the women who haunted the saloons, or simply out of hatred and boredom. For a decade or two, San Francisco became the duelling capital of America, with the local newspapers advertising duels as if they were stage performances, and one duelling editor putting up a notice in his office which read: 'Subscriptions received from 9 to 4, challenges from 11 to 12 only.'

It is to San Francisco that we owe one of the few amusing anecdotes in the history of duelling. A traditional Southerner, Colonel William Gwin, who had come out to California to join the gold rush and had become a senator, quarrelled with a representative called J. W. McCorkle, and the two men agreed to fight a pistol-duel a few miles from Gwin's home. Three times they fired and missed, after which their seconds conferred together and announced that the principals had fought under a 'misunderstanding of the facts'. In the meantime Mrs Gwin had been waiting anxiously for the messengers who had been commissioned to bring her a blow-by-blow account of the fight. After the first exchange one of these messengers rode up and announced breathlessly: 'Ma'am, first fire's over. Nobody hurt!' 'Thanks be to God,' she murmured, and called the family to prayer. A few moments later another messenger arrived and told her: 'Second fire, and both are safe,' obtaining the response: 'Praised be.' But when the first messenger galloped up again and said: 'The third fire's over – nobody's hurt and they've called it off,' Mrs Gwin merely observed: 'That's good.' A surprised neighbour asked her if she didn't think the news was wonderful. 'Yes,' said Mrs Gwin, 'but there's been some mighty poor shooting today.'

Not all Californian duels, of course, were as innocuous or amusing as this, and San Francisco witnessed one fatal encounter which was almost as famous and momentous as the Hamilton-Burr affair. This was the duel fought on September 13, 1859, between David C. Broderick, United States Senator from California, and David S. Terry, former Chief Justice of the Supreme Court of California. The immediate cause of their quarrel was a speech in which Judge Terry called Broderick an arch-traitor, but the underlying reason for it was the political conflict between Terry, who advocated the extension of slavery, and Broderick, who was opposed to slavery in any form. A local correspondent later gave this account of the duel itself:

> All things being in readiness, the pistols were cocked and the hair-triggers set by the seconds. They were then delivered to the combatants. It was observed at this time that Mr Broderick appeared nervous and ill at ease. He repeatedly twitched the skirts of his surtout, as though they were in his way. He was also somewhat out of position, and Mr McKibben corrected him. Broderick closely measured with his eye the ground between himself and Terry. Mr Benham read the conditions of the meeting, and Mr Colton followed with instructions as to the firing. He had won the word. Broderick was still nervous, but Terry stood firm and erect, a silhouette against the early morning light. The men held their weapons muzzle downward. A moment of painful silence ensured.
>
> 'Gentlemen,' said Mr Colton, in a clear voice, 'are you ready?' Both replied, but Broderick delayed a few seconds. He then said, 'I am ready.'
>
> 'Fire! One – ' There was a report from the Senator's pistol. It was answered in a second by Terry's weapon. Broderick's pistol was discharged before he brought it to a level. This was probably caused by the fineness of the hair-trigger and his want of familiarity with that particular weapon. The bullet buried itself in the ground, two-thirds of the distance between himself and his antagonist. It was a splendid line-shot, fallen short of its mark. Broderick had the reputation of being an expert with the pistol, and this result surprised those who knew his skill. With the crack of Terry's weapon Broderick winced, turned half round, and then made an effort to recover himself. 'Hard hit,' his friends murmured. These words were proved by his unavailing efforts to maintain an upright position. He drooped until finally he fell prone on the ground, with his pale face toward the sky. He was hard hit.
>
> Mr Broderick was removed from the ground three-quarters of an hour after he was shot, placed on a mattress in a spring wagon, and taken to the residence of his friend

> Leonidas Haskell, at Black Point. He lingered in great pain until Friday, September 16, and expired at 9.20 in the morning. He did not speak much during his suffering. From his rent and torn breast no breath came without exertion. Words were agony. He felt, to use his own expression, as though a thousand-pound weight was pressing on his chest. But he did utter a sentiment which had great significance a few years after his death. 'They have killed me,' he said, 'because I was opposed to slavery and a corrupt administration.'

As in the case of Burr and Hamilton, this duel was more injurous in the long run to the survivor than to the victim. David Broderick's funeral was attended by over thirty thousand people and became a moving tribute to the 'martyr to the slavocracy'. Terry's slavery party suffered a mortal blow and, though Terry himself was acquitted of murder, he could never hope for high office again, and was pursued to the end of his life by accusations of trickery in his fight with Broderick. In 1889, at Lathrop, California, he attacked his former associate, Judge Stephen Field, and was shot down by a deputy marshal.

By the 1860s, even in California, duelling in America was on the decline, and its history in the second half of the nineteenth century was one of steady retreat in the face of public disapproval and stern legislation. To catalogue the dwindling list of duels which took place in the United States during that period would be merely tedious, but perhaps something should be said about the so-called 'American duel'. This was a duelling method rather similar to 'Russian roulette' and for many years was considered in Europe to be a peculiarly American way of settling a quarrel. As far back as 1894, however, Bronson Howard indignantly repudiated the idea that there was anything American about this particular method, which depended entirely on chance and not at all on skill.

'The Italian', he wrote, 'firmly believes – which belief, by the way, he also shares with the Frenchman – that when two Americans wish to fight a duel, they load one pistol, draw lots for it, and the winner shoots himself. Why this should be supposed to be the American way of duelling I cannot imagine. If there is any such thing as an "American" duel, it is what is familiarly known as "shooting on sight". The challenger sends word to his enemy that he will shoot him the next time he sees him, and thereupon the latter arms himself, and takes his walks abroad with much caution, until the two meet, when both begin a brisk fusillade with their revolvers, and one of them is usually killed, together with from four to six of the bystanders. This sort of duel would never do for a sparsely-populated country like Italy; and as for the other and falsely called "American duel", it lacks everything that could recommend it to the lover of athletic sports.'

9 · Duels in Other Countries

France, Britain and the United States have never, of course, held a monopoly of duelling, and there are a great many duels recorded in the history of other countries, especially in Europe, which deserve to be recalled here.

In Italy, duelling in the form of the trial by combat can be traced back to the seventh century at least, and in 668 we find Grimoald confirming the right of women accused of adultery to appoint a champion to defend their honour. Again, in 713, when Luitprand confirmed the laws governing trial by combat, he declared: 'We are not convinced of the justice of what is called the judgment of God, since we have found that many innocent persons have perished in defending a good cause; but this custom is of such antiquity among the Lombards that we cannot abolish it, notwithstanding its impiety.'

Charlemagne, who succeeded to the crown of Lombardy in 774, tried in Italy as well in France to curb the practice, meeting strong opposition from the Italian nobility; and it was at the request of that nobility that Otto II, in an assembly at Verona in 988, re-established duelling in all its vigour, refusing to exempt the clergy or women from the obligation.

In the thirteenth and fourteenth centuries a spate of works dealing with 'the noble art and science' of duelling appeared in Italy, where Naples became the great centre of the *scienza cavalleresca*. Alberic Balbiano, the Constable of Naples, even established a military order dedicated to St George and pledged to maintain the practice of duelling. Already Italian duels were noted for the cunning tricks and ruses which were to become a characteristic feature of the institution in that country. Most of the leading fencing-masters in Europe were Italians, and Brantôme maintains that Jarnac, before his fatal duel with La Chastaigneraye, had taken lessons from an Italian captain called Caise who had taught him the 'hamstring cut' later known as the *coup de Jarnac*. These fencing-masters were apparently anything but scrupulous with regard to the methods used in killing a man, which they recommended doing *in ogni modo*. Brantôme himself relates that when he was in Milan he took fencing lessons for a month from a famous master called Trappe, and that during this period not a single day passed when he did not see at least twenty *quadrilles* of people fighting in the streets, and leaving the corpses of their antagonists where they fell.

It would seem that the practice of calling in seconds or witnesses to share the dangers of the principals originated in Italy. Brantôme tells the story of a Neapolitan gentleman who was challenged to a duel and killed his opponent; he was leaving the field when the dead man's second stopped him and told him that he could not allow him to depart until he had avenged his friend. The gentleman politely agreed to this proposal and killed the second, whereupon another witness stepped forward and courteously observed that he would be delighted to share in the honour if the victorious duellist did not feel too tired; if, however, he felt at all fatigued, the encounter could be postponed until the following day. To this the gentleman replied that he did not feel in the least tired, and that as he was warm and his hand was in, they might as well set to without delay. Within a few moments the witness's corpse was stretched out beside those of his two friends.

Commenting on this practice, Brantôme observes: 'I have heard a great deal of talk on this matter, and have been informed by great Italian captains that they were the founders of these fights and their punctilios, which were well known in theory and practice. The Spaniards resemble them, but are not so proficient in the art, which nowadays our Frenchmen exercise to perfection. The Italians are rather more cool and deliberate in this business than we are, and somewhat more cruel. In their teaching they have given those who feel disposed to grant or to spare their adversary's life the glorious opportunity of showing their generosity, by maiming their fallen foe, both in his legs and arms, and moreover giving him a fearful cut across the nose and face, to remind him of their condescension and humanity.'

It is hard to make a choice from the *embarras de richesses* which Italy offers the historian of duelling, but perhaps the most characteristic Italian encounter, from the point of view of passion, deceitfulness and treachery, was the duel fought in 1664 at Ostuni between the Duke of Martina and the Count of Conversano. The latter had been in a state of feud for many years with his neighbour the aged Prince of Francavilla, whom he eventually challenged to a sword-fight; the prince refused this form of combat, pleading his age and infirmity, and suggested a pistol-duel instead, but the count insisted on his original proposal and tried to provoke the prince by striking him with the flat of his sword in public. Thirsting for revenge, the prince proposed a

champion in the person of his nephew the Duke of Martina, though insisting that a year should elapse before the duel, since the duke was a young man whose education had not yet been completed. The prince, 'actuated more by fear of shame attendant on defeat than by feelings of affection for his relative', hit upon a stratagem which he hoped would ensure success for his champion. He sent a gentleman attached to his household to the Count of Conversano's castle, to which he gained admission by complaining of wrongs done to him by the Prince of Francavilla. The count received him with splendid hospitality, and, discovering that he was a skilled swordsman, spent several months practising with him the art which he felt sure would bring him victory over his young opponent. A chronicler of the feud recounts the rest of the story as follows:

> A few days previous to the one fixed for the duel, the guest, under pretence of paying a visit to his relatives, withdrew from the Count of Conversano's castle, and secretly returned to his former lord, where he lost no time in communicating to his nephew all the peculiarities and advantages repeated experience had enabled him to remark in the count's manner of fencing. The Duke of Martina was thereby taught that the only chance of success which he could look to was by keeping on the defensive during the early part of the combat; he was instructed that his antagonist, though avowedly the most able swordsman in the kingdom, was extremely violent; and that, if his first passes could be parried, his person, somewhat inclined to corpulency, would speedily be exhausted from the effects of his impetuosity. The Duke of Martina, furnished with this important advice, and strong in the conviction of what he considered a just cause, awaited in calm anxiety the day of battle; and the behaviour of the two combatants on the last morning strongly characterized their different dispositions, as well as the manners and habits of the age they lived in. The duke made his will, confessed himself, and took affectionate leave of his mother, who retired to her oratory to pass in prayer the time devoted to the conflict, while the Count of Conversano ordered a sumptuous feast to be prepared, and invited his friends and retainers after the fight. He then nonchalantly bade his wife farewell, and, brutally alluding to his adversary's youth and inexperience, remarked: '*Vado a far un capretto*,' – 'I am going to kill a kid.'
>
> The parties met at the place appointed. It was an open space, before a monastery of friars, at Ostuni; but these good fathers, by their intercessions and prayers, prevailed upon the combatants to remove to another similar piece of ground, in front of the Capuchin convent, in the same town. Here the bishop and clergy, carrying the host in solemn procession, attempted in vain to dissuade them from their bloody purpose; they were dismissed with scorn, and the duel began.
>
> The conflict was of long duration, and afforded the duke an opportunity of availing himself of the counsels he had received: when he found that the count was beginning to be out of breath, and off his guard, he assumed the offensive, and, having wounded him, demanded if he was satisfied and proposed to desist from any further hostility; but, stung to the soul by this unexpected reverse, he proudly rejected all offers of accommodation; actuated by blind revenge and redoubled animosity, he soon lost all command of himself, and received a second wound, which terminated the contest together with his life.
>
> It appeared afterwards that the Prince of Francavilla, whose principles were as little honourable as those of his adversary, and whose thirst of revenge was no less insatiable, had appointed a band of bravoes to waylay and murder him on his way home, had he been victorious.

At various times Italian rulers tried to suppress the practice of duelling, but the only one to achieve any success was the Prince of Melfe Caraccioli, who commanded the forces of François I from 1545–50; after the failure of various measures, he issued an edict compelling duellists to fight on the parapet of the bridge at Turin, so that both combatants were virtually doomed to fall into the river together. Another prince, Humbert II of Viennois, set a courageous example by refusing to fight a duel; challenged by Amadeus V of Savoy, he replied to his herald: 'My friend, tell your master that the merit of a prince does not lie in physical strength; but that if he wishes to display his prowess, I have not a single bull in my possession that is not stronger than he is; if he wishes to confirm the fact, I shall have pleasure in sending him one to try.'

Neither edicts nor examples, however, succeeded in curbing the practice in Italy, or even in preventing its increase. 'It was due to the necessity of the good opinion of others', Beccaria explains, 'that single combat was resorted to during a state of legal anarchy. It was in vain that this practice was forbidden under pain of death; it was found impossible to check a custom founded upon sentiments which were considered dearer than life.' Going on to ask why the lower classes of society did not imitate their superiors, Beccaria maintains that this was 'simply because they stand in less need of the esteem of others than those who, on account of their position, are subject to more suspicion and distrust'. In fact, the 'lower classes' in Italy were no less susceptible to insult than the nobility, though they generally avenged their wrongs with the stiletto rather than the sword. Occasionally, however, a member of the lower orders who felt in urgent need of 'the esteem of others' made a determined effort to become eligible to fight duels. Such was the case of the artist Michelangelo Caravaggio, who, after Arpino had presumed to criticize some of his pictures and then rejected his challenge on the ground of disparity of rank, went to Malta and had himself dubbed a knight in order to qualify himself for similar occasions in the future. Unfortunately, as might have been expected, he started picking quarrels as soon as he was armed with his new distinction, was forced to leave Malta, killed a critic in Rome, and died in utter destitution on the highway.

Malta, which was Caravaggio's undoing, deserves mention here in passing as one of the few places in the world where duelling was permitted by law. It was, not unreasonably, thought inconsistent to forbid duelling in a place where the entire order was based on the principles of chivalry, but the practice was made subject to certain restrictions intended to lessen its danger. These were that duellists were obliged to settle their quarrel in one particular street on the island, under pain of the severest penalties, and were also obliged, under pain of the same penalties, to put up their swords if ordered to do so by a woman, a priest or a knight. It might be thought that these conditions would have made it impossible to fight a duel at all in the middle of a crowded city, but this was not the case. A cross was always painted on the wall opposite the spot where a duellist had fallen, and in 1770 Brydone counted twenty of these crosses. He was also told of a recent incident in which one knight had struck another in a quarrel but had then refused to accept a challenge. 'The challenge was repeated,' he tells us, 'and, though warned of the consequences, still he refused to fight. He was therefore condemned to make the *amende honorable* in the great church of St Jerome, fifty-five days successively, then to be confined in a dungeon, without light, for five years, after which he is to remain a prisoner in the castle for life. The unfortunate young man who received the blow is also in disgrace, as he has not had an opportunity of wiping it out in the blood of his adversary. This has been looked upon as a very singular affair, and is still one of the principal topics of conversation. The first part of the sentence has already been executed, and the poor wretch is now in his dungeon, nor is it thought that any abatement will be made in what remains. If the legislature in other countries punished with equal rigour those that *do* fight, as it does in this those that do not, I believe we soon should have an end of duelling.'

In Italy, duelling was not encouraged or rather enforced in this way in any of the various states which made up the country, although in Sardinia, where it was legally confined to the army, officers in the nineteenth century were under the same obligation to fight in certain circumstances as officers in the British Army before the reform of 1844. In the Roman states duels had become a rarity by the nineteenth century, in Piedmont and Savoy they were scarcely ever heard of, but in Naples the practice died hard. And although in this century it has fallen into the same general disfavour in Italy as in other European countries, Italy clung to it longer and more passionately than any other country save France. To obtain some idea of its prevalence in Italy as late as the 1880s, one had only to consult the statistics published by a London journal of the duels fought in that country during the decade from 1879 to 1889. This report stated:

> Of course the list is not complete, as many contests took place that were not duly reported. Nevertheless, we have before us full details concerning 2,759 duels which took place in Italy at the period mentioned. Of this number 93 per cent were fought with swords or rapiers, 6 per cent with pistols, and one only with revolvers. Strange to say, no less than 3,901 wounds were inflicted, so that several combatants must have been wounded more than once, and occasionally both combatants were hurt. Of these wounds 1,066 are estimated as serious, and fifty proved fatal. Thus less than 2 per cent of the combatants were killed. The danger of death is therefore not very serious: one man in fifty or sixty may be killed. In analysing the causes of all these encounters, it was found that 30 per cent arose from political divergences of opinion, and newspaper articles concerning the same; 8 per cent only of the duels were fought in consequence of some serious insult; but 10 per cent arose out of discussions on religious topics, and 19 per cent from quarrels over cards and other games. It is also a curious fact that the number of duels is five times greater in summer than in winter – a self-evident proof that heat affects the temper – while in the Lenten season there are hardly any duels at all, which is perhaps an argument in favour of fasting. Out of 100 duellists, it was ascertained that thirty were military men, twenty-nine were journalists, twelve were barristers, four students, three professors, three engineers, and three members of parliament.

In Spain, though duelling never found the general favour it enjoyed in Italy, it was practised intermittently from Roman times until the twentieth century. According to Livy, it existed in Spain before the invasion of the Northern peoples, and the customs of the Goths made it still more frequent. After the Moorish invasion the practice became so widespread that for some

23 · (*a*) *Double duel at Göttingen*, 1816. *An engraving*
23 · (*b*) *Samurais in traditional costume*

24 · *German student duel*

time the Spanish monarchs made no attempt to suppress it but merely tried to regularize it. Thus the edicts issued by the Cortes de Najera were included by King Alfonso the Wise in his *Codigo de las Partidas*, though without much effect.

In 1490 sterner measures were taken in an effort to abolish duelling and the law of the Novissima Récopilacion prescribed the confiscation of the property of anyone who provoked or accepted a duel, death for the provoker if he killed or wounded his opponent, banishment for life for the provoked party if he survived, confiscation of the property of the seconds, and even certain minor penalties for onlookers. Even so, fresh edicts had to be issued during the following centuries, as the Spanish nobility took little notice of the royal prohibitions, and it is only in the present century that duelling has dwindled to insignificant proportions in Spain.

Portugal, on the other hand, has seen very little duelling in her long history, either because of a more pious horror of committing a mortal sin, or because of strict legislation which punished duelling with transportation to Africa, together with confiscation of the offender's goods and chattels.

The Low Countries, which might have been thought to be much less given to duelling than countries with warmer climates, have in fact a long-established duelling tradition, including the legendary combat between Jean le Flamand and the Jew Wilhelm. Duelling in Belgium reached its height in the first decades of the nineteenth century, though in fairness to the Belgians it should be added that most of the duels were between Frenchmen who had slipped across the frontier to escape the attentions of their own police. However, there were a good many native duels, especially in the 1830s when political agitation was at fever-pitch. Disturbed at the frequency of fatal duels fought by Frenchmen on Belgian territory, and roused to indignation by the case of the Belgian Captain Eenens, who was tried for having killed his fellow-officer Captain Pariset in a duel near Waterloo, and acquitted on the plea that no law against duelling existed, the Belgian parliament passed a law in 1841 laying down severe but not impossibly harsh penalties for anyone who caused a duel or killed or wounded an opponent in an affair of honour.

It was Germany which, after Italy, France and Britain, took most enthusiastically, or at least most earnestly, to duelling, a practice to which some Germans are still strongly attached. The first recorded examples of duels in Germany were in the best tradition of the trial by combat or the duel of chivalry. Such a case was the duel fought in 1043 to judge the honour of Gunehilde, wife of the future Henry III and daughter of King Canute of England, who had been accused of adultery. 'No one', writes La Colombière, 'could be found to act as her champion, on account of the gigantic form of her accuser, a certain Rodinger. But the empress finally found a champion in a little English boy, whom she had brought from her country. This youth, by a divine miracle, being unable to strike higher, cut the hamstrings of the slanderer, which was considered a public proof of the innocence of the empress.' According to the same authority, Gunehilde, despite her victory, retired to a convent where she died, and was subsequently canonized.

In more modern times, duelling became so common in the German and Austrian states that various edicts known as 'duel mandates' were issued in the eighteenth century forbidding the practice. One published in Bavaria in 1779 punished a challenge with loss of office, if the offenders held public positions, or with confiscation of property and three years' imprisonment if not, and prescribed the death penalty for both parties if the duel had actually taken place. Similar edicts were issued in Austria and Prussia, and by the turn of the century duelling had been reduced to such an extent that Madame de Staël could obtain the impression that it scarcely existed any longer in Germany. In her work *De l'Allemagne* she wrote:

> Germany, if we except some courts, anxious to imitate the French, was never assailed by that infatuation, immorality and incredulity which, since the Regency, had changed the natural character of the French. Feudality still maintained in Germany some of its chivalric maxims: duels occasionally took place, but they were not as frequent as in France: for the Germans do not possess the same vivacity and petulance as the French nation, nor do they partake of the same notions of courage, public opinion being much more severe on the want of probity and fair dealing. If a man had transgressed the laws of morality, ten duels a day would not have enabled him to recover the esteem he had forfeited.
>
> The spirit of chivalry still reigns among the Germans – but passively. They are incapable of deceit, and in every transaction act loyally; but that energy which exposed men to so many sacrifices, and which exacted from women so many virtues – the chivalric spirit of olden times – has left only faint traces in Germany, where noble actions will only be the result of that liberal impulse which in Europe has succeeded chivalry.

Unfortunately, the beginning of the nineteenth century witnessed the same resurgence of duelling in Germany as in France, and soon affairs of honour were being settled throughout the German states in defiance of the authorities. Three of the most remarkable of these nineteenth-century encounters occurred within a few months of one another, in 1833 and 1834.

In 1833 the corpse of a Lieutenant-Colonel von Keunaw was found in a forest near Dreisen, pierced with a sword-wound. Inquiries revealed that a councillor called von Zahn had proposed to the daughter of a certain Baron Haller, who at the same time was being courted by a friend of von Zahn's, Baron Linsmar. Knowing that Linsmar was totally unskilled in the use of a sword, von Zahn had hit upon the idea of fomenting a quarrel between his rival and another friend of his, von Keunaw, who was reputed to be a master swordsman. His efforts had been successful and a duel had taken place, but, by one of those freaks of chance so common in the history of duelling, the inexperienced swordsman had killed his expert opponent. Von Zahn was brought to trial and condemned to death – a sentence subsequently reduced to twenty years' imprisonment – while Baron Linsmar was sentenced to ten years' imprisonment.

The following year, an even more sensational duel of a highly romantic nature took place. 'A Baron Trautmansdorf', the German papers reported, 'was paying court to the widow of a Polish general, the young Countess Lodoiska R—; he was only waiting for an appointment to an embassy to marry her. In the meantime a Baron von Ropp courted the lady, and in a sonnet poked fun at his more successful rival. The baron immediately sent him a challenge, which Ropp accepted; but on the ground he proposed a champion, who espoused his cause, and Trautmansdorf fell. His second, indignant at this act of treachery, insisted that Ropp should give him satisfaction. The second too was mortally wounded, and it was then discovered that Lodoiska herself had accompanied her betrothed in male attire. Ropp, having recognized her when she fell, felt so deeply the baseness of his conduct that he threw himself on his sword, and expired beside the bodies of Lodoiska and her lover.'

That same year of 1834, Frankfurt witnessed a duel which was historic in that it was the only recorded encounter in which both combatants were killed by one weapon. A ball had been arranged in honour of the arrival of the Grand Duchess Helena of Russia at Baden, and the name of a certain von Haber, a banker's son, was placed on the list of subscribers. Von Goeler, a Baden officer and one of the members of the ball committee, decided that von Haber was not a suitable person to attend the function, and struck his name off the list; and when von Haber called for a duel, the officer corps at Carlsruhe ruled that von Goeler was not required to give satisfaction. Von Haber's second, a captain in the Russian service called Verefkin, now took up the matter, and a duel was arranged between him and von Goeler. The first exchange of shots had no effect, but Verefkin's second shot wounded von Goeler so seriously that he could scarcely remain on his feet. Thinking that his antagonist was *hors de combat*, Verefkin tossed his pistol on to the ground, only to see von Goeler take aim at him three times, his pistol missing fire on each occasion. Meanwhile von Goeler's second had picked up Verefkin's

pistol and loaded it, and he now handed it to his principal. With a final desperate effort, the wounded man fired at Verefkin, killing him on the spot. Von Goeler later died of his wound, killed by the same pistol which had been responsible for his opponent's death.

Most duels in Germany, however, were not fought between officers or private citizens but between university students or *Burschen*. The chief purpose of these encounters was, and still is, to receive cuts on the face, these being left open to form duelling scars which were regarded as marks of courage and honour. Since the eyes were protected by a peaked cap or iron spectacles, the throat enclosed in a thick stock, the right arm swathed in bandages so heavy that it had to be supported when not in action, and the legs and trunk encased in leather, it might reasonably be argued that these student combats were not really duels at all, but elaborate ritualistic facial operations. Sometimes, however, in spite of all the protective clothing worn by the combatants, a student would be killed in a duel, whereupon his adversary would be advised to leave the university, receiving from the senate what was called a *consilium abeundi*; he could then pursue his studies at another university, but if he killed a second man, every academic door was closed against him.

A special weapon was of course required for the aesthetic purposes of German student duelling, and this was the *Schläger*, a sword with a blade three and a half feet long, and triangular like a bayonet, with the handle pro-

tected by a tin plate, ten inches in diameter, and humorously known as 'the soup plate of honour'. Handle, soup-plate and blade could all be unscrewed and hidden by the duellist, the hilt and guard under his cloak, and the blade inside a hollow walking-stick. Explaining how this weapon was used, an English authority wrote at the end of the nineteenth century that 'German students never thrust. The hand which holds the weapon is raised above the level, and well in front of the head, and the blade comes down somewhat diagonally in front of the body. The cuts are delivered with the wrist alone. At one university, and one alone, has the point been used in my time, and there, I believe, it is no longer employed. That university is Jena, and the reason why the use of the small sword was allowed is an odd one. Jena was the great resort of theological students, and a theological student with a sword-cut on his face was not admitted into the ministry. Permission was therefore given by the student code to Jenaites to settle their disputes by running one another through the body.'

In 1890 the Emperor called for a report on the extent of duelling in the German army, and it was widely reported that he meant to take stern measures to suppress duelling, not only in the army, but also in the universities. The next year, however, at the opening of the summer term at Bonn University, he appalled the University authorities by praising the duelling clubs as 'providing the best education which a young man can get for his future life'. The humanizing, reforming work of decades was undone by those words in a few moments. Even now, though duelling and duelling clubs have been prohibited in Germany for many years, the corps have been formed once more and duels are again being fought in secret.

Going north from Germany, we find that the Scandinavian countries have long ago abandoned duelling, but still treasure the tradition of a picturesque duelling past. A nineteenth-century authority on the subject has left us this account of single combat in Scandinavia in ancient times:

> By an ancient law of Sweden, if a man told another that he was inferior to any other man, or had not the heart of a man, and the other replied: 'I am as good a man as yourself,' a meeting was to follow. If the aggressor came to the ground, but did not find the offended, the latter was to be considered dishonoured, and held unfit to give testimony in any cause, and deprived moreover of the power to make a will. But if, on the other hand, the insulted party came forward, and the offending party did not make his appearance, the former was to call him aloud by his name three times, and, if he did not appear, make a mark upon the ground, when the offender would be held as infamous and false. When both parties, met, and the offended was killed, his antagonist had to pay a half compensation for his death; but, if the aggressor succumbed, his fate was to be attributed to temerity and an unguarded expression, therefore his death called for no compensation. In Norway, any gentleman who refused satisfaction to another was said to have *lost his law*, and could not be admitted as evidence upon oath. According to the Danish laws, it was held that force is better arbiter in contestations than words; and in the judicial combats, which frequently arose on the slightest provocation, no champion was allowed to fight in the cause of another, however feeble or unskilled in arms he might be: women were not even allowed a proxy to defend them, but obliged to defend their honour personally. In such cases, to afford the woman a better chance, the man who had offended her was obliged to get into a pit up to his waist, by which means his Amazonian opponent could wheel round him and strike him on the head with a sling or leather thong to which was suspended a heavy stone; the male combatant was armed with a club, and if he missed her three times, or struck the ground instead of her, he was declared to be vanquished.

The ancient Scandinavians displayed the same practical ingenuity when it came to selecting suitable sites for their duels, for in order to prevent either of the parties from fleeing they usually chose small islands called *Holms*, the duels themselves taking the name of *Holmsgang*. Sometimes a hide seven ells long was spread out on the ground; at other times the lists were marked out with stakes or stones; whichever party stepped outside these limits, or was driven outside them, was considered conquered.

At an early stage the Scandinavian countries turned against duelling, and stringent measures were taken to enforce the ban placed on the practice. Thus it is recorded that Gustavus II of Sweden, a contemporary of Louis XIII of France, hearing that two of his officers were planning a meeting, went to the ground before them. Finding him there when they arrived, they were about to withdraw when he pointed to a gallows, with the hangman waiting at its foot, and said grimly: 'Now gentlemen, you may proceed.' Later rulers and parliaments in Norway, Sweden and Denmark instituted rigorous laws which effectively abolished duelling in those countries. Only Iceland had no need of such legislation, for she had done away with duelling centuries before. Icelandic tradition had it that two poets, Gunnlang and Rafn, had once fought for the hand of the beautiful Helga of the Golden Locks, and had both fallen in the encounter, whereupon the greatest popular assembly Iceland had ever known had gathered together and prohibited duelling in perpetuity.

In Russia, the situation with respect to duelling has varied considerably over the centuries. For a long period there was virtually no duelling in Russia on account of the stringent laws against it. The military penal code of Peter I, for instance, ruled that anyone who provoked another to fight a duel should be hanged, whether the duel took place or not, and that the seconds should suffer the same punishment unless they did their utmost to prevent the encounter. In the case of a quarrel in which a blow was given, the aggressor was compelled to ask the forgiveness of the offended party in front of a military tribunal, and submit to a public retaliation. Again, in the code of Catherine the Great it is stated that 'as to duelling, the best means of preventing it is to punish the aggressor, and to declare the innocence of the man who, without any fault of his own, has found himself under the necessity of avenging his honour'.

In the nineteenth century, however, under the influence of European fashion and with the encouragement of Alexander I, duelling came into vogue in Russia; and soon there were few young Russian officers or aristocrats who had not engaged in an affair of honour. Probably the most notorious of all Russian duellists was a certain Count Tolstoy, who had a long list of victories to his credit. The oddest of the duels which he fought and won was an encounter with a naval officer who had at first refused his challenge on the ground of the count's well-known skill in the use of arms. Tolstoy then suggested fighting with pistols muzzle to muzzle, but the officer rejected this proposal too, insisting on fighting in what he called the naval manner – namely seizing each other and jumping into the water, victory going to the party who escaped drowning. The count in his turn rejected this suggestion, pleading that he could not swim, but when the naval officer taunted him with cowardice he rushed at him and threw himself with his adversary into the sea. Both men were pulled out of the water, but the naval officer was so seriously injured that he died a few days later.

Another curious Russian duel fought between an old general called Zass and Prince Dolgoroucki bore some resemblance to what later became known as 'Russian roulette'. Zass had refused to obey an order from the prince which would have nullified his plan of cperations, and the two men had agreed to fight a duel. At that moment, however, the enemy artillery was heard and news came that a near-by redoubt was being attacked. 'Prince,' said the general 'we cannot fight a duel when our duty calls us to meet the enemy; but let us both stand in an embrasure of that battery, against which the enemy are directing their fire, and let us remain there until one of us is struck.' Dolgoroucki agreed to this suggestion, and the two antagonists stood in full view of the enemy, hand on hip and glaring fiercely at each other, until the prince was cut in two by a cannon-ball.

Duelling in Russia received increased impetus in 1894, when the Tsar promulgated a new law according to which it was obligatory upon army officers, not only whenever they themselves fancied they had been insulted, but also whenever anybody else thought they had. 'Detailed accounts', wrote an English correspondent, 'reach St Petersburg every other day of duels between young officers who are intimate friends, and never dreamt of offending each other, simply because, when joking among themselves, one of the party said or did something which in the opinion of somebody else ought to prove insulting. Thus, we read of one young man being shot by another, whose best friend he is, and with whom he had no quarrel of any kind, being compelled to call him out by the officers' "Court of Honour", which had been instituted in accordance with the recent imperial law; and of another promising young fellow in the south, who is now disabled for the rest of his life because forced to fight with a comrade who never said a cross word to him. In all these cases the alternative is fight or leave the army, and no one dares to

choose the latter.' This state of affairs could not be changed, however, except by the Tsar himself, and it was only with the Revolution that duelling was finally and utterly abolished in Russia.

Lastly, brief mention must be made here of duelling in Japan, for the duel is not an exclusively Western institution and was once practised in that country. The duel for private reasons was generally considered an unworthy act, but an offence directed against a man in his capacity as a *samurai* or soldier was unpardonable. A challenge was promptly given by word of mouth, and later in writing; the opponent had to be a *samurai* himself; and there were no seconds, for it was regarded as inconceivable that a knight might commit any action contrary to honour while engaging in a duel of honour.

According to an account of one highly characteristic Japanese duel, the opposing parties in an affair of honour did not always have to fight in order to obtain satisfaction. Two officers belonging to the Emperor's staff met one day on the imperial staircase, where their swords happened to tangle. When one of the officers protested, the other coolly replied: 'It is only an accident, and at the most it is only a quarrel between two swords.' 'We shall see about that,' cried the first, and with these words he drew his sword and plunged it into his own breast. The other, impatient to obtain the same advantage, hurried away on the errand he was performing, and then returned to his antagonist, who was at the point of death. After satisfying himself that the other man was still breathing, he in turn plunged his sword into his body, with these last words:

'You would not have had a start on me if you had not found me engaged in the service of the Emperor. I die content, however, since I have had the satisfaction of convincing you that my sword is as good as yours.'

10 · Unusual Duels

While the sword or pistol duel, fought on foot and in daylight, attended by seconds, and governed by a strict code of rules, has for a long time been the normal way of settling an affair of honour in Europe and America, there have been a great many encounters distinguished by unusual weapons or circumstances.

Countless weapons of every sort, ranging from the brutally simple to the diabolically complicated, have been used in mortal combat. Persians used to fight each other with maces, Zulus with assagais, and the natives of Patagonia with slings carrying round stones generally weighing a pound each. Brantôme tells of two Corsicans who were armed not only with swords, but also with short sharp-pointed daggers fixed to the front of their helmets; after fighting for some time without result, they threw away their swords and began to wrestle together, butting each other's face, neck and arms, and causing such profuse bleeding that they had to be separated and one of them died within a month. An even more ingenious piece of equipment was devised by a diminutive young soldier who had been insulted by a tall Gascon: he insisted that they should both wear a steel collar round their necks, bristling with pointed blades, ostensibly as an additional weapon, but in fact to prevent his opponent from looking down at him without cutting his own chin.

Duellists with no fancy for either sword or pistol have been known to choose gentler but no less lethal weapons. Thus Cagliostro, called out by a physician whom he had described as a quack, proposed, on the ground that a medical question should be settled medicinally, that the opponents should each swallow one of two pills, one of which was poisonous and the other innocuous. But the most unusual duel ever fought, from the point of view of the weapons employed, was an encounter which took place in France in September 1843, in the Commune of Maison Fort (Seine-et-Oise). Two gentlemen called Lenfant and Mellant, having quarrelled over a game of billiards, drew lots as to who should first throw a red ball at his adversary's head. Chance favoured Mellant, who threw the ball with such force and accuracy at Lenfant's forehead as to kill him on the spot.

Unarmed combat has of course always been common in all countries, but it is generally so unpremeditated, unceremonious and non-lethal that it

scarcely qualifies as duelling. An exception is the 'forehead fight', a brutal form of combat inherited from the ancient Turks and still practised in the Crimea: the two opponents are forbidden to use blows or kicks, and simply butt each other with their foreheads until one of them falls to the ground exhausted, whereupon he draws a knife from his belt and slits his own throat. Again, in the west, there have also been occasional examples of an unarmed combat conducted with a certain ceremony and fought to the point of death. Such a fight occurred towards the end of the last century between two young farmers in the Missouri valley, Duggan Points and Will Moss, for the love of a girl called Sallie Craig. A year later, when news of the affair percolated to Sioux City, the local paper gave the following report of the encounter:

The place of the fight was agreed upon as half-way between the respective residents. A man from Loveland seconded Moss, and Points' brother acted as his second. The fight was not to be conducted according to any specified rules, but in the most approved rough-and-tumble style. About sixty people were on the ground, among whom was the girl over whom the contest was caused, to witness the brutal affair. The seconds stood with cocked revolvers in hand and warned no one to interfere. The men commenced fighting fiercely. They used fists, heels and teeth; and in clinching and tumbling about rolled over a large area of ground. The fight lasted fifty-five minutes, and throughout was one of the most brutal character. It was brought to a fatal conclusion by Points' strength entirely giving way, and then Moss, with the last efforts of his madness, stamped upon his prostrate foe and crushed in his breast and kicked in his head. The spectators at this overpowered the seconds and dragged the men apart. Points was dying when picked up, and expired soon afterwards. Moss had been severely bitten by his antagonist, having had two fingers, an ear and his nose taken off, and was in a deplorable condition from other injuries.

Even when unarmed, duellists are usually adequately clothed. Hence the astonishment of the seconds and onlookers at Brighton in 1806, when Humphrey Howarth, the Member of Parliament for Evesham, arriving on the ground for a duel with Lord Barrymore, deliberately took off his clothes and presented himself stark naked to his opponent's pistol. 'The fact was,' explains Thomas Raikes, 'he had been a surgeon in the Company's army in India, and knowing professionally that gunshot wounds are often aggravated by parts of the clothing being driven by the ball into the orifice, he had determined to avoid at least this risk by divesting himself of all incumbrances. The precaution, however, was needless as no blood was spilt, and the matter arranged by a random shot from each party.' Another version of this incident is given by Samuel Rogers, who denies that any shots were exchanged. 'Howarth's antagonist', he writes, 'declared that fighting with a man in *puris naturalibus* would be quite ridiculous; and accordingly they parted without further discussion.'

Only very rarely have duels been fought during the hours of darkness, it being argued that daylight is essential if the fight is to be properly conducted and the combatants given a fair chance. Brantôme cites the case of a gentleman who provided a less noble but just as practical reason for refusing a challenge to fight in his shirt on a winter's night. He replied 'that he would not expose himself to catch a cold or a purging, which he dreaded more than his antagonist's valour'. But the most striking defence of the daylight tradition was undoubtedly that put up on very personal grounds by the great duellist

Bussy. 'Bussy,' he replied, when challenged to fight by night, 'is not wont to display his valour to the stars or even to the moon, since they are unable to contemplate him properly, or to appreciate his skill. Let those whose deeds are obscure and darkling seek the shades of night that knows no shame. But tomorrow morning, as soon as the sun is risen, I will be at the spot you mention, or any other which your friend prefers. Come with him and bring a couple of sextons with you, for before leaving the spot I should like to see each of you buried with all due ceremony.'

Sometimes, however, one of a pair of duellists has insisted on the encounter taking place in a dark room, and there are two such duels on record. The first known instance occurred under the Empire in France, when one of Napoleon's generals was challenged by a young officer, and accepted the glove on condition that the duel should take place in a dark room, and with pistols. The two parties were positioned, pistol in hand, at opposite corners of the room, the light was put out, the signal to fire was given, and two unequal explosions were heard. When the lamp was lighted again, both combatants were found to be unscathed, and the old general explained to his abashed subordinate: 'Look here, young man. On the floor there you see the charge of the pistol which I drew, only reserving the powder in the pan for a flash; but just come here and see for yourself. If I had not taken good care to step out of your line of fire, you see your bullet would have gone right through me. The Emperor would have lost a man I have reason to believe he can't well spare, and he would have played the devil with you for the misfortune. Well, you've had the satisfaction of making me do what I have never done before, shrink from death; and that's a great deal. Now let's be friends; here's my hand.'

In the other recorded instance of a duel in the dark, which was fought between two Americans, the choice of a darkened room as the duelling-ground would seem to have been inspired by a somewhat unworthier motive. Describing the affair, a contemporary chronicler wrote:

> The two Yankees took up their position at the distance of the corners of the apartment. One fired and missed. 'Now, you rascal,' cried the other, 'I'll track you till I send my bullet through you.' Thereupon he began sidling about stealthily, groping for the intended victim. After a while, not finding him, nor hearing the least sound of footsteps or breathing, he began to think that his man had 'absquatulated'; but, at length, a notion struck him, and he exclaimed: 'Oh! I know where you are! Capital! Just the thing!' Thereupon, going to the fireplace, he poked his pistol up the chimney, saying:

'Now for it!' – 'For God's sake, don't fire! I'll pay the bet,' said a voice up the chimney, whilst the other Yankee kept his muzzle close to the speaker's seat of honour. 'Will you pay me 800 dollars?' asked the latter. 'Oh, yes. Do take away that damned pistol!' – 'Stop a bit,' said the other. 'I must have a voucher.' Thereupon he took out his knife, and cut off the seat of the fellow's breeches, saying: 'Now I have got your bond. You may come down.' The chimney-groper descended, paid the money, and was glad to slink off, minus his money and the piece of his outer integument.

There have, of course, been pistol duels in which the combatants, far from aiming haphazardly at an adversary they could not see, were so close that they could almost touch each other. One such duel was fought in 1796 at Cobham, between Major Sweetman and Captain Watson. The two officers were posted by their seconds at a distance of ten yards; but when Major Sweetman, who was short-sighted, complained that he could not see clearly,

Captain Watson called out to him to advance until he was satisfied. He walked forward to within four yards of his adversary, whereupon both parties fired together. The major paid dearly for his short-sightedness, for he was killed instantly, while the captain was wounded in the thigh. Three months later, Watson was tried for the 'murder' of the major, but was acquitted, the surgeons refusing to be examined for fear of being incriminated.

Some pistol duels were fought at even closer quarters than the Sweetman-Watson affair, not for optical reasons, but because the duellists' hatred for each other was so great that they wanted the encounter to be a fight to the death. One of these duels *au mouchoir* – so-called because the combatants had only a handkerchief between them, one end of it held by the left hand of each – was fought in France during the reign of Louis XVIII, between two close friends, one of whom had maligned the character of the other's mistress. An English contemporary has left us the following vivid account of the affair, which began as a sword duel:

> In spite of the earnest attempts of the seconds at the last moment to effect a reconciliation, the parties set to with the utmost fury and determination; but they were too equally matched to be able to do each other much harm; and at length, getting tired of the useless weapons, they flung them away by mutual consent, and rushed to a case of pistols on the sward. 'This will settle the matter more expeditiously,' said one of them. 'Ah, I'll let you know, my roung rake, what it is to calumniate my *chère amie*!' Posted on the ground, and ready to fire, the one who had been thus addressed suddenly exclaimed: 'We shall fight *au mouchoir*!' Hereupon the seconds interposed: they could bear it no longer, and exclaimed that it would be an assassination, adding that such a procedure would show more ferocity than courage. 'It matters not,' they furiously replied. 'The outrage has been too deadly,' added he of the mistress. 'Well then, gentlemen,' said the seconds, 'if there must absolutely be a victim to your vengeance, let us not lose at one fell stroke both of our dear friends together; let us follow the regulation in such cases. Let one of the pistols only be primed, and let chance decide the rest.'
>
> This murderous compact being made, the seconds prepared the pistols, enveloping them in a handkerchief, and then presenting them to one of the combatants; he took his weapon, and the other was delivered to his antagonist. The ends of the handkerchief were respectively placed in their hands; they raised their pistols; the word was given; they fired, and the slanderer fell back, shot through the breast, a torrent of blood gushing at the instant from his mouth and nostils!
>
> 'Virtuous Amelia!' exclaimed the other antagonist with cruel exultation, 'receive this incense in expiation; it is not worthy of all thy merit!'
>
> The seconds proceeded to examine the pockets of the dying man, whilst the echoes of the forest repeated the frightful death-rattle of his agony amid fitful convulsions; they removed his watch, his papers, everything that might give any clue to the actors in the hideous tragedy, and then all disappeared, like assassins after a murder, already pursued by the pangs of remorse.

The duel *au mouchoir* was, by its very nature, so dangerous that both parties were usually killed. It is therefore scarcely surprising that one such duel which was arranged in 1817 at Kingston, Jamaica, should have taken place in a grave deep enough to receive the bodies of both combatants. The offender was one Henri d'Egville, a French Creole and notorious duellist from Santo

25 · *Duel on horseback. An eighteenth-century oil-painting*

26 · (*a*) *'I don't mind being killed, but I'm damned if I'll catch cold.'*
An engraving of Sainte-Beuve's duel with Dubois

26 · (*b*) *Sabre duel*, 1900, *resulting in a decapitation*

Domingo, who at a dinner party at Kingston had peremptorily insisted on a Scots captain called Stewart singing a Gaelic song, despite the captain's protests that he did not know one. Stewart had finally sung one of Anacreon's odes, to his own amusement and the Creole's triumphant satisfaction, and it was only later that d'Egville had learnt of the trick which had been played on him. He had promptly sought out Stewart, struck him with a horse-whip, and galloped away. The Scot inevitably challenged him to a duel, but, haunted by the memory of another affair of honour in which he had killed his opponent, decided that on this occasion he would make certain that both parties died. When d'Egville appeared at the rendezvous, he therefore proposed that they should fight a duel *à outrance* standing in a grave which two members of his crew had just dug. His proposal was accepted, and the two men descended into the grave, where the handkerchief was placed in their hands – to be grasped firmly by the Scot and tremblingly by the Creole. 'The word "fire" was about to be given', records a chronicler of the affair, 'when the ruffian fainted, and fell at the feet of his adversary, the pistol and handkerchief dropping from his hands as though he had been suddenly struck dead. Stewart spurned him with his foot as a dastardly coward, and exclaiming: "Cowardly cut-throat, you are too pitiable an object to excite my anger," left him to the care of his worthy companion and friend.'

Even when the encounter took place in a grave, the duellists *au mouchoir* did at least fight on foot with a certain degree of immobility. But other duellists have been known to settle their differences on horseback, on bicycles, and even in balloons. The most famous example of a duel fought under these last conditions was the encounter over Paris, early in the nineteenth century, between a Monsieur de Grandpré and a Monsieur de Pique. These two gentlemen had quarrelled over Mademoiselle Tirevit, a famous dancer who was the mistress of the former but had been discovered in compromising circumstances with the latter. They decided to fight it out in balloons – according to contemporary wits because they were both 'of elevated mind' – and on May 3, 1808, they met close to the Tuileries, where their balloons were waiting to receive them. Watched by a huge crowd which had been drawn by the sight of the balloons but little imagined the purpose they were meant to serve, each combatant climbed into his car, armed with a blunderbuss, since pistols would obviously have been ineffective in the circumstances. At nine o'clock the cords were cut, and the balloons rose majestically into the air, keeping within about eighty yards of each other. When they had risen some 2,000 feet, Monsieur de Pique fired his blunderbuss without result. His fire was returned almost immediately by Monsieur de Grandpré, whose shot punctured his adversary's balloon, so that it hurtled to the ground, dashing Monsieur de Pique and his second to pieces on a rooftop. The triumphant Grandpré then drifted happily away from the scene of his victory to land safely at a distance of seventeen miles from Paris.

Compared with aerial encounters of this sort, duelling on horseback might seem almost commonplace, but it was in fact one of the most lethal as well as one of the most exciting forms of single combat. Nearly every western country has known at least one duel of this nature since the Age of Chivalry. Thus in Spain, during the reign of Ferdinand and Isabella, Don Pedro Velasco and Ponce de Leon fought a duel on horseback on a narrow causeway near Madrid, the former being run through the body with a spear. In France, in 1589, there was a duel between the young Comte de Luz, mounted on a white palfrey, and the Duc de Guise, on a black stallion; the duke, who had already killed de Luz's father in a duel, won this encounter by seizing the count's swordarm with one hand and driving his own weapon through his antagonist's throat with the other. In England, Sir Matthew Brown, of Beechwood Castle, and Sir John Townshend met in 1603 on Hounslow Heath, where they fought a savage duel on horseback which was fatal to them both. And in America, in 1883, two young cousins called Austin Guthrie and Franklin Meyers, who were in love with the same girl, engaged in a mounted duel with knives near Black Creek in Arkansas; both men were terribly cut about the head and body, Meyers' left arm being almost severed, and they died after falling from their horses.

It was in Ireland, however, that duelling on horseback was most common – so common in fact that special fields were set aside for the Irish gentry to do battle on their chargers in the best possible conditions. Tradition, according to a noted Irish duellist, laid down that 'the combatants should gallop past each other at a distance marked out by posts, which prevented a nearer approach. They were at liberty to fire at each other at any time from the commencement to the end of their course, but they were compelled to do so at a hard gallop, their weapons having been previously charged alike with a certain number of balls, slugs or whatever was most convenient, as agreed upon. The posts were usually placed eight or nine yards apart, being the nearest points from which the combatants might fire. If neither party were hit during one course the combatants proceeded to a second; and if it was decided to continue the fight after the pistols were discharged, they then either finished with broadswords on horseback or with smallswords on foot.'

One of the most interesting and best recorded of these mounted duels in Ireland took place at Maryborough in 1759, between Colonel Jonah Barrington and a neighbour called Gilbert. There had been bad blood between the two men for some time, and finally, we are told, 'some judicious friends interfered, and, from a fear that the feud might descend by way of a vendetta to the innocent offspring, pressed that the matter should be cleared up in the open, honest, legitimate way'. The ground was fixed at one hundred yards of race on the Maryborough Green; and it was agreed that the weapons should be two holster pistols charged with ball and swan-drops, broadswords with basket-handles, and skeens, or long, broad-bladed daggers. Publicly announced six months in advance, the duel drew spectators from all over the country, and what with the huge crowds, the mounted gamekeepers and huntsmen keeping the ground clear, and the county trumpeter in all his glory, the Maryborough Green looked more like a racecourse than a duelling-ground.

When the signal to begin the duel was given, the two combatants galloped towards each other, both firing before they came abreast, and both missing. During the second course, Barrington received most of Gilbert's shot full in his face, but the large bullet missed him and the swandrops penetrated no deeper than his temple and cheekbones. A fierce hand-to-hand battle ensued, which Barrington's grandson, Sir Jonah Barrington, has described as follows:

> My grandfather got three cuts, which he used to exhibit with great glee: one on the thick of the right arm, a second on his bridle-arm, and a third on the inside of the left hand. His hat, which he kept to the day of his death, was also sliced in several places; but both had iron skull-caps under their hats, which probably saved their brains from remaining upon the green of Maryborough. Gilbert had received two pokes from my grandfather on his thigh and his side, but neither dangerous. I fancy he had the best of the battle, being as strong as, and less irritable than, my grandfather, who, I suspect, grew towards the last a little ticklish on the subject – for he rushed headlong at Gilbert, and instead of striking at his person, thrust his broadsword into the horse's body as often as he could, until the beast dropped his rider underneath him; my grandfather then leaped off his horse, threw away his sword, and putting his skeen, or broad dagger to the throat of Gilbert, told him to ask his life or die, as he must do either one or the

other in half a minute. Gilbert said he would ask his life only upon the terms that, without apology or conversation, they should shake hands heartily and be future friends and companions, and not leave the youths of two old families to revenge their quarrel by slaughtering each other. These terms being quite agreeable to my grandfather, as they breathed good sense, intrepidity, and good heart, he acquiesced; and from that time they were the most intimately attached and joyous friends and companions of the county they resided in.

While there have been a good many duels on horseback, particularly in Ireland, there is only one case on record of a duel fought inside a horse-drawn carriage. This encounter took place in France under the Restoration, at the time when officers of Napoleon's Army on half-pay were constantly picking

quarrels with officers of the Royal Guard. The most formidable and obstreperous member of the Imperial party was a certain Colonel Barbier-Dufai, who one day set out to provoke a herculean young officer of the Royal Guard whom he saw in the Palais-Royal. He first trod on the toes of his chosen victim, whose name was Raoul, and then dug his elbow into his side; but he obtained no response until he told the young man in so many words that he was not insulting him but his cockade. Sharp words were exchanged and it was agreed that only a duel could settle the quarrel. However, when the Colonel asked Raoul to name his weapon, and the young officer admitted that as he was only eighteen he was equally unskilled with rapier, sword or pistol, Dufai refused to fight 'a mere child' and walked away. Taking the only possible course to make a duel inevitable, Raoul ran after him and slapped his face. A furious Dufai demanded instant satisfaction, rapiers were obtained, and the duel began.

Four times over, the colonel disarmed his adversary, sending his rapier spinning out of his hand. Finally, losing patience with this unequal fight, he suggested some other weapon. Pistols were out of the question in a Paris street, but then, seeing a hackney carriage approaching, Dufai had an idea. Stopping the carriage, he suggested to Raoul that they should use it as a mobile duelling-ground for a fight to the death.

'Here is my proposal,' he said. 'We will enter that coach, each armed with a poignard. These gentlemen will tie us together, only leaving free our right arms; thus there will be no means of escape. The doors of the coach shall be closed, and at a given signal the coach will set off and go twice round the Place du Carrousel.'

The young man agreed to this suggestion, and he and the colonel were accordingly tied together and shut up in the carriage. The coachman was ordered to get down, and his place was taken by two of the seconds, while the other two climbed up behind. At a shout from Dufai, the carriage moved off and was driven swiftly round the square to the accompaniment of cries from within. A contemporary English chronicler has left us this account of the grisly conclusion of the affair:

> At the end of the second round the seconds jumped down and opened the door of the coach. The silence of death was within, mid a sea of blood. Raoul was dead, and Dufai also seemed to be dead; but he recovered from the frightful wounds he had received. Raoul had driven his poignard four times through the Colonel's chest, and had hacked the lower part of his person with his teeth.
>
> 'Why did he slap me?' muttered the colonel. 'At least, gentlemen, you will do me the justice to declare that I killed him fairly. All the chances were in his favour. His athletic constitution gave him a great advantage over me; but his hour had come. . . .'

Bizarre though this duel was, it cannot be accounted the most unusual ever fought. That was almost certainly the protracted encounter between two French officers called Fournier and Dupont. It began in 1794 at Strasbourg, where Captain Fournier, a fanatical duellist endowed with remarkable skill, had just challenged and killed, on the most frivolous of pretexts, a young man called Blum. The killing had aroused tremendous indignation in the town, and General Moreau, who was giving a ball to the citizens of Strasbourg on the very evening of the funeral, gave instructions to his aide-de-camp, Captain Dupont, to prevent Fournier from entering the ballroom. This Dupont did, with the inevitable result that Fournier promised to 'pay him handsomely for the commission of doorkeeper which he had accepted'.

The duel was fought, and Fournier was laid on the grass with a vigorous sword-thrust.

'That's the *first* touch,' he said, as he sank to the ground.

'Then you want another bout, do you?' asked Dupont.

'I certainly do, my dear fellow,' replied Fournier, 'and before long, I hope.'

A month later, he had recovered, and the two men fought again. This time, Dupont was seriously wounded, but as he fell he cried: 'That's the *second*. Next time we shall have the *finish*.'

The next time, however, the *finish* was not forthcoming, for each of the two inflicted a slight wound on the other. The fact was that they were equally matched with the sword, and Dupont not unreasonably refused to fight with pistols, as Fournier proposed, for the latter was a crack shot and was reputed to amuse himself by smashing the short pipes of his fellow hussars between their lips when they galloped past smoking. The two men therefore resolved to continue the contest with swords until one of them confessed that he was beaten or 'satisfied'. They drew up a formal contract governing their private war, in the following terms:

1. Every time that Dupont and Fournier shall be a hundred miles from each other, they will each approach from a distance to meet sword in hand.
2. Should one of the contracting parties be prevented by service duties, he who is free must travel the entire distance, so as to reconcile the obligations of service with the demands of the present treaty.
3. No excuse whatever, excepting those resulting from military obligations, will be admitted.
4. The present being a *bona fide* treaty, no alteration can be made to the conditions agreed upon by the contracting parties.

This contract was religiously observed in every detail, and soon the state of war between the two officers became a normal condition for them. They were as eager and impatient to meet after a long separation as two lovers, and they never crossed swords without first exchanging a warm handshake. Their correspondence consisted entirely of letters in this vein:

'I have been invited to breakfast with the officers of the Regiment of Chasseurs at Lunéville. I hope to be able to accept this invitation. As you are on leave in that town, we will take the opportunity, if you are agreeable, to have a thrust at each other.'

From time to time the promotion of one of the two interrupted the duel for a while: this was one of the eventualities provided for by Article 3 of the treaty. As soon as equality of rank was restored between them, the one who had just been promoted would receive from the other a message similar to this letter written by Fournier:

'My dear Dupont: I hear that the Emperor, doing justice to your merit, has just promoted you to the rank of Brigadier-General. Accept my sincere congratulations on a promotion which your ability and courage rendered inevitable, a mere matter of course. I have two reasons to be delighted at this appointment. First, the satisfaction afforded by your advancement; and secondly, the facility now vouchsafed to us to have a thrust at each other at the first opportunity.'

The duel nearly ended fatally in Switzerland, at a time when both men were generals. Dupont arrived in a village occupied by the Staff, to find no light except in the window of a small cottage. Opening the door, he found himself face to face with Fournier, and the two generals delightedly set to, conversing as they fought. Suddenly Dupont drove his sword through Fournier's neck and held him against the wall, only to be warned by his adversary that as soon as he lowered his arm he would receive a thrust in the belly before he had time to parry. Luckily some other officers, attracted by the noise they were making, came up and separated them, saving Fournier from a slow and painful death spitted on Dupont's sword.

The contest might have gone on like this indefinitely if Dupont had not decided to get married. Calling on Fournier in Paris one day, he informed him of his project and, in order to obtain a final result, offered to substitute the pistol for the sword. In reply to Fournier's objection that he was courting certain death, he outlined a plan he had devised to equalize the conflict.

'Near Neuilly,' he said, 'there is a little wood which is at my disposal. My proposal is this. We shall enter the wood, each armed with a pair of horse-pistols, and then, having separated, and being out of sight of each other, we shall track each other as best we can, and fire at our convenience.'

Fournier agreed to this proposal, though warning Dupont not to go too far with his marriage arrangements, as he was sure to die a bachelor. On the appointed day, after separating as agreed, they crept about the wood trying to catch a glimpse of each other. All of a sudden, as if on purpose, they both came in sight together, and promptly took cover behind two trees. For a few minutes there was no sound or movement. Then Dupont raised the flap of his coat and allowed one end to project past the tree: a bullet immediately cut through the cloth. A little later, Dupont repeated his stratagem, this time on the other side of the tree. Holding his pistol in his left hand, he presented the barrel as if on the point of firing, and at the same time held out his hat in his right hand. Another explosion was heard, and the hat was carried away into the bushes.

'It's all up with you now, my good fellow!' exclaimed the triumphant Dupont, emerging from cover with both his pistols cocked, and walking over to Fournier. 'Your life is at my disposal . . . but I won't take it.'

'Just as you please,' Fournier muttered sullenly.

'No, but you must remember that I retain my rights over it. Take care never to cross my path again, for if you do, I shall probably send my two bullets into your brain, as I am entitled to at this moment.'

Thus ended, after a total period of nineteen years, the longest, friendliest and most mobile duel in history.

11 · Women Duellists

Of the thousands of duels on record, a vast number were fought over the honour or love of some woman. There have, however, been a few rare cases in which women, not content to have their cause championed by a man, set out to avenge their own wrongs.

One of the first duels in which women are known to have engaged took place near Bordeaux in 1650, and was fought between two sisters. The discreet contemporary chronicler who has left us the story of this encounter tells us that they came from 'one of the most illustrious families in Gascony, the name of which I shall pass over in silence, not to revive a sorrow which is not yet extinguished', and that the elder sister was married to a count 'unequalled in courage and generosity', while the younger sister's husband was a counsellor who had been considered the best swordsman of his time before circumstances had forced him to 'take the long robe'. We are also informed that the younger sister had learnt from her brother, who later became a Capuchin under the name of Father Clement, how to use a sling with such deadly effect that she could kill the smallest of birds with it. The chronicler continues:

> Although the younger sister had been married only a few years, she had already received several visits from her elder sister. Not wishing to appear illbred, she in her turn went to visit her elder in a castle near Bordeaux. After spending a few days there in various worthy pastimes, they conversed together on the affairs of the times. On such an occasion, the younger sister having shown her elder a most delicately fashioned sling, the elder took the opportunity to mock the robe and the pen and praise the sword, which she did with more warmth than reason. The younger, who had a quick mind, supported her opinion with some good reasons, among others that when

> Justice was depicted, she was given scales in her right hand and a sword in her left, to teach us that the sword was inferior to the robe. Seeing herself defeated by the younger sister's arguments, the elder was so surprised and carried away by anger that she seized a sword which happened to be there and said to her in a fury: 'We shall see whether deeds will match words.' Pulling her younger sister after her, she led her to a piece of land very close to the castle, took her sword in her hand, and belaboured her severely, so that she received a wound in one arm. But she did not go much further, for the younger sister, noticing two or three maidens coming towards her, and supposing them to be her sister's ladies-in-waiting, as seemed quite likely, seeing herself already wounded and unarmed, made, as they say, a virtue of necessity, taking the sling from her pocket, putting a pebble in it, and aiming it at her sister's head. The young ladies who had come to separate them were very astonished to see the countess in such a sorry condition; but if this caused them astonishment, imagine the count's anger when he learnt of his wife's injury.

The count, in fact, promptly wrote an indignant letter to the counsellor declaring that 'since your wife has had the effrontery and the temerity to attack me by killing my wife, for we consider her as good as dead, having already had her trepanned, I hereby break with you, no longer regarding you as a relative, but as an enemy.' That same evening the two husbands met in single combat and the count was mortally wounded, dying in the arms of his brother-in-law, Father Clement. Adding that his wife soon followed him to the grave, our chronicler concludes with an unexceptionable moral: 'Consider this story and moderate your passions.'

The next noteworthy duel involving a woman was probably that fought by the Comtesse de Saint-Belmont. When her husband, who had been fighting against the King, was taken prisoner, the countess remained on his estates to take care of them. A cavalry officer having taken up his quarters there without invitation, Madame de Saint-Belmont sent him a polite letter of complaint about his discourtesy, which he ignored. Annoyed at this, she resolved that he should give her satisfaction, and sent him a challenge signed: 'Le Chevalier de Saint-Belmont.' The officer promptly accepted the challenge, and went to the appointed place, where Madame de Saint-Belmont met him dressed in male attire. Within a few moments, the countess had disarmed her opponent, after which she reduced him to utter shame and confusion by saying: 'You thought, Monsieur, that you were fighting the Chevalier de Saint-Belmont, but you are mistaken. I am Madame de Saint-Belmont. I return you your sword, Monsieur, and politely beg you to pay proper respect to any request made by a lady in future.'

Another sword duel of this period, this time between two women, brought together Molière's Henriette Sylvie and a rival of hers, both of them dressed in male costume. In the letters of Madame Dunoyer, we are told of a lady of Beaucaire and a young lady of rank who, after a regular challenge, fought with swords in their garden, and would have killed each other if they had not been separated. Saint-Foix mentions the case of a Mademoiselle Durieux, who fought her lover, a man called Antinotti, in the open street; and La Colombière recounts a duel which took place on the Boulevard Saint-Antoine between two ladies of doubtful virtue, in which, so he says, 'they inflicted several wounds on each other's face and bosom, two points at which female jealousy would naturally aim'. But the most famous female duellist of the time

was undoubtedly the actress Maupin, a performer at the Opera. One of her lovers was the great fencing-master Serane, and he gave her a great many valuable lessons in his art, which she was impatient to put into practice. Insulted one day by an actor by the name of Dumény, she called him out; and when he refused to give her satisfaction, she carried off his watch and his snuff-box as trophies of her victory. Another performer who offended her and refused a meeting was forced to kneel down before her and beg her forgiveness. Then, one evening at a ball, after behaving offensively to a lady and being asked to leave the room, she agreed to do so only on condition that those gentlemen who had stood up for the outraged lady should accompany her. She led them outside, killed them one after another, and then calmly returned to the ballroom. Louis XIV granted this remarkable woman a pardon, and she retired to Brussels, where she became the mistress of the Elector of Bavaria. Paris, however, had not seen the last of her, for she eventually returned to the Opera there and died in 1707 at the age of thirty-seven.

Under the Regency, the most celebrated female duel took place between the Comtesse de Polignac and the Marquise de Nesle, and was fought over the Duc de Richelieu, himself one of the greatest duellists and lovers of his day. By one of those unfortunate accidents which can mar the career of even the most methodical of philanderers, Richelieu's secretary is said to have arranged a *rendezvous galant* for the duke with each lady at one and the same hour. The duke, immensely flattered and amused that two women should risk their lives for his sake, has left us this complacent account of the affair:

These are the circumstances in which an unprecedented duel between two women, well known for their love of pleasure, preoccupied the whole capital, and above all the Regent's court. It was stated that Madame de Polignac and Madame de Nesle had fought a pistol duel in the Bois de Boulogne, to decide which should have me if they were not both killed. It was in vain that I had repeatedly rebuffed Madame de Polignac, for she was madly enamoured of my coquetry and my infidelities did not hurt her; all that troubled her was my mockery of her whenever she returned to me, for I had fallen in love with her in 1715 when I was only nineteen and had been running away from her ever since. Jealous of all the innumerable ladies who had succeeded her, not one after another but all together, she picked on Madame de Nesle one day and called her out to the Bois de Boulogne, telling her that she must come there with a pistol.

The Marquise de Nesle, my aunt, was absolutely determined to kill her rival and did not care if she herself was left dead on the field. She imagined that my love would henceforth go to her who so nobly scorned death for my sake, and did not wait for the challenge to be repeated. When they met, in the Bois de Boulogne, the two ladies, dressed in riding-habit, gave a preliminary curtsy and then exchanged pistol shots. People came running up when they saw Madame de Nesle fall to the ground, with blood flowing over her bosom. But on examination, it was found that the blood was coming from a scratch on her shoulder, the bullet having only grazed Madame de Nesle's skin. Herself recovering from her terror, she gave thanks to heaven, saying that she had defeated her rival. This remark informed the onlookers, dismayed by a fight of this sort, that some lover was concerned, and led them to ask Madame de Nesle if the lover in question was worth fighting for. 'Yes, yes,' said the wounded lady, 'he is worthy of having even finer blood shed for him.' They stopped her blood with nettles rubbed between two stones, bandaged the wound with compresses made from her handkerchief, and removed her from the field of battle in her carriage. And when they asked her who the happy mortal was for whom she had shed her blood, she replied: 'He is the most charming nobleman at court, and I am prepared to shed all my blood for him down to the last drop. All the ladies at court set traps for him, but I am sure that the proof which I have just given him of my love will win me his undivided affection. I am too greatly obliged to you,' she added, 'to keep his name from you; he is the Duc de Richelieu, yes, the Duc de Richelieu, the eldest son of Mars and Venus.'

Fifty years later, on January 31, 1772, an even bloodier encounter occurred between Mademoiselle de Guignes and Mademoiselle d'Aiguillon, two ladies of quality who had quarrelled about precedence at a *soirée*. There seem to have been no seconds and very little decorum attending the affair, for the pair fought with knives until both were wounded, the former in the arm and the latter in the neck. The next encounter in which a woman was involved, in August 1777, though also unattended by seconds, did at least bear a greater resemblance to the traditional duel. It occurred when a certain Mademoiselle Leverrier, a young lady of good family who had been jilted by a naval officer called Duprez, met the latter in a street in Paris. Instead of shooting the man down, as she could have done, she generously handed him a pistol and told him to defend himself. There, however, her consideration for him stopped, for while he chivalrously fired his pistol into the air, she shot him full in the face.

By the end of the century, not to be outdone, the ladies across the Channel had taken to duelling, or at least to calling each other out. Thus the *Western County Magazine* published a brief but angry correspondence which passed between two London ladies in 1790:

St. J——s P——,
Thursday morning.

The Hon. Miss —— cannot longer exist under the public insults she has received from the Hon. Miss ——. *Honourable men* demand and receive satisfaction for similar injuries. Why are *Maids of Honour* to be proscribed on such occasions? My further sentiments will be conveyed to you by Ensign —— of the Coldstream, who is charged with the delivery of this letter.

Yours, etc.

Answer:

Madam,

You may give yourself what appellation you please. When the laws of honour declare it right that a *gentleman* should meet a notorious *blackleg*, I shall think it my duty to obey the summons of a ——! The Ensign who bore your commission is a *creature* of *fine feelings*, for he would have fainted before he left my apartment but for the timely application of my *eau de luce*.

Yours, etc.

If this duel got no further than a challenge and a refusal, two other angry English ladies did reach the field in that same year of 1790. Known to us only as Mrs A. and Mrs B., they had a heated exchange of words at a ball after a gentleman they both admired had shown a marked preference for Mrs A.

The next morning, her rival called upon her before she was up and demanded satisfaction in a duel. 'With all my heart,' answered Mrs A. 'As soon as I am dressed I will attend you.' So saying, she rang for her maid Betty to come and dress her, after which she went into her closet and returned with a brace of pistols, which she calmly proceeded to load. 'Madam,' she asked her visitor, 'shall we settle the matter here or in the field?' 'In the field, madam,' answered Mrs B. 'Well then,' said the other, 'I will attend you immediately.' And off they went to the field, where they were on the point of taking their ground when a constable who had been fetched by Betty intervened and stopped the encounter, to the fury of the frustrated rivals.

At last, in 1792, a petticoat duel actually took place in England, and blood was shed – even if only a few drops. The occasion of this encounter was a call paid upon Lady Almeria Braddock by a certain Mrs Elphinstone, who in the course of a somewhat unfriendly conversation told her hostess: 'You have been a very beautiful woman.' Lady Almeria was shaken by this unflattering use of the past tense, but worse was to follow. 'You have a very good autumnal face even now,' Mrs Elphistone went on, 'but you must acknowledge that the lilies and roses are somewhat faded. Forty years ago, I am told, a young fellow could hardly gaze upon you with impunity.' Lady Almeria indignantly retorted that she was not yet thirty years old, only to hear her visitor cite Collins, the Burke of the day, to the effect that she had been born in 1732 and was therefore over sixty. After that, there was no course open to the two ladies but to adjourn to Hyde Park and have it out about Mr Collins's accuracy. To begin with, they set to with pistols at a range of ten yards, Mrs Elphinstone putting a bullet through her opponent's hat while going unscathed herself. The seconds then proposed a reconciliation, but Lady Almeria would have none of it unless her opponent admitted that she had been in the wrong, and this Mrs Elphinstone indignantly refused to do. A sword duel ensued, in which Mrs Elphinstone was slightly wounded in the right arm. Having drawn blood, Lady Almeria declared that she was satisfied, and after a convention agreeable to both combatants had been drawn up and signed, the ladies curtsied to each other and, in the words of a contemporary chronicler, quitted the field with honour.

Often, of course, measures were taken by the seconds or other parties to reduce or remove the danger to which petticoat duellists exposed themselves. A case in point was a duel in the Bois de Boulogne between a dancer at the Paris Opera, Mademoiselle Théodore, and a singer at the same theatre. They were on the point of taking aim with their pistols when their lover arrived on the scene and rushed between them. He treated them to an impassioned speech which only made them more determined to shoot it out; but while declaiming and gesticulating, he succeeded in getting hold of the pistols, which he deposited 'in a wet place', with the result that they failed to go off. Similar precautions were taken before a duel which took place in 1828 between a young girl and a *garde du corps* who had deceived her. The girl, as the offended party, chose the weapons, and two shots were exchanged, but without any result, as the seconds had not loaded with ball. 'The young lady,' writes a contemporary chronicler, 'ignorant of this precaution, fired first, and received the fire of her adversary with the utmost coolness, when, to try her courage, after taking a long and deliberate aim, he fired into the air, and thus terminated the meeting, which no doubt led to many others of a less hostile nature.'

As duelling became prevalent in the United States, American women were naturally led to imitate their menfolk. Occasionally the police succeeded in stopping the duel in time, as when they arrested Catherine Hurley and Jane

27 · *'Duel between two ladies.' An etching by Henri Lefort*

28·(*a*) *Duel 'entre deux soeurs proche de Bordeaux'. An early woodcut*

28·(*b*) *'An Affair of Honour.' A painting by Emile Bayard*

Hall of Buffalo, New York, 'who had met on the toll-bridge on Ohio Street, in the presence of a vast assemblage, to fight a duel with Allen's revolvers'. But more often than not the encounter took place as arranged, generally ending as decisively and as bloodily as this duel described in a Georgia newspaper in 1817:

> Last week a point of honor was decided between two ladies near the South Carolina line, the cause of the quarrel being the usual one – love. The object of the rival affections of these fair champions was present on the field as the mutual arbiter in the dreadful combat, and he had the grief of beholding one of the suitors for his favor fall dangerously wounded before his eyes. The whole business was managed with all the decorum and inflexibility usually practised on such occasions, and the conqueror was immediately married to the *innocent second*, conformably to the previous conditions of the duel.

Towards the end of the nineteenth century, with the spread of the campaign for female emancipation, it was inevitable that the more bellicose of the 'new women' should insist on members of their sex fighting their own battles instead of relying on the championship of mere males. Thus, in September 1890, at a meeting in Paris of the League for the Emancipation of Women, the assembly passed a vote of censure on the woman journalist Séverine for having allowed a colleague to fight on her behalf in defence of an article she had written. The resolution proposed by Madame d'Estoc (a name which, very suitably, means 'rapier') declared that any woman who did not assume responsibility for her actions, and who allowed a man to champion her cause, was guilty of a 'deed of inferiority'. Madame d'Estoc would no doubt have thoroughly approved of a completely emancipated duel which was fought in August 1892 at Vaduz, the capital of Liechtenstein, between Princess Pauline Metternich, the Honorary President of the Vienna Musical and Theatrical Exhibition, and Countess Kilmannsegg, the President of the Ladies' Committee of the Exhibition. The cause of the difference between these two ladies was no commonplace love affair but some arrangements at the Exhibition, and no male was even remotely connected with the encounter itself. The duel, which resulted in the princess being slightly wounded on the nose and the countess on the arm, was attended by two female seconds, Princess Schwarzenberg and Countess Kinsky, and the combatants' wounds were dressed by Baroness Lubinska, a Polish lady who held a degree in medicine and whom they had prudently summoned from Warsaw to minister to them.

However, in spite of the enormous progress made by female emancipation, women, never much given to duelling, have shown even less enthusiasm for 'affairs of honour' in the present century than men. A leading authority on duelling wrote over a hundred years ago that 'when we consider the bitter animosity that frequently exists between women, who are not in the habit of repairing their real or supposed wrongs by having recourse to a personal satisfaction, which may be considered the safety-valve of passions, and which not unfrequently supersedes assassination, one may be surprised that duels are not more frequent between them'. The only reason which he could suggest to account for this circumstance was 'their natural timidity as regards personal danger', to which he maliciously added 'the greater certainty of avenging their injuries by intrigue and slander, whose edge is sharper than the sword'.

A kinder and no less plausible explanation would surely be that they have more sense than the opposite sex.

12 · The Pen and the Sword

So many men of letters have fought duels and so many have described duels in their writings that a mere chapter on the relationship between pen and sword in the history of duelling cannot hope to do justice to the subject. But a brief consideration of the duelling experience and duelling literature of a few famous writers may none the less prove of some interest and amusement.

The most striking thing which emerges from any such consideration is an impression of a fundamental hostility between pen and sword. Most men of letters who have written about duels and duelling have been hostile to the practice to a greater or lesser degree: Shakespeare, for example, seems to be poking fun at it on most of the occasions when he presents a duel. But even authors who approved of duelling and engaged in single combat themselves have left us writings or personal anecdotes which highlight the basic absurdity of the institution.

The seventeenth-century French poet Voiture, for example, who fought at least four duels, is remembered nowadays not so much for these combats or his poetry as for his famous reply on being challenged by a formidable swordsman about whom he had composed an epigram. 'The game is not equal', he wrote. 'You are big, I am little; you are brave, I am a coward; however, if you want to kill me – well, *I consider myself dead*.'

Again, the story of the duel which La Fontaine once reluctantly fought with an officer called Poignant, not out of genuine indignation but simply because public opinion required him to do so, might have been intended as one of his own fables. A chronicler has left us the following account of the incident:

> It was during the reign of King Louis XIV that a curious meeting took place between La Fontaine the fabulist, whose meekness and apathy had acquired him the name of 'the Good', and an officer. Although generally blind to the irregularities of his wife, he once took it into his head to become jealous of a captain of dragoons, of the name of Poignant. La Fontaine had not himself observed the intimacy with his wife; but some kind friends had drawn his attention to its impropriety, telling him that it was incumbent on him to demand satisfaction. La Fontaine, reluctantly persuaded, contrary to his usual habits, got up early one morning, took his sword, and went out to meet his antagonist. When the parties were in presence, the worthy poet said: 'My dear sir, I must fight you, since I am assured that it is absolutely necessary.' He then proceeded to acquaint him with the reasons that induced him to call him out, and drew his pacific sword. The dragoon, thus obliged to defend himself, whipped the weapon out of the inexperienced hand of the fabulist, and, having disarmed him, proceeded quietly to point out to him the absurdity of the reports circulated in regard to his wife, and the folly of his having thus exposed his valuable life; adding that since his visits had been the occasion of scandal, he would from that hour cease to call at his house. *Le bon* La Fontaine was so affected by this sincere explanation that he not only insisted that the captain should pay more frequent visits than ever, but swore that he would fight him over again if he discontinued them.

In England too, writers who profoundly disapproved of duelling were occasionally compelled by public opinion to engage in single combat. A case in point is that of Steele, who, in the early years of the eighteenth century, joined Addison in attacking duelling in the *Spectator* with the twin weapons of persuasion and ridicule. Addison cited a duelling club of the time of Charles II 'which consisted only of men of *honour*' and 'did not continue long, most of the members being put to the sword, or hanged, a little after the institution'; and in a later paper retailed an anecdote about a French gentleman who called on an English peer very early one morning, 'and after great professions of respect, let him know that he had it in his power to oblige him, which in short amounted to this, that he believed he could tell his Lordship the person's name who had jostled him as he came out of the Opera; but before he would proceed, he begged his Lordship that he would not deny him the honour of making him his second . . .' Steele for his part, in an essay on duelling, wrote feelingly: 'Alas! in the Dominions of Pharamond, by the Force of a Tyrant Custom, which is misnamed a Point of Honour, the Duellist kills his Friend whom he loves; and the Judge condemns the Duellist, while he approves his Behaviour. Shame is the greatest of all Evils; what avail Laws, when Death only attends the Breach of them, and Shame Obedience to them?' Yet in spite of these admirable sentiments Steele was drawn into a quarrel which nearly proved fatal. Accused of having compromised a friend's honour by dissuading him from calling out a person who had offended him, he was himself challenged, and, after trying in vain to avoid the encounter, finally accepted the cartel. On the duelling-ground he again tried to avoid a fight on the pretext that his buckle had broken while he was tightening his shoe, but his opponent insisted on satisfaction. Obliged to fight, he felt sure that his superior

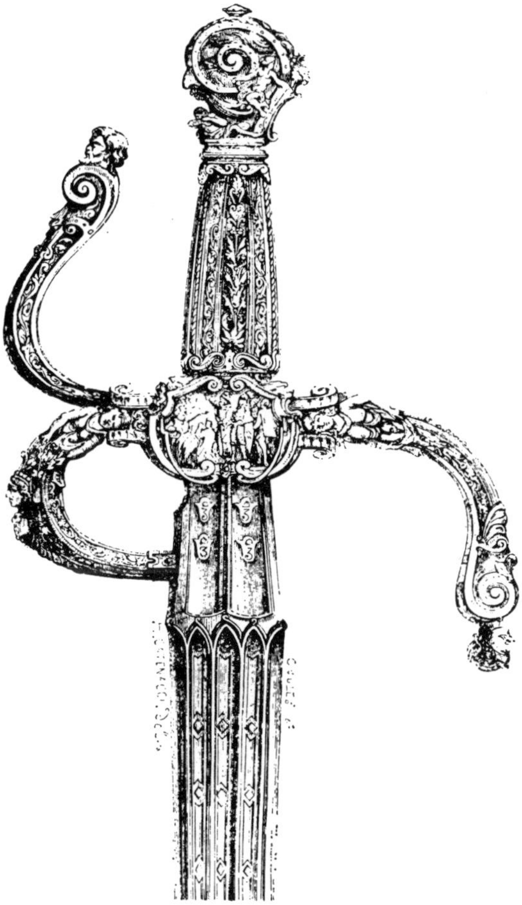

swordsmanship would allow him to disarm his antagonist without harming him. Again, however, his hopes were disappointed, for after a few lunges the man spitted himself on Steele's sword, and it was only by an extraordinary chance that he eventually recovered from his wound.

Sheridan may be cited as a similar case, for he nearly lost his life in the sort of encounter which he ridiculed so brilliantly in *The Rivals.* No playwright has ever drawn greater comedy from the representation of a bloodthirsty, omniscient master-duellist than Sheridan in this scene between Sir Lucius O'Trigger and the reluctant Acres:

ACRES: By my valour! then, Sir Lucius, forty yards is a good distance. Odds levels and aims! – I say it is a good distance.

SIR LUCIUS: Is it for muskets or small field-pieces? Upon my conscience, Mr Acres, you must leave those things to me. Stay now – I'll show you. (*Measures paces along the stage.*) There now, that is a very pretty distance – a pretty gentleman's distance.

ACRES: Z——ds! we might as well fight in a sentry-box! I tell you, Sir Lucius, the farther he is off, the cooler I shall take my aim.

SIR LUCIUS: Faith! then I suppose you would aim at him best of all if he was out of sight!

ACRES: No, Sir Lucius, but I should think forty or eight-and-thirty yards——

SIR LUCIUS: Pho! pho! nonsense! three or four feet between the mouths of your pistols is as good as a mile.

ACRES: Odds bullets, no! – by my valour! there is no merit in killing him so near: no, my dear Sir Lucius, let me bring him down at a long shot: a long shot, Sir Lucius, if you love me!

SIR LUCIUS: Well – the gentleman's friend and I must settle that. But tell me now, Mr Acres, in case of an accident, is there any little will or commission I could execute for you?

ACRES: I'm much obliged to you, Sir Lucius – but I don't understand ——

SIR LUCIUS: Why, you may think there's no being shot at without a little risk, and if an unlucky bullet should carry a quietus with it – I say it will be no time then to be bothering you about family matters.

ACRES: A quietus!

SIR LUCIUS: For instance, now – if that should be the case – would you choose to be pickled and sent home? – or would it be the same to you to lie here in the Abbey? I'm told there is very snug lying in the Abbey.

ACRES: Pickled! – snug lying in the Abbey! Odds tremors! Sir Lucius, don't talk so!

SIR LUCIUS: I suppose, Mr Acres, you never were engaged in an affair of this kind before?

ACRES: No, Sir Lucius, never before.

SIR LUCIUS: Ah! that's a pity! – there's nothing like being used to a thing. Pray now, how would you receive the gentleman's shot?

ACRES: Odds files! – I've practised that – there, Sir Lucius – there. (*Puts himself in an attitude.*) A side-front hey? Odds! I'll make myself small enough; I'll stand edgeways.

SIR LUCIUS: Now – you're quite out – for if you stand so when I take my aim—— (*Levelling at him.*)

ACRES: Z——ds! Sir Lucius – are you sure it is not cocked?

SIR LUCIUS: Never fear.

ACRES: But – but – you don't know – it may go off of its own head!

SIR LUCIUS: Pho! be easy. Well, now if I hit you in the body, my bullet has a double chance – for if it misses a vital part of your right side, 'twill be very hard if it don't succeed on the left!

ACRES: A vital part!

SIR LUCIUS: But, there – fix yourself so (*placing him*) – let him see the broad-side of your full front – there – now a ball or two may pass clean through your body, and never do any harm at all.

ACRES: Clean through me! – a ball or two clean through me!

SIR LUCIUS: Aye – may they – and it is much the gentlest attitude into the bargain.

ACRES: Look'ee! Sir Lucius – I'd just as lieve be shot in an awkward posture as a genteel one – so, by my valour! I will stand edgeways.

Duelling did not appear to Sheridan in such an amusing light in 1772, when he felt obliged to call out Captain Thomas Mathews, a gentleman who had cast aspersions on the character of his bride, the singer Alicia Linley. A first duel was fought in London, at the Castle Tavern in Henrietta Street, and according to Sheridan Mathews was forced to beg for his life. However, Mathews, infuriated by the publicity which was given to this duel, refused to accept his defeat as final, so that another encounter took place in August 1772, on Kingsdown, near Bath. This time both men were wounded, Sheridan dangerously, 'being borne from the field with a portion of his antagonist's weapon sticking through an ear, his breast-bone touched, his whole body covered with wounds and blood, and his face nearly beaten to a jelly with the hilt of Mathews' sword'. Fortunately his remarkable constitution pulled him through, and eight days after this bloody affair the *Bath Chronicle* was able to announce that he was out of danger.

In that same year of 1772, at a dinner-party at General Oglethorpe's, Dr Johnson expressed his considered opinion on the subject of duelling. This was in reply to a question put by Boswell, who in his Life of the doctor writes:

I started the question, whether duelling was consistent with moral duty. The brave old General fired at this, and said with a lofty air, 'Undoubtedly a man has a right to defend his honour.' GOLDSMITH (turning to me): 'I ask you first, Sir, what would you do if you were affronted?' I answered, I should think it necessary to fight. 'Why then (replied Goldsmith) that solves the question.' JOHNSON: 'No, Sir, it does not solve the question. It does not follow, that what a man would do is therefore right.' I said, I wished to have it settled, whether duelling was contrary to the laws of Christianity. Johnson immediately entered on the subject, and treated it in a masterly manner; and so far as I have been able to recollect, his thoughts were these: 'Sir, as men become in a

> high degree refined, various causes of offence arise; which are considered to be of such importance, that life must be staked to atone for them, though in reality they are not so. A body that has received a very fine polish may be easily hurt. Before men arrive at this artificial refinement, if one tells his neighbour – he lies, his neighbour tells him – he lies; if one gives his neighbour a blow, his neighbour gives him a blow: but in a state of highly polished society, an affront is held to be a serious injury. It must, therefore, be resented, or rather, a duel must be fought upon it; as men have agreed to banish from their society one who puts up with an affront without fighting a duel. Now, Sir, it is never unlawful to fight in self-defence. He, then, who fights a duel, does not fight from passion against his antagonist, but out of self-defence; to avert the stigma of the world, and to prevent himself from being driven out of society. I could wish there was not that superfluity of refinement; but while such notions prevail, no doubt a man may lawfully fight a duel.'

However much Boswell respected Johnson's opinions, this pronouncement was not enough to satisfy him on a problem which he had taken very much to heart, and only nine days later we find the doctor returning to the subject, no doubt at his prompting. 'He this day again defended duelling', Boswell wrote on April 19, 'and put his argument upon what I have ever thought as the most solid basis; that if publick war be allowed to be consistent with morality, private war must be equally so. Indeed we may observe what strained arguments are used to reconcile war with the Christian religion. But, in my opinion, it is exceedingly clear that duelling, having better reasons for its barbarous violence, is more justifiable than war in which thousands go forth without any cause of personal quarrel, and massacre each other.'

Boswell's anxious interest in the subject of duelling seems to have been due to the conflict between his reluctance to shed blood unnecessarily and a conviction that it was sometimes essential to fight, between the approval of the practice expressed by Johnson in private conversation and the passionate indictment of duelling made by Rousseau in the *Nouvelle Héloïse*. In an effort to solve his dilemma, he had written to Rousseau in 1764 as follows:

> You know me well, sir, for you have read the sketch of my life. But I forgot to tell you an anecdote that has troubled me. Last summer I was in a large company in Germany. It was a very disagreeable company, and I was vexed at having to waste time in it. They were all praising the French, and I declaimed against that nation in the rudest terms. An officer rose, came to my side, and said: 'Sir, I am French, and no one but a scoundrel would speak so of that nation.' We were still at dinner. I made a bow. I had half an hour to reflect. After dinner was over, I took the Captain into the garden. I said to him: 'Sir, I am deeply embarrassed. I was very impolite; I am sincerely sorry

> for it. But you have made use of an expression which a man of honour cannot put up with, and I must have satisfaction for it. If it is possible to avoid a quarrel, I should be happy, for I was wrong. Will you be good enough to apologize to me before the company? I will apologize to you first. If you cannot agree to my proposal, we must fight, though I confess that I shall do it with repugnance.' I spoke to him with the sang-froid of a philosopher determined to do his duty. The officer was a worthy man. He replied: 'Sir, I will do everything you wish.' We went back into the company. We made our apologies to each other. We embraced. The affair was over. Yet I could not be at ease until I had consulted two or three Scotsmen. I said to them: 'Gentlemen, I am a simple man; I am not acquainted with the rules you follow in society, but I think I acted like a man. You are my country-men. I ask your opinions.' They assured me that the affair had been honourably adjusted on both sides. They advised me to take the scrape as a lesson for the future. Forgive me, Sir, for having told you this story. As I hope to be truly reckoned among your friends, I wish you to know all the good and all the bad of my character, so that you may cherish the one and correct the other. I am timid by temperament, and my education did everything to make me the slave of fear. But I have a soul capable of breaking these vile chains and forcing myself to feel the noble courage that belongs to a man. What is your serious opinion as to duels? You have not said enough on the subject in the *Héloïse*. There are people who would have us believe that the Gospel teaches us to be too delicate. I am a little of that way of thinking myself.

Neither Rousseau nor Johnson ever succeeded in convincing Boswell what course a Christian who was a man of honour should adopt if insulted or challenged, and he went on worrying over the problem – a very real and urgent one in his day for a thinking man – until the end of his life.

In contrast, an almost total unconcern about the rights and wrongs of duelling was shown by the poet Tom Moore, one of the combatants in the famous encounter of 1806 immortalized by Byron in his *English Bards and Scotch Reviewers:*

> Can none remember that eventful day,
> That ever glorious, almost fatal fray,
> When Little's leadless pistols met his eye,
> And Bow Street myrmidons stood laughing by?

Tom Moore was the challenger in this affair, and his grievance arose from an attack made in the *Edinburgh Review* by the critic Jeffrey on his *Odes and Epistles*. Hearing that Jeffrey had observed in company that he doubted if the poet would 'show much amenity' to him if they met, Moore decided to fulfil his apprehensions, apparently simply for the fun of the thing. 'However boyish it might have been of me', he wrote later, 'to consider myself bound to take this sort of notice of the attack, there was certainly but little, if any, mixture either of ill-temper or mere personal hostility, with my motives. That they were equally free from a certain *Irish* predilection for such encounters, or wholly unleavened by a dash of *vanity*, I will not positively assert.'

An encounter was arranged at Chalk Farm, where the two antagonists strolled up and down together, making friendly conversation, while their seconds busied themselves loading the pistols. Catching sight of this operation slowly going on behind some trees, Moore, who was in excellent spirits, reminded Jeffrey of what the Irish barrister Billy Egan had once said in similar circumstances: 'Sure, isn't it bad enough to take the dose without being by at the mixing up?'

'Jeffrey had scarcely time to smile at this story', Moore wrote in his account of the affair, 'when our two friends, issuing from behind the trees, placed us at our respective posts – the distance being, I suppose, previously measured by them – and put the pistols into our hands. They then retired to a little distance, the pistols were on both sides raised, and we waited but the signal to fire, when some police-officers whose approach none of us had noticed, and who were within a second of being too late, rushed out from a hedge behind Jeffrey, and one of them striking at Jeffrey's pistol with his staff, knocked it to some distance into the field, while another running over to me, took possession of mine. We were then replaced in our respective carriages, and conveyed crestfallen to Bow Street.'

They were almost immediately released on bail, but when Moore went back for the pistols, which he had forgotten, he was told that the police had found no bullet in Jeffrey's pistol. The missing bullet was later found, according to Moore, but in the meantime its disappearance had been made public and, as Byron put it, 'gave occasion to much waggery in the daily prints'. Moore issued indignant statements to the Press, but all in vain: instead of reaping honour and glory from his duel with Jeffrey, he was held up to ridicule as a hero who had only courage enough to face a 'leadless pistol'. In his anger and disappointment, the poet seems to have forgotten the suspicious slowness with which the seconds had loaded the pistols, and the no less suspicious punctuality with which the Bow Street runners had appeared – circumstances which suggest that, whether the pistols were loaded or not, steps had been taken to ensure that no blood should be shed between English bard and Scotch reviewer.

Fate was not, of course, always so kind to men of letters who engaged in duelling, and several writers died in affairs of honour during the nineteenth century alone. Probably the greatest loss to literature occasioned by a duel was that of Alexander Pushkin in 1837. Pushkin had fought a great many duels as a young man – almost every day during one period – and had even accepted a challenge from his old friend Kiukhelberker, who had been offended by one of his cruel epigrams. That particular duel had been bloodless, for Kiukhelberker had missed with his shot, while Pushkin had either fired into the air or, according to one report, refused to fire at all, saying: 'It's all utterly ridiculous, my dear fellow – let's go and drink some tea.' But the duel which Pushkin fought in January 1837 with Baron Heckeren, to defend his honour and that of his wife, was a far more serious affair, in which the poet was bent on killing his antagonist.

By an irony of fate, as Pushkin was driving out to the duelling-ground from Petersburg in the late afternoon, the sleigh in which he and his second, Danzas, were sitting passed his wife's carriage coming in the opposite direction. Danzas silently hoped that Natasha Pushkin would see her husband, hear about the duel from him, and persuade him to come home. But Natasha was short-sighted, and Pushkin deliberately turned his head away. The two vehicles passed within a few yards of each other without either husband or wife giving any sign of recognition, and Pushkin drove on to his fatal rendezvous.

When the two parties arrived at the duelling-ground, they found that the snow was knee-deep, and the seconds, helped by Heckeren, had to trample down a narrow lane before they could measure out the agreed twenty paces. At last the principals took up their positions, Danzas gave the signal to begin, and the two antagonists advanced towards their respective barriers. Pushkin reached his first and raised his pistol, but Heckeren fired after walking only four paces, and the poet fell to the ground, seriously wounded. His adversary came towards him, but after a few moments he raised himself on one elbow and said: 'Wait, I have enough strength to take my shot.'

Heckeren returned to his post and stood sideways, covering his breast with his right arm, so that when Pushkin eventually fired and hit him, the bullet went through his arm and merely bruised his ribs. Pushkin collapsed in a faint immediately after firing, but quickly recovered and asked after his enemy. 'It is strange,' he said to his second. 'I thought it would give pleasure to kill him, but I do not feel that now.' Even so, when Heckeren's second suggested a reconciliation he curtly rejected the idea. 'In the end it is all the same,' he said; 'if we both recover, we shall try again.' But Alexander Pushkin did not have the opportunity to try again: he died two days later.

Most of the duels fought in France in the nineteenth century by men of letters were innocuous affairs in comparison, often relieved by some amusing incident or witty remark. Thus when the critic Sainte-Beuve arrived at the duelling-ground to fight Dubois, the editor of the *Globe*, he took his pistol in his right hand but kept his open umbrella in his left, to protect himself from the pouring rain. 'I don't mind being killed,' he said, 'but I'll be damned if I'm going to catch a cold.'

Again, at the end of the century, George Moore used to fascinate friends of his who called to see him in Paris with an exciting account of a duel he had fought there. One day Sir William Geary asked him how far he had been from his opponent – ten or fifteen paces. 'No,' replied Moore, 'that would have been dangerous. We were thirty-five paces apart; each of us went unscathed.'

Perhaps the most amusing story, however, of an affair of honour in which a man of letters was involved during this period is that concerning the Sâr Joséphin Péladan, a mystical novelist who considered himself a high priest of the revived Rosicrucian movement. In the spring of 1891 Péladan quarrelled with Rodolphe Salis, the proprietor of the Chat Noir cabaret and the satirical magazine of the same name, who sent two of his friends to call on the Sâr to challenge him to a duel. They returned with a categorical refusal, the reasons for which were subsequently published in all the Paris newspapers, to their readers' great amusement:

My dear Salis,

Following a letter signed by the Sâr Péladan and published in *La France*, which you considered insulting to yourself, you instructed us to ask the aforementioned Sâr for a retraction or reparation by arms.

We accordingly called upon the Sâr Péladan this morning and explained to him the purpose of our visit. The Sâr replied to us that he owed you no apology, because you had priority in the matter of insults. As for reparation by arms, the Sâr did not agree to this either, for the following reasons:

1. Although a good Catholic, his relations with Rome are somewhat strained, so that in the event of a duel he would infallibly incur papal excommunication.

2. On account of certain occult powers, he is sure to kill you, and this would constitute a murder.

3. This murder would involve Hermetic Impurity for him, and as at the moment there is no College of Magic in existence which could purify him, the Sâr has no desire to incur such a stain.

Having taken note of these reasons, my dear Salis, we regard our mission as terminated, and we beg you to accept our respects.

Alphonse Allais.
Maurice Donnay.

So many tales of duelling were written by men of letters of all countries in the nineteenth century that any choice is bound to be arbitrary and unfair. But no consideration of the duel in literature would be complete without some mention of two outstanding fictional affairs of honour – one the abortive duel in Maupassant's short story *A Coward* and the other Pechorin's horrifying duel in Lermontov's *A Hero of our Time*.

Maupassant's story, which represents better than any other piece of fiction or indeed any autobiographical work the feelings of a sensitive young man on the eve of his first duel, tells the story of the Vicomte Gantran-Joseph de Signoles, who slaps a stranger for staring offensively at a lady in his company and who, in the waiting period between challenge and duel, begins to go to pieces at the thought that he might show fear in the face of death. The story continues as follows:

He kept repeating to himself, as he walked along:
'I must be forceful, very forceful. I must prove that I am not afraid.'

His seconds, the marquis and the colonel, placed themselves at his service and, after shaking him warmly by the hand, discussed the conditions of the duel.
The colonel asked:
'Do you want a serious duel?'
The vicomte replied:
'Very serious.'
The marquis went on:
'You insist on pistols?'
'Yes.'

'Do you leave it to us to arrange the rest?'

The vicomte said in a dry, jerky voice:

'Twenty paces, at a given signal, raising the weapon instead of lowering it. An exchange of shots until one of the combatants is seriously wounded.'

The colonel declared in a satisfied voice:

'Those are excellent conditions. You are a good shot, and all the chances are in your favour.'

And they left. The vicomte went home to wait for them. His agitation, which had been calmed for a moment, was now growing every minute. Along his arms, along his legs, and in his chest, he could feel a sort of quivering, a continuous vibration; he could not remain still sitting or standing. There was not a trace of saliva left in his mouth, and every few moments he made a noisy movement with his tongue, as if he were detaching it from his palate.

He tried to have some lunch, but he could not eat. Then the idea occurred to him of drinking to give himself courage, and he sent for a bottle of rum and drank six small glasses one after the other.

A warmth like a burning sensation invaded him, followed immediately afterwards by a dazed feeling. He thought:

'This is the way. Now everything is all right.'

But after an hour he had emptied the bottle and his agitation was becoming unbearable again. He felt a mad impulse to roll on the floor, to scream, to bite. Dusk was falling.

A ring at the bell gave him such a shock that he had not the strength to stand up to greet his seconds.

He no longer even dared to speak to them, to bid them good evening, to utter a single word, for fear that they should guess everything from the change in his voice.

The colonel said:

'Everything has been arranged in accordance with the conditions you laid down. To begin with, your adversary demanded the privileges of the offended party, but he gave way almost immediately and accepted everything. His seconds are two officers.'

The vicomte said:

'Thank you.'

The colonel went on:

'Forgive us if we don't stay, but we still have a host of things to see to. We need a good doctor, since the duel is to go on until one of the combatants is seriously wounded, and you know that there's no joking with bullets. We have to decide on the place, near a house so that we can take the wounded man there if necessary, and so on. Altogether, we still have two or three hours' work before us.'

Once again the vicomte said:

'Thank you.'

The colonel asked:

'You are all right? You are quite calm?'

'Yes, very calm, thank you.'

The two men withdrew.

When he felt that he was alone again, it seemed to him that he was going mad.

Once his servant had lit the lamps, he sat down at his table to write some letters. After writing, at the top of one page: 'This is my last will . . .' he jumped to his feet, and walked away, feeling incapable of putting two ideas together, of taking a decision, of deciding anything whatever.

So he was going to fight! He could no longer avoid it. So what was happening inside him? He wanted to fight; that intention and that resolution were quite definite; yet he was aware that in spite of all the efforts of his mind and all the tension of his will, he could not keep even the strength required to go as far as the duelling-ground. He tried to imagine the fight, his own attitude and his opponent's bearing.

Now and then his teeth chattered with a small brittle sound. He wanted to read something and picked up Châteauvillard's code of duelling. Then he asked himself:

'Has my adversary practised shooting? Is he well-known as a shot? Is he in a special class? How can I find out?'

He remembered the Baron de Vaux's book about crack shots, and went through it from cover to cover. Georges Lamil's name was not in it. But if this man was not a crack shot, surely he wouldn't have accepted straight away this dangerous weapon and these mortal conditions?

Going past a small table, he opened a Gastinne-Renette box which was lying on it and took out one of the pistols. Then he placed himself as he would in order to fire, and raised his arm. But he was trembling from head to foot, and the barrel moved in every direction.

Then he said to himself:

'It's impossible. I can't fight like this.'

He looked at the end of the barrel, at that little deep black hole which spits death, and he thought about dishonour, about the whispers in the clubs, about the laughter in the drawing-rooms, about the women's contempt, about the allusions in the papers, about the insults cowards would throw in his face.

He was still looking at the weapon, and, lifting the hammer, he suddenly saw a a cartridge-cap shining underneath like a little red flame. The pistol had been left loaded by chance, out of forgetfulness. And he felt a vague inexplicable joy at the discovery.

If, facing the other man, he did not have the calm, noble bearing that was required, he would be ruined for ever. He would be stained, marked with an infamous sign, expelled from society! And that calm, bold bearing was something he would not have – he knew it, he felt it. Yet he was not a coward, since. . . . The thought which occurred to him did not even take shape in his mind; but, opening his mouth wide, he suddenly thrust the barrel of his pistol down into his throat, and pressed the trigger. . . .

When his valet came running in, attracted by the noise of the shot, he found him dead, lying on his back. A jet of blood had splashed the white paper on the table and made a big red stain below these five words:

'This is my last will.'

Maupassant himself, with his endless affairs with married women, should by rights have been engaged in an affair of honour every other morning. In

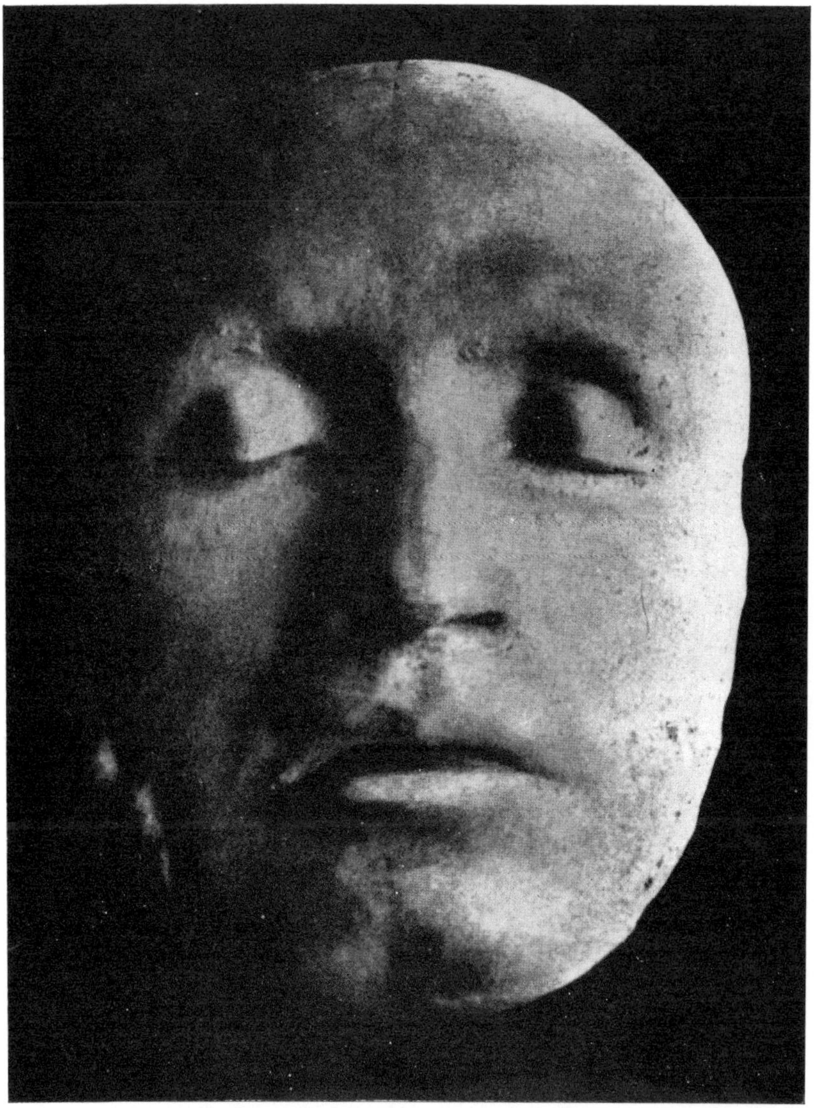

29 · *Pushkin's death-mask*

30 · (*a*) *Drawing of Lermontov's character, Pechorin, taken from a Russian edition of 'A Hero of Our Time'*

30 · (*b*) *A Forain cartoon, taken from an edition of Maupassant's 'Bel Ami'*

31 · *A modern French duel between Serge Lifar and the Marquis de Cuevas:*
(a) The offence
(b) The duel

(*c*) *'First blood'*
(*d*) *Reconciliation*

fact, however, he fought very few duels, and those were never made public, for if he accepted a challenge it was invariably on condition that nothing should be sent to the papers. His immunity at the hands of all the countless husbands he had cuckolded was almost certainly due to his reputation as a master in the use of arms, particularly of the pistol – as a man capable of shooting a given leaf off a tree at a distance of twenty-eight paces. This reputation not only saved him from many a duel, but on one occasion enabled him to rescue a friend from an encounter which might well have proved fatal to him.

The painter Henri Gervex had quarrelled with the Baron de Vaux, who, being the offended party and knowing Gervex to be a good swordsman, had announced his intention of calling him out for a pistol duel. Hearing of this and not wanting his friend to be killed or wounded, Maupassant hurried round to Gastinne-Renette's shooting gallery, where he spent the morning firing at a number of target cards, scoring bull's-eye after bull's-eye. He then took the cards home and scattered them casually on a table in his smoking room. The Baron de Vaux, who came to lunch with him that day, saw them and expressed his admiration at the writer's fantastic skill as a marksman. 'But those aren't my cards,' said Maupassant. 'They are the work of Henri Gervex. He shoots at Gastinne's every morning.' The baron changed colour, and the next day Gervex learned to his relief that the threatened duel had been called off.

As for the duel in Lermontov's *A Hero of our Time*, it is fought between the arrogant, successful Pechorin and his envious brother officer Grushnitski, whom he has overheard plotting with a captain of dragoons, the plot being to put a bullet in Grushnitski's pistol alone. Pechorin gives this exciting account of the duel itself:

> Three horses were tethered in the bushes at the foot of the cliff. We tethered ours there too and climbed up a narrow path to the place where Grushnitski was waiting for us. With him were the captain of dragoons and his other second, who was called Ivan Ignatyevich. I never heard his surname.
>
> 'We've been waiting a long time for you,' said the captain of dragoons with a sarcastic smile.
>
> I took out my watch and showed it to him. He apologized, saying that his watch was fast. There was an embarrassing silence lasting several minutes. At last the doctor broke it, turning to Grushnitski.
>
> 'It seems to me,' he said, 'that since you have both shown a readiness to fight and

thus have done what your honour demands, you may be able, gentlemen, to clear up the misunderstanding and end the matter to your mutual satisfaction.'

'I am ready to do so,' I said.

The captain winked at Grushnitski and the latter, thinking that I was scared, assumed disdainful expression, although until that moment he had looked as white as a sheet. For the first time since we had arrived he looked straight at me, but there was a certain uneasiness in his glance which indicated an inner struggle.

'Explain your conditions,' he said, 'and you may be sure that everything I can do for you. . . .'

'These are my conditions: you will take back your slander and will ask my forgiveness.'

'My dear sir, I'm surprised that you dare to make such proposals.'

'What can I suggest to you apart from that?'

'We shall fight.'

I shrugged my shoulders.

'As you like. But you must realize that one of us is certain to be killed.'

'I hope it will be you.'

'But I am sure of the contrary. . . .'

Taken aback, he reddened, then gave a forced laugh.

The captain took him by the arm and led him aside. They whispered together for a long time. I was quite calm, but all this was beginning to annoy me.

The doctor came up to me.

'Listen,' he said, with obvious concern, 'you seem to have forgotten about their plot. I don't know how to load a pistol, but in this case. . . . You're a strange fellow! Tell them you know what they intend to do and they won't dare. . . . What an idea, to shoot you down like a sitting bird!'

'Don't worry, doctor, be patient. . . . I'll handle things so that they'll obtain no advantage. Let them whisper.'

'Gentlemen, this is getting tedious!' I told them loudly, 'if we're going to fight we're going to fight; you had plenty of time to talk yesterday.'

'We're ready,' replied the captain. 'Take your places, gentlemen! Doctor, please be good enough to measure out six paces.'

'Take your places,' repeated Ivan Ignatyevich in a shrill voice.

'One moment, please,' I said. 'There's one more condition. Since we're going to fight to the death, we must do everything possible to keep this a secret so that our seconds are not held responsible. Do you agree?'

'We agree entirely.'

'Well then, I have thought of this; you see the little space at the top of that sheer cliff there on the right? It's about two hundred feet, if not more, from there to the bottom and there are sharp rocks below. Each of us will stand at the very edge of the space – like that even a light wound will be fatal. That should be consistent with your wishes, for you yourself stipulated six paces. Whoever is wounded is bound to fall down and be smashed to pieces. The doctor will extract the bullet, and then it will be easy to ascribe the death to an unlucky fall. We'll throw lots for who is to be the first to fire. I inform you in conclusion that if these conditions are not fulfilled I shall not fight.'

'Very well then,' said the captain, looking meaningfully at Grushnitski, who nodded his head in agreement. His face was changing every instant. I had put him in a difficult position. Fighting a duel under normal conditions, he could shoot me in the leg, wound me slightly and thus obtain his revenge without burdening his conscience. But now he had to fire into the air, or make himself a murderer, or abandon his underhand scheme and face danger on equal terms with me. I would not have liked to be in his shoes at that moment. He called the captain aside and spoke urgently to him. I saw that his lips were blue and trembling. But the captain turned away from him with a contemptuous smile. 'You're a fool!' he told Grushnitski quite loudly, 'you don't know a thing! Let's begin, gentlemen!'

A narrow path led up the incline, between the bushes. The precarious steps of this natural staircase consisted of pieces of rock. We started scrambling up, holding on to the bushes for support. Grushnitski went first, followed by his seconds and the doctor, and I brought up the rear.

'You amaze me,' said the doctor, taking hold of my wrist. 'Let me feel your pulse. Ah! Feverish! But there's nothing unusual about your face . . . except that your eyes are sparkling more brightly.'

Suddenly some small stones rolled down under our feet. What was it? Grushnitski had stumbled; a bough he was holding on to had broken and he would have fallen, if his seconds had not held him up.

'Be careful,' I called out to him, 'don't fall beforehand, it's a bad omen. Remember Julius Caesar!'

At last we came to the top of the overhanging cliff. The ground was covered with fine sand as if it had been planned for a duel. The mountain tops were crowded together like a great herd, lost in the golden morning mists. To the south Elbrus rose up in a white mass, the main link in the chain of icy peaks. Thin clouds coming over from the east were beginning to filter between them. I walked up to the edge and looked down. I felt almost giddy. It looked as dark and cold as the grave down below. Mossy crenellations, eroded by storms and time, were waiting for their prey.

The space on which we had to fight was an almost equilateral triangle.

Six paces were measured out from the projecting corner and it was decided that the one who had to receive the other's fire first would stand at the very tip with his back to the precipice. If he was not killed, the opponents would change places.

I was determined to let Grushnitski have every advantage. I wanted to test him; a generous spark might kindle in his heart, and then everything would be settled for the best. But his pride and weakness of character had to triumph. I wanted to give myself the right to be merciless to him, if fate spared me. Who has not made such bargains with his conscience?

'Toss the coin, doctor,' said the captain.

The doctor took a silver piece out of his pocket and flicked it into the air.

'Tails!' Grushnitski called out promptly, like a man suddenly aroused by a friendly pat on the shoulder. 'Heads!' I said.

The coin spun and fell with a tinkling sound. Everyone rushed towards it.

'You're lucky,' I told Grushnitski, 'you have the first turn. But remember that if you don't kill me, I won't miss – I give you my word of honour.'

He turned red; he was ashamed to kill an unarmed man. I watched him closely; for a moment I thought he was going to throw himself at my feet and beg my forgiveness, but how could he confess to such an ignoble plan? He had one course left – to fire into the air; I was sure that he would fire into the air! Only one thing could stop him doing that: the thought that I would insist on another duel.

'The time's come!' the doctor whispered to me, tugging at my sleeve, 'everything's lost if you don't say now that we know their intentions. Look he's already loading . . . if you won't say anything, then I will myself. . . .'

'Not for anything in the world, doctor,' I replied, holding him back by his arm; 'you'll spoil everything. You gave me your word not to interfere. . . . What concern is it of yours? Perhaps I want to be killed.'

He looked at me in surprise.

'Oh, well, that's another matter! . . . But don't blame me when you're in the next world.'

Meanwhile the captain had loaded his pistols, and gave one to Grushnitski, whispering something to him with a smile. The other he gave to me.

I stood at the corner of the triangle, bracing my left foot firmly against a stone, and bent forward slightly, so as not to fall back if I were slightly wounded.

Grushnitski stood facing me, and at a given signal began to raise the pistol. His knees were shaking. He was aiming straight at my forehead.

I started to boil with an inexplicable fury.

Suddenly, he lowered the muzzle of the pistol, and white as a sheet, turned to his second.

'I can't,' he said dully.

'Coward!' replied the captain.

A shot rang out. The bullet grazed my knee. Involuntarily I took a few paces forward, so as to get away from the edge as quickly as I could.

'Well, Grushnitski, I'm sorry you missed,' said the captain. 'Now it's your turn. Take your place! But embrace me first – we won't see each other again.' They embraced. The captain could scarcely refrain from laughing. 'Don't be afraid,' he added with a sly glance at Grushnitski, 'nothing has any significance in this world. Nature's an idiot, fate is a fool, and life isn't worth a brass farthing.'

After this tragic phrase, pronounced with suitable solemnity, he took up his position. Ivan Ignatyevich also embraced Grushnitski with tears in his eyes, and at last he remained there, alone, facing me. I am still trying to explain to myself what the feeling was that surged up inside me at that moment. It was anger at the insult to my pride, and hatred and contempt at the thought that this man, who was looking at me now with such self-assurance, with such calm insolence, had tried to kill me like a dog two minutes before,without exposing himself to any danger at all. For if the wound in my leg had been any worse, I would undoubtedly have fallen from the cliff.

I stared at him in the face for a while, trying to find even the slightest trace of remorse. But it seemed to me that he was suppressing a smile.

'I advise you to pray to God before you die,' I said.

'Don't bother about my soul any more than you do about your own. I have only one request to make: shoot quickly.'

'So you won't withdraw your slander? You won't apologize? Think carefully – doesn't your conscience worry you at all?'

'Mr Pechorin,' the captain cried, 'allow me to point out that you're not here to hear confession. Let's get it over with. Someone might ride through the ravine and see us.'

'Very well. Doctor, come here.'

The doctor walked up to me. Poor doctor! He looked paler than Grushnitski had ten minutes before.

I intentionally pronounced the following words as a judge pronounces sentence of death – loudly, clearly and deliberately:

'Doctor, these gentlemen, probably in their haste, have forgotten to place a bullet in my pistol. I ask you to load it again – and properly!'

'That's impossible,' cried the captain, 'impossible! I loaded both pistols. Perhaps the bullet fell out of yours. . . . It's not my fault! And you have no right to reload . . . no right at all . . . it's quite against the rules. I won't allow it.'

'Very well!' I told the captain. 'If that's the case, then I shall fight a duel with you under the same conditions.'

He stopped short.

Grushnitski was standing with his head sunk on his breast. He was terribly embarrassed.

'Let them be!' he said at last to the captain, who was trying to tear the pistol out of the doctor's hands. 'You know perfectly well that they're right.'

The captain made various signs to him in vain. Grushnitski did not even look at him.

Meanwhile the doctor loaded the pistol and gave it to me.

When he saw this, the captain spat and stamped his foot.

'You're a fool, my friend,' he said, 'an absolute idiot! If you'd relied on me and done everything I told you. . . . It serves you right! Get yourself swatted like a fly. . . .' He turned aside, muttering as he walked away: 'And it's quite against the rules anyway.'

'Grushnitski,' I said, 'there's still time. Withdraw your slander, and I shall forgive you everything. You haven't succeeded in fooling me, and my pride is satisfied. Remember, we were friends once.'

His face lit up and his eyes flashed.

'Shoot!' he replied, 'I despise myself but I hate you. If you don't kill me, I'll lie in wait for you one night and cut your throat. There isn't room for the two of us on this earth.'

I fired.

When the smoke cleared, Grushnitski was no longer there. A light cloud of dust hung above the edge of the precipice.

They all cried out at the same time.

'*Finita la commedia!*' I said to the doctor.

He did not reply and turned away in horror.

I shrugged my shoulders and took my leave of Grushnitski's seconds. On my way down the path, I caught sight of Grushnitski's bloody corpse in a cleft of the rock. I closed my eyes involuntarily.

I untethered the horse and rode him home slowly. My heart was heavy. The sun seemed pale and its rays gave me no warmth.

This story represents one of the most hideously ironical passages in the whole literature of the duel. For in July 1841, at Pyatigorsk, Mikhail Yuryevich Lermontov fought a duel with an old acquaintance called Martynov who had generally been identified as the model for Grushnitski in *A Hero of our Time*. The duel took place in much the same circumstances as in the novel, but the man whom the author had killed off in fiction shot Lermontov dead in fact.

13 · The Decline of Duelling

After over a thousand years of life in various forms, the duel is now virtually extinct, a state of affairs which, only a century ago, would have struck most Europeans and Americans as inconceivable.

The decline of duelling may be attributed in part to the stern legislation against the practice introduced and enforced in many countries. Anti-duelling laws, however, proved totally ineffective in earlier times in suppressing the practice in countries such as France and Italy, and it seems probable that a more potent antidote has been a growing concern at the waste of human life effected by duels over matters of comparatively little importance. A writer in *Vanity Fair* in 1891 might hanker nostalgically after the days when a gentleman guilty of some slight discourtesy 'might be punished by a bullet in a soft part of his body', but most people today would consider the risk of death or serious injury too high a price to demand for the satisfaction of wounded vanity or offended susceptibility.

The most effective weapon used against duelling, however, has undoubtedly been ridicule. As Hunt wrote in the last century in his *Table-Talk*, 'the diffusion of knowledge seems to be conspiring with the increased activity and practical good sense of the age to discountenance duelling, and render it ridiculous; and as the occasions of it are in general really so, while the consequences are tragical to the persons concerned, it is to be hoped that every brave and considerate man will do what he can to assist in proving it superfluous. Did anyone ever write a serious panegyric on a duel? It has received hundreds of banters, and (consequences apart) has a natural tendency to the burlesque.'

Another writer of the late nineteenth century made much the same point when he regretted that the London correspondent of the *Figaro*, who had joined a duelling party on a journey into Holland, had not had a camera with him to record the fight. 'I believe', he wrote, 'that if the correspondent of the *Figaro* had not been taken by surprise when the new functions were imposed upon him, he would have had with him an instantaneous photographic apparatus, which would have caught the combatants in their various postures, and supplied the public with the means of almost witnessing the fight. A special photographic apparatus will no doubt be added next to the special correspondent, and the newspaper Press will have the means of criticizing duels just as it criticizes artistic, musical or dramatic entertainments. The process is one that should be encouraged, for when duelling has in this way been made ridiculous it will be abandoned. At present the practice is only barbarous, a logical conclusion which does not suffice to extinguish it.'

No institution, in fact, can survive indefinitely prolonged and general ridicule, and duelling has proved no exception. Even when the practice was at its height, in the late eighteenth and early nineteenth century, its more intelligent opponents were using ridicule in order to curb it, and their method was later steadily extended. Thus when one of Ney's staff officers informed the marshal that he had challenged a brother-officer who had slapped him in the face, Ney told him: 'Go to him and say you have washed your face, as it was easier to get rid of the effects of blackguardly conduct by water than by fighting.' Again, when a gentleman told Talleyrand that he had sent a challenge to an officer who had thrown him out of an upper-story window for allegedly cheating at cards, Talleyrand replied: 'Let me give you a word of advice. Don't fight over such a small affair, and don't play cards again with that officer, except on the ground floor.' Another man who did a great deal to bring duelling into ridicule was the great Judge Dooly of Georgia, who laughed his way out of countless duels with a pleasant wit which disarmed his bitterest enemies; thus a man who warned him that if he did not fight his name would fill the columns of a newspaper was told that he 'would rather fill ten newspapers than one coffin'; and a duel with a man suffering from St Vitus's dance was called off after Dooly had solicitously planted a forked stick in front of his opponent to serve as a pistol-rest, remarking: 'If you shoot at me with your hand shaking like that, you'll pepper me full of holes at the first fire.' And finally, in England, the balloon of the affair of honour was amusingly pricked by a lawyer called Mann, who declined a challenge from a bachelor colleague called Fleet in the following terms:

In the first place, unless I am grossly deceived,
I myself am in conscience the party aggrieved;
And therefore, good sir, if a challenge *must* be,
Pray wait till that challenge be *tendered* by *me*.
Again, sir, I think it by far the more sinful
To stand and be shot than to sit for a skinful;
From whence you'll conclude (as I'd have you indeed)
That fighting composes not part of my creed –
And my courage (which, though it was never disputed,
Is not, I imagine, too, too deeply rooted)
Would prefer that its fruit, sir, whate'er it may yield,
Should appear at '*the table*', and not in '*the field*'.
And lastly, *my life*, be it never forgot,
Possesses a value which *yours*, sir, does not;
So I mean to preserve it as long as I can,
Being justly entitled 'a family *Mann*',
With three or four children (I scarce know how many),
Whilst *you*, sir, have not, or *ought* not to have any.
Besides, that the contest would be too unequal,
I doubt not will plainly appear by the sequel:
For e'en *you* must acknowledge it would not be meet
That one small '*Mann* of war' should engage 'a whole *Fleet*'.

Banned by the law, ridiculed by the Press, and frowned upon by the public, duelling was gradually abandoned in one country after another, until it now survives only in Germany, and then under cover and within a restricted milieu. In France, where it once flourished more than anywhere else in the world, it has become nothing more than an infrequent and picturesque practice, indulged in with the minimum of risk and the maximum of publicity. The last noteworthy duel fought in that country, in March 1958, between Serge Lifar and the Marquis de Cuevas, is a case in point. Every stage in this duel, from the offence to the reconciliation, was witnessed and recorded by a host of reporters and photographers. The quarrel began at the Théâtre des Champs-Élysées, where Lifar, whose ballet *Noir et Blanc* had just been performed in defiance of his instructions, threw his handkerchief in the marquis's face and was slapped in return. The duel was fought at Blaru, near Vernon, after the participants had been chased by the world's Press at ninety miles an hour from the Bois de Boulogne, and was stopped when Lifar suffered a slight scratch on the forearm. The reconciliation took place in the local doctor's house, where the seventy-three-year-old marquis clasped Lifar in his arms, sobbing: 'I thought I had killed my son.' One cannot help thinking that the great French duellists of the past must have turned in their graves.

In Britain, duelling is practised only at the ancient universities, where undergraduates occasionally cross swords in a self-conscious attempt to revive an old tradition, and also, one suspects, to win a little amusing publicity in the national Press. The latest duel of this kind, at the time of writing, was fought at Oxford on St Valentine's Day, 1964, between two Magdalen College undergraduates, Rory Donellan and Adam Poynter. The latter had allegedly described a certain young lady as 'thick in mind and body', and had been called out by Donellan, a former fencing champion of Natal and at this time captain of the ominously entitled University Assassins. Poynter, who knew nothing about fencing, was reported to have been 'roughed up a bit and his arms cut about', but after the fight the two antagonists drank the young lady's health in whisky. Her name was then furnished to the Press and circulated to all the leading news agencies in the world. She rather surprisingly went on record as saying that she was flattered, but the university newspaper dismissed the whole affair as 'silly'.

As for the United States, that other great bastion of duelling, the practice died there in the first half of the twentieth century. Indeed, in 1945, a writer in *Atlantic* pleaded for a revival of duelling as a defence against libel – 'with such safeguards around it as to prevent it from becoming the plaything of expert pistol shots in search of stranger diversion than softball games' – thus offering a sure indication that the institution was already extinct in his country.

It was one of the world's most celebrated duellists, the Frenchman Saint-Foix, who once unwittingly voiced one of the most simple and forceful arguments against the practice to which he was so devoted. He had told an officer of the Guard that he smelt like a goat, and the man had promptly drawn his sword to avenge the insult. 'Put up your sword, you fool,' said the great duellist; 'for if you kill me you will not smell any better, and if I kill you you will smell a damn sight worse.'

It has taken the world a long time to appreciate the simple logic of that remark and behave accordingly, but the lesson seems at last to have been learnt.

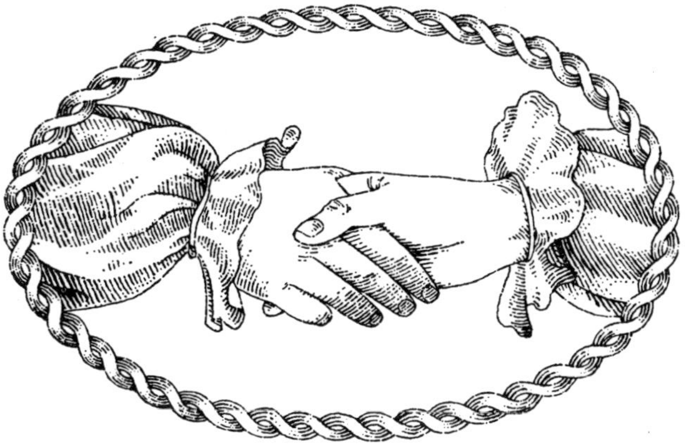

Bibliography

The following is a selection of the most interesting or useful works consulted in the preparation of this book.

ALMBER (Alfred d'): *Physiologie du duel*, Paris, 1867.
AUDIGUIER (Vital d'): *Le vray et ancien usage des duels*, Paris, 1617.
BATAILLARD (C.): *Du Duel*, Paris, 1829.
BEAUVOIR (Roger de): *Duels et duellistes*, Paris, 1864.
BOSQUETT (A.): *The Young Man of Honour's Vade-Mecum*, London, 1817.
BOSTON (Noel): *Old Guns and Pistols*, London, 1958.
BOSWELL (James): *Boswell on the Grand Tour*, London, 1953.
BRANTÔME (Pierre de Bourdeilles, Seigneur de): *Oeuvres complètes*, 8 vols., Paris, 1822–3.
BRYSKETT (Lodowick): *A Discourse of Civill Life*, London, 1606.
CAMPIGNEULLES (Fougeroux de): *Histoire des duels anciens et modernes*, 2 vols., Paris, 1835.
COUSTARD DE MASSI (A. P.): *The History of Duelling in all Countries*, London, 1880.
DOUGLAS (William): *Duelling Days in the Army*, London, 1887.
GODDARD (Henry): *Memoirs of a Bow Street Runner*, London, 1956.
GRISIER (Augustin): *Les armes et le duel*, Paris, 1847.
HEY (Richard): *A Dissertation on Duelling*, Cambridge, 1784.
KANE (Harnett T.): *Gentlemen, Swords and Pistols*, New York, 1951.
LETAINTURIER-FRADIN (Gabriel): *Le Duel à travers les ages*, Paris, 1892.
MOORE (Charles): *Two Treatises on Duelling and Gaming*, London, 1790.
SELDEN (John): *The Duello, or Single Combat*, London, 1610.
TAVERNIER (Adolphe): *L'Art du duel*, Paris, 1884.
THIMM (Carl A.): *A Bibliography of Fencing and Duelling*, London, 1896.
'TRAVELLER, A': *The Art of Duelling*, London, 1836.
TRUMAN (Ben C.): *The Field of Honor*, New York, 1884.
VALLÉE (Henri): *Le Duel*, Paris, 1877.
VAUX (Ludovic de): *Les duels célèbres*, Paris, 1884.

Index